ITALY, THE MAGIC LAND

ITALY
THE MAGIC LAND

BY

LILIAN WHITING

AUTHOR OF "THE FLORENCE OF LANDOR," "THE LAND OF
ENCHANTMENT," "THE WORLD BEAUTIFUL," ETC.

" And, under many a yellow star,
We dropped into the Magic Land! "

Illustrated from Photographs

BOSTON
LITTLE, BROWN, AND COMPANY
1907

THE GRIFFITH-STILLINGS PRESS, BOSTON, U.S.A.

TO

ELLA

(Mrs. Franklin Simmons)

WHOSE EARTHLY FORM REPOSES IN THE BEAUTIFUL ROMAN CEMETERY,
WHERE POETIC ASSOCIATIONS WITH KEATS AND SHELLEY HAUNT
THE AIR, — UNDER THE SCULPTURED "ANGEL OF THE RES-
URRECTION," WITH ITS MAJESTIC SYMBOLISM OF THE
TRIUMPH OF IMMORTALITY, — BUT WHOSE RADIANT
PRESENCE STILL TRANSFIGURES THE LIFE THAT
HELD HER IN IMMORTAL DEVOTION, —
THESE PAGES ARE INSCRIBED,

WITH THE UNFORGETTING LOVE OF

LILIAN WHITING.

ROME, ITALY, May Days, 1907.

" Nor Life is ever lord of Death,
And Love can never lose its own."

PREFATORY NOTE

THAT Florence, the "Flower City," receives only a passing allusion in this record of various impressions that gleam and glow through the days after several visits to the Magic Land, is due to the fact that in a previous volume by the writer — one entitled "The Florence of Landor" — the lovely Tuscan town with its art, its ineffable beauty, and its choice social life, formed the subject matter of that volume. Any attempt to portray Florence in the present book would savor only of the repetition of loves and enthusiasms already recorded in the previous work in which Walter Savage Landor formed the central figure. For that reason no mention of Florence, beyond some mere allusion, is attempted in these pages, which only aim to present certain fragmentary impressions of various sojourns in Italy, refracted through the prism of memory. Whatever inconveniences or discomfort attend the traveller swiftly fade, and leave to him only the precious heritage of resplendent sunset skies, of poetic association, of artistic beauty. In spirit he is again lingering through long afternoons in St. Peter's till the golden light through the far windows of the tribune is merged into the dusk of twilight in which the vast monumental groups gleam wraith-like. Again

vii

PREFATORY NOTE

he is ascending the magnificent *Scala Regia*, and lingering in the Raphael Stanze, or in the wonderful sculpture galleries of the Vatican, or sauntering in the sunshine on the Palatine. In memory he is again spellbound by ancient and mediæval art. In the line of modern sculpture the work of Franklin Simmons in Rome is a feature of Italy that haunts the imagination. No lover of beauty would willingly miss his great studios in the Via San Nicolo da Tolentino, with their wealth of ideal creations that contribute new interest to the most divine of all the arts.

> " The world of art is an ideal world, —
> The world I love, and that I fain would live in;
> So speak to me of artists and of art,
> Of all the painters, sculptors, and musicians
> That now illustrate Rome."

The mystic charm of the pilgrimage to Assisi; the romance that reflects itself in the violet seas and flaming splendors of the sky on the shores of Ischia and Capri; the buried treasures of Amalfi; the magnetic impressiveness of the Eternal City, — all these enter into life as new forces to build and shape the future into undreamed-of destinies.

L. W.

The Brunswick, Boston,
October Days, 1907.

CONTENTS

LIST OF ILLUSTRATIONS

LIST OF ILLUSTRATIONS

"*Rest we content if whispers from the stars*
In wafting of the incalculable wind
Come blown at midnight through our prison-bars."

THE MAGIC LAND

By woodland belt, by ocean bar,
　The full south breeze our forehead fanned;
And, under many a yellow star,
　We dropped into the Magic Land.

　　　．　　　．　　　．　　　．　　　．

We heard, far-off, the siren's song;
　We caught the gleam of sea-maids' hair;
The glimmering isles and rocks among
　We moved through sparkling purple air.

Then Morning rose, and smote from far
　Her elfin harps o'er land and sea;
And woodland belt, and ocean bar
　To one sweet note sighed — "Italy!"

OWEN MEREDITH.

ITALY, THE MAGIC LAND

I

THE PERIOD OF MODERN ART IN ROME

> But ah, that spring should vanish with the Rose!
> That youth's sweet-scented manuscript should close!
> The nightingale that in the branches sang,
> Oh, where and whither flown again, — who knows?
>
> OMAR KHAYYAM.

ROME, as the picturesque city of the Popes in the middle years of the nineteenth century, was resplendent in local color. It was the Rome of sunny winters; the Rome of gay excursions over that haunted sea of the Campagna to pictorial points in the Alban and Sabine hills; the Rome of young artist life, which organized impromptu festas with Arcadian freedom, and utilized the shadow or the shelter of ruined temples or tombs in which to spread its picnic lunches and bring the glow of simple, friendly intercourse into the romantic lights of the poetic, historic, or tragic past. There were splendid Catholic processions and ceremonials that seemed organized as a part of the stage scenery that ensconced itself, also, with the

3

nonchalance of easy possession, in the vast salons of historic palaces where tapestried walls and richly painted ceilings, arched high overhead, with statues dimly seen in niches here and there, and the bust of some crowned Antoninus, or radiant Juno, gleaming from a shadowy corner, all made up the *mise-en-scène* of familiar evenings. There were lingering hours in the gardens of the Villa Medici into whose shades one strolled by that beguiling path along the parapet on Monte Pincio, through the beautiful grove with its walks and fountains. The old ilex bosquet, with its tangled growth and air of complete seclusion, had its spell of fascination. Then, as now, the elevated temple, at the end of the main path, seemed the haunt of gods and muses. In all the incidental, as well as the ceremonial social meeting and mingling, art and religion were the general themes of discussion. This idyllic life —

> "Comprehending, too, the soul's
> And all the high necessities of art" —

has left its impress on the air as well as its record on many a page of the poet and the romancist. The names that made memorable

4

those wonderful days touch chords of association that still vibrate in the life of the hour.
For the most part the artists and their asso-
ciates have gone their way — not into a Silent
Land, a land of shadows and vague, wandering ghosts — but into that realm wherein is the
"life more abundant," of more intense energy
and of nobler achievement; the realm in which
every aspiration of earth enlarges its conception and every inspiration is exalted and endowed with new purpose; the realm where, as
Browning says, —

"Power comes in full play."

The poet's vision recognizes the truth: —

"I know there shall dawn a day,
— Is it here on homely earth?
Is it yonder, worlds away,
Where the strange and new have birth,
That Power comes in full play?"

The names of sculptor, painter, and poet
throng back, imaged in that retrospective mirror
which reflects a vista of the past, rich in ideal
creation. Beautiful forms emerge from the
marble; pictorial scenes glow from the canvas;
song and story and happy, historic days are in

the very air. To Italy, land of romance and song, all the artists came trooping, and

"Under many a yellow Star"

they dropped into the Magic Land. If the wraiths of the centuries long since dead walked the streets, they were quite welcome to revisit the glimpses of the moon and contribute their mystery to the general artistic effectiveness of the Seven-hilled City. All this group of American idealists, from Allston and Page to Crawford, Story, Randolph Rogers, Vedder, Simmons, and to the latest comer of all, Charles Walter Stetson, recognized something of the artist's native air in this Mecca of their pilgrimage.

It was, indeed, quite natural, on account of the stupendous work of Michael Angelo and the unrivalled museums of the Vatican, that Rome should have become pre-eminently the artistic centre of the ninteenth century and should have attracted students and lovers of art from all parts of the world. The immortal works of the two great periods, the Greek and the Renaissance, — the art that was forever great because it was the outgrowth of profound religious conviction, — were enshrined in the

churches and the galleries of Rome. The leading countries of Europe sent here their aspiring
students and established permanent academies
for their residence. Germany, France, and
England were thus represented. Thorwaldsen
came as a pensioner from the Academy of Fine
Arts in Copenhagen; and it was during his life,
and that of the noble Canova, that Rome began
to be recognized as the modern world-centre of
art. Was it not a natural sequence that the
early painters and sculptors who came to study
under the stimulating influences of the great
masterpieces of the past should linger on in
the city whose very air became to them the
breath of inspiring suggestion? Where but in
Rome would have come to Crawford the vision
of his "Orpheus" and of his noble Beethoven?
or to Story his "Libyan Sibyl," and that exquisite group, "Into the Silent Land"? or to Vedder
his marvellous creations of "The Fates Gathering in the Stars," the "Cumæan Sibyl," or the
"Dance of the Pleiades"? to Simmons his triumphant "Angel of the Resurrection," and
"The Genius of Progress Leading the Nations"? or to Stetson that ineffable vision of
"The Child," and that wonderful group called

"Music"? whose coloring Titian or Giorgione might well mistake for their own.

Under the Pontifical *régime* the general character of Rome was mediæval and religious. The perpetual festas of the church made the streets constantly picturesque with their processions of monks, and friars, and priests, and these wonderful blendings of color and scenic effect stimulated the artistic sense. The expenses of living in Rome were then only a fraction of what the cost is at the present time; and as the city was the resort of the wealthy and cultured few, the artists were surrounded by the stimulus of critical appreciation and of patronage. Their work, their dreams, were the theme of literary discussion, and focussed the attention of the polite world. Their studios were among the important interests to every visitor in the Eternal City. In those days the traveller did not land with his touring car at Naples, make "the run" to Rome in a record that distanced any possibilities of railroad trains, pass two or three days in motoring about the city and its environs, seeing the exterior of everything in a dissolving view and the interior of nothing, — as within this time, at least, he must flash on in his touring car to Florence. On the contrary, the traveller proceeded to Rome with serious deliberation, and with a more realizing sense of undertaking a journey than Walter Wellman experiences in attempting to fly in his aero-car to the North Pole and send his observations across the polar seas by wireless telegraphy. The visitor went to Rome for a winter, for a year, and gave himself up to leisurely impressions. Rome was an atmosphere, not a spectacle, and it was to be entered with the lofty and reverent appreciation of the poet's power and the artist's vision.

In Rome, Thomas Cole painted some of his best pictures; and in Rome or Florence wrought a long list of painters and sculptors. Whether in the Eternal City or in the Flower City, their environment was alike Italy—the environment of the Magic Land. Among the more prominent of all these devotees of Beauty several nationalities were represented. Each might have said of his purpose, in the words of William Watson:—

> "I follow Beauty; of her train am I,
> Beauty, whose voice is earth and sea and air;
> Who serveth, and her hands for all things ply;
> Who reigneth, and her throne is everywhere."

ITALY, THE MAGIC LAND

Among these artists there flash upon memory the names of Vanderlyn, Benjamin West, Allston, Rauch, Ange, Veit, Tenerani, Overbeck, Schadow, Horace Vernet, Thorwaldsen, John Gibson, Hiram Powers, Crawford, Page, Clark Mills, Randolph Rogers, William Rinehart, Launt Thompson, Horatio and Richard Greenough, Thomas Ball, Anne Whitney, Larkin G. Mead, Paul Akers, William Wetmore Story, Harriet Hosmer, J. Rollin Tilton, and, later, Elihu Vedder, Moses Ezekiel, Franklin Simmons, Augustus St. Gaudens, and Charles Walter Stetson, the name of Mr. Stetson linking the long and interesting procession with the immediate life of to-day. Of these later artists Story, Miss Hosmer, Ezekiel, Vedder, Simmons, and Stetson are identified with Rome as being either their permanent or their prolonged residence. Mr. St. Gaudens was a transient student, returning to his own country to pursue his work; and of two young sculptors, Hendrick Christian Anderson and C. Percival Dietsch, time has not yet developed their powers beyond an experimental stage of brilliant promise.

The Rome of the artists of clay and canvas was also the Rome of the poets and romancists, of authors in all lines of literary achievement. How the names of the procession of visitors and sojourners in the Eternal City, from Milton, Goethe, and Mme. de Staël to Henry James, Marion Crawford, Richard Bagot, and Grace Ellery Channing (Mrs. Charles Walter Stetson), gleam from that resplendent panorama of the modern past of Rome! Like the words in electric fire that flash out of the darkness in city streets at night, there shine the names of Shelley and of Keats; of Gladstone, on whom in one memorable summer day, while strolling in Italian sunshine, there fell a vision of the sacredness and the significance of life and its infinite responsibility in the fulfilment of lofty purposes. What charming associations these guests and sojourners have left behind! Hawthorne, embodying in immortal romance the spirit of the scenic greatness of the Eternal City; Margaret Fuller, Marchesa d'Ossoli, allying herself in marriage with the country she loved, and living in Rome those troubled, mysterious years that were to close the earthly chapter of her life; Robert and Elizabeth Browning, the wedded poets, who sang of love and Italy; Harriet Beecher Stowe, finding on

the enchánted Italian shores the material which
she wove with such irresistible attraction into
the romance of "Agnes of Sorrento;" Longfellow, with his poet's vision, transmuting every
vista and impression into some exquisite lyric;
Lowell, bringing his philosophic as well as his
poetic insight to penetrate the untold meaning
of Rome; Thomas William Parsons, making the
country of Dante fairly his own; Thackeray,
with his brilliant interpretation of the *comédie
humaine;* Emerson, who, oblivious of all the
glories of art or the joys of nature, absorbed
himself in writing transcendental letters to his
eccentric, but high-souled aunt, Mary Moody
Emerson; Ruskin, translating Italian art to
Italy herself; Dr. Samuel Gridley Howe and
his poet wife, Mrs. Julia Ward Howe, in the
first flush of their bridal happiness, when Mrs.
Howe's impassioned love for the Seven-hilled
City inspired many a lyric that mirrors the
Roman atmosphere of that day; Kate Field,
with a young girl's glad enthusiasm over the
marvellous loveliness of a Maytime in Rome,
and her devotion to those great histrionic
artists, Ristori and Salvini; George Stillman
Hillard, leaving to literature the rich legacy of

ANGEL, CHURCH OF SAN ANDREA DELLE FRATTE, ROME
Giovanni Lorenzo Bernini
Page 32

his "Six Months in Italy," — a work that to this day holds precedence as a clear and comprehensive presentation of the scenic beauty, the notable monumental and architectural art, and the general life and resources of this land of painter and poet. Other names, too, throng upon memory — that of William Dean Howells, painting Italian life in his "Venetian Days," and charming all the literary world by his choice art; and among later work, the interesting interpretations of Rome and of social life in Rome, by Marion Crawford, Henry James, and Richard Bagot, — in chronicle, in romance, or in biographical record. During the last quarter of the nineteenth century, indeed, the visitors to Rome — authors, artists, travellers of easy leisure — defy any numerical record. Mrs. Louise Chandler Moulton, poet, romancist, and delightful *raconteur* as well, has recorded some charming impressions of her various sojourns in Rome both in her "Random Rambles" and in "Lazy Tours." Of the Palatine Hill we find her saying: —

"Sometimes we go to the Palace of the Cæsars, and look off upon the heights where the snow lingers and the warm light rests, making them shine like the Delectable Mountains. Nearer at hand are the almond trees, in flower, or the orange trees, bright at once with their white, sweet blossoms and their golden fruit."

Mrs. Moulton writes of the "stately dwellers" in Rome whom time cannot change; and to whom, whenever she returns, she makes her first visit; some of whom are in the mighty palace of the Vatican and some of whom dwell in state in the Capitol.

"The beautiful Antoninus still wears his crown of lotus in Villa Albani and the Juno whom Goethe worshipped reigns forever at the Ludovisi," she writes; "I can never put in words the pleasure I find in these immortals." Mrs. Moulton loved to wander in the Villa Borghese "before the place is thronged with the beauty and fashion of Rome as it is in the late afternoon. I do not wonder that Miriam and Donatello could forget their fate in these enchanted glades," she wrote, "and dance as the sunbeams danced with the shadows. Some-

times I seem to see them where the sun sifts
through the young green leaves, and her beauty
— her human, deep-souled beauty — and his
fantastic grace are the only things here that
cannot change.

"The walls will crumble; the busts of kings
and heroes and poets will lose their contours,
the lovely Roman ladies also grow old and
fade, and vanish from sight and from memory;
but still these two, hopeless yet happy, will
dance in these wild glades immortally beyond
the reach of the effacing years."

The visit to Rome of the Rev. Dr. Phillips
Brooks — later the Bishop of Massachusetts —
is immortalized in the most lifelike portrait
bust of the great preacher ever modelled; a
bust in which the genius of the sculptor, Franklin Simmons, found one of its noblest expressions, and has perpetuated, with masterly
power, the energy of thought, at once profound
and intense, in the countenance of Bishop
Brooks. These, and many another whom the
gods have loved and dowered with gifts, rise
before any retrospective glance over the comparatively recent past of Rome. Bishop Brooks

passed there the Holy Week of one Lenten season, and of the Miserere in the Sistine Chapel he wrote that it was certainly the most wonderful music to which he had ever listened; and he added: —

"The Miserere in the Sistine, the Benediction from the balcony, the solemn moment of the elevation of the Host on Easter, and the illumination of St. Peter's, these all seem to reach very remarkably the great ideal of the central religious commemoration of Christendom."

It was in the winter of 1828 that Mr. Longfellow first visited Rome, which "is announced," he wrote, "by Nero's tomb," and he quotes Dupaty's lines: —

"Quoi! c'est là Rome? quoi!
C'est le tombeau de Neron qui l'annonce."

Mr. Longfellow expressed his love for the Eternal City, and in a personal letter[1] he said: —

[1] Henry Wadsworth Longfellow: Houghton, Mifflin & Co.

ITALY, THE MAGIC LAND

"I have been so delighted with Rome that I have extended my residence much beyond my original intention. There is so much in the city to delay the stranger; the villages in the environs are so beautiful, and there is such a quiet and stillness about everything that, were it in my power, I should be induced to remain the whole year round. You can imagine nothing equal to the ruins of Rome. The Forum and the Coliseum are beyond all I had ever fancied them; and the ruined temples and the mouldering aqueducts which are scattered over the Campagna; I do not believe there is a finer view in the world than that from the eastern gate of the city, embracing the Campagna, with its ruined aqueducts diverging in long broken arcades, and terminated by the sweep of the Albanian hills, sprinkled with their white villages, and celebrated in song and story! But the great charm of the scene springs from association; and though everything in Italy is really picturesque, yet strip the country of its historic recollections, — think merely of what it is, and not of what it has been, — and you will find the dream to be fading away.

"You would be shocked at the misery of the

people, especially in the Pope's dominions: but their element seems to be in rags and misery; and with the ceremonials of their religion and the holidays of the church, which average nearly three a week, they are poor — and lazy and happy. I mean, happy in their way."

In a later visit the poet was domiciled in an hotel on the Piazza Barberini, where the wonderful view included then the entire city "to where St. Peter's dome darkens against the sunset." Of this visit his brother, Rev. Samuel Longfellow, writes: —

"Here Mr. Longfellow became for the season the centre of the group of American visitors and resident artists, whose well-known names need not be recounted. Here he made, also, acquaintances among the Italians, — especially the Duke of Sermoneta, the Dantean scholar, and Monsignore Nardi, of the papal court. The Pope himself he did not visit. An interesting acquaintance was that made with the Abbé Liszt, who was spending the winter in Rome, having rooms in the abandoned Convent of Santa Francesca, in the Forum. Call-

ing there one evening, in company with Mr.
Healy the artist, the inner door of the apartment
was opened to them by Liszt himself, holding
high in his hand a candle which illuminated his
fine face. The picture was so striking that Mr.
Longfellow begged his companion to put it
upon canvas, — which he did; and the painting now hangs in the library of Craigie House.
At a morning visit, Liszt delighted the party
with a performance upon his Chickering piano-
forte.

"To see Rome, as all travellers know, is a
work for many months; and it was pursued with
tolerable diligence. But Mr. Longfellow was
never a good sight-seer. He was impatient of
lingering in picture galleries, churches, or ruins.
He saw quickly the essential points, and soon
tired of any minuter examination."

But long, indeed, before nineteenth-century
artists and authors laid siege to the Eternal
City, in the far-away years of 1638, Milton
visited Rome, and there still remains the tablet,
on the wall of the *casa* in the Via delle Quattre
Fontane in which he stayed, a tablet bearing
an inscription giving the date of his visit; as,

also, in Via Machella, there is an inscription marking the place where Scott lived during his visit to Rome. Goethe made his memorable tour to Italy in 1786 — fourteen years before the dawn of the nineteenth century — and wrote: "I feel the greatest longing to read Tacitus in Rome;" and again (an observation with which every visitor to the Eternal City will sympathize) he noted: —

"It grows more and more difficult for me to render an account of my residence in Rome, for as we always find the sea deeper the further we go, so it is with me in observation of this city. . . . Wherever we go and wherever we stand, we see about us a finished picture, — forms of every kind and style; palaces and ruins; gardens and wastes; the distant and the near houses; triumphal arches and columns, — often all so close together that they might be sketched on a single sheet. One should have a thousand points of steel with which to write, and what can a single pen do? and then in the evening one is weary and exhausted with the day of seeing and admiring. Here one reads history from within outward."

ITALY, THE MAGIC LAND

Chateaubriand, who in his earliest youth had visited America as the guest of Washington, passed the winter of 1803–4 in Rome, and his pictorial transcriptions of the city and its environs are among the most exquisite things in literary record. As, for instance, this description of a sunset from Monte Mario: —

"I was never weary of seeing, from the Villa Borghese, the sun go down behind the cypresses of Monte Mario, and the pines of the Villa Pamphili planted by Le Notre. I have stood upon the Ponte Molle to enjoy the sublime spectacle of the close of day. The summits of the Sabine hills appeared of lapis lazuli and pale gold, while their bases and sides were bathed in vapors of violet or purple. Sometimes lovely clouds, like fairy cars, borne along by the evening wind with inimitable grace, recall the mythological tales of the descent of the deities of Olympus. Sometimes old Rome seems to have spread all over the west the purple of her consuls and her Cæsars, beneath the last steps of the god of day. This rich decoration does not vanish so quickly as in our climate. When we think the hues are about to disappear they revive on some other point of the horizon; one twilight follows another and the magic of sunset is prolonged."

It was in the same year that Mme. de Staël visited Rome and recorded, in her glowing romance, "Corinne," the impressions she received. In the spring of 1817 Lord Byron found in Rome the inspiration that he transmitted into that wonderful line in "Childe Harold": —

"The Niobe of Nations! There she stands."

It was two years later that Shelley passed the spring in the Seven-hilled City, retiring to Leghorn later, to write his tragedy of "The Cenci."

In Rome the visitor follows Michael Angelo and Raphael through the various churches and museums. The celebrated sibyls of Raphael are in the Santa Maria della Pace; his "Isaiah" is in San Agostino and his "Entombment" in the Casino of the Villa Borghese. While the sublime work of Michael Angelo in the Sistine Chapel is always one of the first things in Rome to which the traveller goes to study that incomparable work portraying the Creation — the Prophets and the Sibyls, the Angels and the Genii, that record the impassioned power of the master — yet all footsteps turn quickly, too, to the church called San Pietro in Vincoli, near the house in which Lucrezia Borgia lived, in which is the colossal Moses of Michael Angelo. As it stands, it fails to convey the first design of the great sculptor. Originally intended for the tomb of Pope Julius II, the plan included a massive block of marble (some forty by twenty feet) surmounted by a cornice and having its niches, its columns, and its statues, of which the Moses was to have been one. It would then have been judged relatively to the entire group, while now it is seen alone, and thus out of the proportions that were in the mind of the artist. The entire conception, indeed, was to unite sculpture and architecture into one splendid combination. "Thus the statue of Moses was meant to have been raised considerably above the eye of the spectator," writes Mr. Hillard, "and to have been a single object in a colossal structure of architecture and sculpture, which would have had a foreground and a background, and been crowned with a mass at once dome-like and pyramidal. Torn, as it is, from its proper place; divorced from its proportionate companionship; stuck against the wall of a church; and brought face to face with the observer, — what wonder that so many of those who see it turn away with no other impressions than those of caricature and exaggeration!"

Mr. Hillard adds: —

"But who that can appreciate the sublime in art will fail to bow down before it as embodied in this wonderful statue? The majestic character of the head, the prodigious muscles of the chest and arms, and the beard that flows like a torrent to the waist, represent a being of more than mortal port and power, speaking with the authority, and frowning with the sanctions of incarnate law. The drapery of the lower part of the figure is inferior to the anatomy of the upper part. Remarkable as the execution of the statue is, the expression is yet more so; for notwithstanding its colossal proportions, its prominent characteristic is the embodiment of intellectual power. It is the

DETAIL FROM STUART MONUMENT, ST. PETER'S, ROME
Antonio Canova
Page 33

great leader and lawgiver of his people that we see, whose voice was command, and whose outstretched arm sustained a nation's infant steps. He looks as if he might control the energies of nature as well as shape the mould in which the character of his people should be formed. That any one should stand before this statue in a scoffing mood is to me perfectly inexplicable. My own emotions were more nearly akin to absolute bodily fear. At an irreverent word, I should have expected the brow to contract into a darker frown, and the marble lips to unclose in rebuke."

William Watson condenses his impressions of this majestic sculpture in the following quatrain. —

> "The captain's might, and mystery of the seer —
> Remoteness of Jehovah's colloquist,
> Nearness of man's heaven-advocate — are here:
> Alone Mount Nebo's harsh foreshadow is miss'd."

The impressive group of sculptures and buildings on the Campidoglio — where once the shrine of Jupiter Capitolinus stood — owes its present picturesque scheme largely to Michael Angelo. The fascination of the long flights of

steps leading from the Piazza Aracöeli to the
Capitoline, where the ancient bronze equestrian
statue of Marcus Aurelius forever keeps guard,
is indescribable. The historic statues of Castor
and Pollux mark the portals; on either hand
there are seen the Muses of ancient sculpture,
the Palazzo Sentoriale and the Palazzo dci
Conservatore. There is in the entire world
no more classic ground than is found in this
impressive grouping of art and architecture.

The genius of Raphael has recorded itself in
those brilliant and imperishable works that en-
thrall the student of art in the Raphael *stanze* in
the Vatican. He was imbued with the spirit
of Greek art, and while Titian is a greater colorist, while Correggio, Botticelli, Perugino, and
other artists that could be named equal or exceed Raphael in certain lines, yet as the interpreter of the profoundest thought, and for his
philosophic grasp and his power to endow his
conceptions with the most brilliant animation,
he stands alone. The religious exaltation of
"The Transfiguration" reveals the supreme degree of the divine genius of Raphael. That
this painting was the last work of his life, that
it was placed above his body as it lay in state,

and was carried in his funeral procession, invests it with peculiar interest.

As a draftsman Raphael was second only to Michael Angelo, with whom he must forever share the immortality of fame. The Academy in Venice holds some of his choicest drawings, and in the Venetian sketch-book in the National Gallery in London are many of his small pictures, including that of the "Knight's Dream."

It was in the autumn of 1508, when Raphael was in his twenty-fifth year, that he was called to Rome in the service of the Pope. The Pontiff at this time was Pope Julius II, whose successor was Leo X, and under their pontificates (from 1508 to 1520) Raphael produced these masterpieces which stand unrivalled in the world save by the creations of Michael Angelo in the Capella Sistina. The celebrated "Four Sibyls" of Raphael are not, however, in the stanze of the Vatican, but in the Church of San Maria della Pace. In the Palazzo Vaticano these four wonderful stanze entrance the visitor; the Stanza della Signatura, the Stanza d' Eliodoro, the Stanza della Incendio and the Sala di Constantino.

ITALY, THE MAGIC LAND

For the decoration of these stanze several painters from Umbria had been summoned,— Perugino, Sodoma, Signorelli, and others; but when Raphael had produced the "Disputa" in the Sala della Signatura, Pope Julius II recognized the work as so transcendent that he ordered the other artists to cease and even had some of their paintings obliterated that there might be more space for the exercise of Raphael's genius. In the "Disputa" are glorified the highest expressions of the human intellect — the domain portrayed being that of Theology, Philosophy, Poetry, and Justice. The splendor of this creation transcends all attempts of interpretation in language. Against a background of gold mosaic are portrayed these typical figures enthroned on clouds where genii flit to and fro bearing tablets with inscriptions. Theology holds in the left hand a book, while the other points to the vision of angels; Poetry, laurel-crowned, is seen seated on a throne with books and lyre; Philosophy wears a diadem, and Justice, with her balance and her sword, is also crowned. The title of this marvellous work is misleading. Its message is not that of disputation but of beatitude.

ITALY, THE MAGIC LAND

At the altar are grouped the congregation; the mystic spell of heavenly enthusiasm enfolds the scene as an atmosphere, as above the heavens open and the glorified Christ, surrounded by the saints who have kept the faith, is disclosed to the devotees kneeling below, while a choir of listening angels bend over them from the distant clouds in the background.

Under Poetry are grouped Apollo and the Muses, and the figures of Homer, Dante and Virgil, of Petrarcha, Anacreon and Sappho, of Pindar and of Horace are recognized. The great scholars seen in the Philosophy include Plato and Aristotle, while in the groups under Justice, Moses and Solon are seen.

"Raphael seems to have never known despair," remarked Franklin Simmons of the work of this divine genius. "His paintings reveal no struggle, but seem to have been produced without effort, as if brought into existence by an enchanter's wand."

No observation could more vividly interpret the wonderful effect produced on the student by Raphael, and he cannot but recall the truth expressed in these lines of Festus:—

ITALY, THE MAGIC LAND

"All aspiration is a toil;
But inspiration cometh from above
And is no labor."

The inspiration of Raphael was of the noblest order. His genius, his kindling enthusiasm, his ecstasy of religious devotion, have left an imperishable heritage to art. By his transcendent gifts he represents the highest manifestation of the art of painting in the Renaissance. For the true note in art lies in spiritual perception. Not so brilliant a colorist as Titian, he was more the interpreter of the extension of human activity into that realm of the life more abundant, and with his extraordinary facility of execution he united exquisite refinement and unerring sense of beauty and the masterly power in composition that fairly created for the spectator the visions that his soul beheld. "I say to you," said Mr. Bryce recently in a press interview, — "I say to you, each oncoming tide of life requires and needs men of lofty thought who shall dream for it, sing for it, who shall gather up its tendencies, formulate its ideals and voice its spirit." One of those men of lofty thought who thus dream for the ages was Raphael, and his power and glory have left an ineffaceable impress upon human life. He was the divinely appointed messenger of beauty, and he was never disobedient to the heavenly vision.

> "Time hath no tide but must abide
> The servant of Thy will;
> Tide hath no time, for to Thy rhyme
> The ranging stars stand still."

The decline of art after Michael Angelo and Raphael was marked. The very splendor and power of their creations, instead of inspiring those who immediately followed them, produced almost the inertia of despair. In the reverence and awe and admiration with which these transcendent masterpieces were approached any power to originate seemed futile by contrast. Imitation rather than creation became the method adopted, resulting in an increased poverty of design and feeble execution. The art of the sixteenth century deteriorated rapidly till the baroco style was in evidence. One reason, too, for the decline was in that art was no longer so exclusively dedicated to the high service of religion, but aimed, instead, to please and to procure patrons, and thus were all worthy standards lowered to pernicious levels.

A sculptor who left his impress upon the sixteenth-century art was Lorenzo Bernini, a Neapolitan (born in 1598) who died in Rome in 1685. The work of Bernini has a certain fascination and airy touch that, while it sometimes degenerates into the merely fantastic and even into tawdry and puerile affectations, has at its best a refinement and grace that lend to his sculptures an enduring charm, as seen in his "Apollo and Daphne" (a work executed in his eighteenth year) which is now in the Casino of the Villa Borghese. Bernini's name is perpetuated in the colossal statues on the colonnade of St. Peter's, the great bronze angels with their draperies streaming to the winds on the Pont San Angelo, and in the vast fountain in the Piazza Navona. In the court of the Palazzo Bernini is one of the most interesting of his works — a colossal figure, allegorical in significance, illustrating "Truth Brought to Light by Time." One of the most important works of Bernini — now placed in the Music Nazionale — is the group of "Pluto and Proserpine."

TOMB OF CLEMENT XIII, ST. PETER'S, ROME
Antonio Canova
Page 42

ITALY, THE MAGIC LAND

The influence that was to reform and regenerate the art of sculpture in the sixteenth century came with the great and good Canova, with which was united that of Flaxman and of Thorwaldsen. The heavenly messengers are always sent and appear at the time they are most needed. Neither Truth nor Art is ever left without a witness.

> "God sends his teachers unto every age,
> To every clime, and every race of men,
> With revelations fitted to their growth
> And shape of mind; nor gives the realm of truth
> Into the selfish rule of one sole race."

Canova's genius and services were widely recognized. In 1719 he was made a Senator; he was ennobled with the title of Marchese of Ischia and granted a yearly allowance of three thousand scudi; and his noble and generous enthusiasms, not less than his genius, have left their record on life as well as on art. When he died (in Venice, Oct. 3, 1822) his work included fifty-nine statues, fourteen groups, twenty-two monuments, and fifty-four busts. The statue of Pius V and the tomb of Clement XIII are his greatest works, and the latter is perhaps even increasingly held as a master-piece of the ages.

Canova, warned by the fatal influence of imitation in art in the sixteenth century, frequently counselled his pupils against copying his own style and constantly urged them to study from the Greeks. He advised them to visit frequently the studios of other artists, "and especially," he would add, "the studios of Thorwaldsen, who is a very great artist."

In the early part of the nineteenth century contemporary sculpture in Rome was led by the three great artists, — Canova, Thorwaldsen, and Gibson. In 1829 Gibson had the honor of being elected a member of the Accadémia di San Luca in place of the sculptor Massimiliano, who had then just died. Cammuccini, the historical painter, proposed Gibson, and with the ardent assistance of Thorwaldsen he was elected resident Academician of merit. "Like Canova, Thorwaldsen was most generous to young artists," says Gibson of the great Danish master, "and he freely visited all who required his advice. I profited greatly by the knowledge which this splendid sculptor had of his art. On every occasion when I was modelling a new work he came to me, and corrected whatever he thought amiss. I also often went to his studio and contemplated his glorious works, always in the noblest style, full of pure and severe simplicity. His studio was a safe school for the young, and was the resort of artists and lovers of art from all nations. The old man's person can never be forgotten by those who saw him. Tall and strong, — he never lost a tooth in his life, — he was most venerable looking. His kind countenance was marked with hard thinking, his eyes were gray, and his white locks lay upon his broad shoulders. At great assemblies his breast was covered with orders."

Thorwaldsen (born in Copenhagen, Nov. 19, 1770) went to Rome in 1797 — sent by the government of Denmark as a pensioner. It is said that, in his enthusiasm for Rome, Thorwaldsen dated his birth from the hour he entered the Eternal City. "Before that day," he exclaimed, "I existed; I did not live." For nearly fifty years — until his death in 1844 — he lived and worked in Rome, occupying at one time the studio in Via Babuino that had formerly been that of Flaxman.

ITALY, THE MAGIC LAND

John Gibson, who went to Rome in 1817, — twenty years after Thorwaldsen first arrived, — had the good fortune to be for five years a pupil of Canova, whose death in 1822 terminated this inestimable privilege. The elevation of purpose that characterized the young English student made his progress and development a matter of peculiar interest to the master. Gibson, also, bears his testimony to the stimulus of the Roman environment. "Rome above all other cities," he says, "has a peculiar influence upon and charm for the real student; he feels himself in the very university of art, where it is the one thing talked about and thought about. Constantly did I feel the presence of this influence. Every morning I rose with the sun, my soul gladdened by a new day of a happy and delightful pursuit; and as I walked to my breakfast at the Caffè Greco and watched with new pleasure the tops of the churches and palaces gilt by the morning sun, I was inspired with a sense of daily renovated youth, and fresh enthusiasm, and returned joyfully to the combat, to the invigorating strife with the difficulties of art. Nor did the worm of envy creep round

my heart whenever I saw a beautiful idea skilfully executed by any of my young rivals, but
constantly spurred on by the talent around me
I returned to my studio with fresh resolution."
Again to a friend Gibson writes: —

"I renewed my visits to the Vatican, refresh-
ing my spirits in that Pantheon of the gods,
demigods, and heroes of Hellas. . . . In the
art of sculpture the Greeks were gods. . . .
In the Vatican we go from statue to statue,
from fragment to fragment, like the bee from
flower to flower."

These five years in which Canova, Thorwaldsen, and Gibson lived and wrought together —
although the youngest of this trio was still in
his student life — form a definite period in
the history of modern art in Rome. The
dreams, the enthusiasm, the devotion to ideal
beauty which characterized their work left its
impress and its vitality of influence — a mystic
power ready to incarnate itself again through
the facility of expression of the artists yet to
come. To the young men whose steps were
turned toward Rome in these early years of

the century just passed, how great was the privilege of coming into close range of the influence of such artists as these; to study their methods; to hear the expression of their views on art in familiar meeting and conversation! These artists were closely in touch with that "lovely and faithful dream which came with Italian Renaissance in the works of Pisani, Mino di Fiesole, Donatello, Michael Angelo, and Giovanni da Bologna — all who caught the spirit of Greek art." Artistic truth was the keynote of the hour, and it is this truth which is the basis of the highest conception of life.

> "Art's a service, — mark:
> A silver key is given to thy clasp
> And thou shalt stand unwearied night and day,
> And fix it in the hard, slow-turning wards
> To open, so that intermediate door
> Betwixt the different planes of sensuous form
> And form insensuous, that inferior men
> May learn to feel on still through these to those,
> And bless thy ministration. The world waits for help."

In their true relation art and ethics meet in their ministry to humanity, for only in their union can they best serve man. All the nobler

culture has its responsibility in service. "Many
a man has a blind notion of stewardship about
his property, but very few have it about their
knowledge," said Bishop Phillips Brooks, and
he added: "One grows tired of seeing culti-
vated people with all their culture cursed by
selfishness." To the true idealist — as distinct
from the mere emotionalist with æsthetic tastes
— selfishness is an impossible prison. The only
spiritual freedom lies in the perpetual sharing
of the fuller life. The gift shared is the gift
doubled. Art is the spiritual glory of life; the
supreme manifestation, the very influence of
spiritual achievement. Mr. Stillman, discussing the revival of art, has questioned: "Does
the world want art any longer? Has it,
in the present state of human progress, any
place which will justify devotion to it?"

He questions as to whether man is still

"Apparelled in celestial light,"

or whether he has lost "the glory and the freshness" of his dreams.

"No one can admit," continues Mr. Stillman, "that the human intellect is weaker than

it was five or twenty centuries ago; but it is certain that if we take the pains to study what was done five centuries ago in painting, or twenty centuries ago in sculpture, and compare it with the best work of to-day, we shall find the latter trivial and 'prentice work compared with the ordinary work of men whose names are lost in the lustre of a school.

"Then, little men inspired by the Zeitgeist, painted greatly; now, our great men fail to reach the technical achievement of the little men of them. There is only one living painter who can treat a portrait as a Venetian artist of 1550 A.D. would have done it, and how differently in the mastery of his material! If we go to the work of wider range, the Campo Santo of Pisa, the Stanze, the Sistine Chapel, the distance becomes an abyss; the simplest fragment of a Greek statue of 450 B.C. shows us that the best sculpture of this century, even the French, is only a happy child-work, not even to be put in sight of Donatello or Michael Angelo. The reason is simple, and already indicated. The early men grew up in a system in which the power of expression was taught from childhood; they acquired method as the musician does now, and the tendency of the opinion of their time was to keep them in the good method."

Is this not too narrow and sweeping a judgment? The art of portraiture certainly did not die with the Venetian painters of 1550, however great their work; and if there be but "one living painter" who can treat portrait art like the early Venetians, there are scores of artists who achieve signal success by other methods of treatment.

At all events, these three men, Canova, Thorwaldsen, and Gibson, worked with the conviction that art is service. With Victor Hugo, Canova could have said: "Genius is not made for genius; it is made for men. . . . Let him have wings for the infinite provided he has feet for the earth, and that, after having been seen flying, he is seen walking. After he has been seen an archangel, let him be still more a brother. . . . To be the servant of God in the march of progress — such is the law which regulates the growth of genius."

They worked and taught by this creed. Thorwaldsen, on first arriving in Rome, wandered for three years, it is said, among the statues of gods and heroes, like a man in a dream. The atmosphere of the earlier day when Titian was employed by the king of Portugal and Raphael by the Pope to create works of great public importance still lingered and exerted over Thorwaldsen, and over all artists susceptible to its subtle influence, a peculiar spell. Its power was revealed in his subsequent works — the "Christ;" the sculptured groups for tombs in St. Peter's and in other churches; the poetic reliefs symbolizing "Day" and "Night;" "Ganymede Watering the Eagle;" the "Three Graces," "Hebe," and many others.

Among Canova's works his immortal masterpiece is the monumental memorial group for the tomb of Pope Clement XIII in St. Peter's. The Pope is represented as kneeling in prayer. The modelling of the entire figure is instinct with expression. The fine and beautiful hands express reverence and trust. The countenance is pervaded with that peace only known to the soul that is in complete harmony with the divine power. The Holy Father has taken the tiara from his head and it lies before him on

"THE GENIUS OF DEATH," DETAIL FROM TOMB OF CLEMENT XIII,
ST. PETER'S, ROME
Antonio Canova
Page 43

the cushion on which he kneels. Although the entire portrayal of the figure reveals that devotion expressed in the solemn and searching words of the church service, "And here we offer and present unto thee, O Lord, ourselves, our souls and bodies to be a reasonable, holy, and living sacrifice unto thee," — although it is the very utmost rendering of the soul to God, it is yet the deliberate, the joyful, the living acceptance of divine love and no mere trance of ecstasy. No more wonderful figure in all the range of sculpture has been created than the Clement XIII of Canova.

The group is completed by two symbolic figures representing Religion and Death. The former is personified as a female figure holding a cross; the latter sits with his torch reversed. Grief, but not hopeless and despairing sorrow, is portrayed; it is the grief companioned by faith which ever sees

"The stars shine through the cypress trees."

The base of the monument represents a chapel guarded by lions. Pistolesi, the great Italian authority on the sculpture of St. Peter's and the Vatican galleries, notes that the lions typify the firmness and the force and the courage, "*la fortezza dell' anima*," that so signally characterized Clement XIII. There is probably no sacred monument in the realm of all modern art which can equal this creation in its delicacy, its lofty beauty, and the noble message that it conveys.

The oldest art school, the Accadémia di San Luca, founded in 1507 by Sixtus, when he called to Rome all the leading artists of Europe to assist in the decoration of the Sistine Chapel, is an organization that magically links the present with the days of Canova, Thorwaldsen, and Gibson, as it linked them, also, with the remote and historic past. The father of the present custodian of the Academy knew Thorwaldsen well. The grandfather of the gifted Italian sculptor, Tadolini (who has recently completed the tomb for Pope Leo XIII, placed in the Basilica of San Giovanni Laterano), modelled the bust of Thorwaldsen, and in one gallery hangs the great Danish sculptor's portrait, painted by himself. The first director of San Luca was Federigo Zuccaro. In the early years of the nineteenth century this Academy was a vital centre of art life, and it is still a school that draws students, although the visitor who does not loiter and linger in his Rome may fail to know of this most alluring place. The San Luca is in the Via Bonella, one of the old, dark, narrow, and gloomy streets of the oldest part of Rome, — a short street of hardly more than two blocks, running between the Via Alessandra and the Forum. Hawthorne vividly pictures all this old Rome when he speaks of the "narrow, crooked, intricate streets, so uncomfortably paved with little squares of lava that to tread over them is a penitential pilgrimage; so indescribably ugly, moreover; so cold, so alley-like, into which the sun never falls and where a chill wind forces its deadly breath into our lungs; the immense seven-storied, yellow-washed hovels, or call them palaces, where all that is dreary in domestic life seems magnified and multiplied; those staircases which ascend from a ground floor of cook shops and cobblers' stalls, stables and regiments of cavalry, to a middle region of princes, cardinals, and ambassadors, and an upper tier of artists just beneath the unattainable sky: . . . in which the visitor becomes

sick at heart of Italian trickery, which has up-
rooted whatever faith in man's integrity had
till then endured;" the city "crushed down in
spirit by the desolation of her ruin and the
hopelessness of her future;" one recalls these
words when passing through the unspeakable
gloom and horror and desolation and squalor
of ancient Rome. In these surroundings one's
cab stops at "No. 44," and ringing the bell the
door is open, whether by super-normal agency
or by some invisible terrestrial manipulation
one is unable to determine; but in the semi-
darkness of the narrow hall he discerns before
him a flight of steep stairs, and, as no other
vista opens, he reasons that, by the law of
exclusion, this must be the appointed way.
Along the wall are seen, here and there, some
antique casts from Trajan's Column, and reliefs from Canova and Thorwaldsen. The galleries above hold only a small and a comparatively unimportant collection of pictures. There
are marines from Vernet and Claude Lorraine;
a "Venus Crowned by the Graces" from Rubens;
Giulio Romano's copy of Raphael's "Galatea,"—
the original of which (in the Villa Farnesina)
represents Galatea surrounded by Nymphs,

"LA FORTUNA," ACCADÉMIA DI SAN LUCA, ROME
Guido Reni
Page 47

Cupids, and Tritons, being carried in a shell across the sea. There is a Cupid, and also the "Fortuna" of Guido Reni, — the latter a figure of ineffable grace floating in the air. One of Raphael's early works representing "St. Luke Painting the Madonna" is here. There are several works by Titian, but these have less than would be expected of the glory usually associated with his name; and a Vandyke representing the Virgin and Child, with two angels playing, the one on a lute, the other on the violin.

One salon filled with portraits of artists is especially interesting, and that of Thorwaldsen is so feminine in its costume and the parting of the hair, that it is almost inevitably mistaken for that of a woman. Guido's graceful "Fortuna" is represented as a female figure flying through the air, her long hair streaming in the wind, and the picture recalls to one the Greek legend of Opportunity, as told by Kainos. The legend runs: —

> "'Of what town is thy sculptor?'
> "'Of Lukzon.'
> "'What is his name?'
> "'Lysippos.'

"'And thine?'

"'Opportunity, controller of all things.'

"'But why standest thou on tiptoe?'

"'I am always running.'

"'Why, then, hast thou wings on both feet?'

"'I fly like the wind.'

"'But wherefore bearest thou a razor in thy right hand?'

"'As a sign to men that I am sharper than any steel.'

"'And why wearest thou thy hair long in front?'

"'That I may be seized by him who approaches me.'

"'By Zeus! And thou art bald behind?'

"'Because once I have passed with my winged feet no one may seize me then.'"

From one landing, on the steep narrow staircase of San Luca, opens the Biblioteca Sarti, an art library of some fifteen thousand volumes. The sculpture gallery is now closed and can only be entered by special permission. This is the more to be regretted as it contains the principal collections in Rome of the original casts of the works of Thorwaldsen and Canova.

ITALY, THE MAGIC LAND

The latter-day artists who have been setting up their Lares and Penates in Rome at various periods during the early and into the later years of the nineteenth century have found the Eternal City in strong contrast with its twentieth-century aspects, however it may have differed from the Rome of the Popes. The earlier American artists to seek the Seven-hilled City were painters; and Allston, Copley, and Stuart had already distinguished themselves in pictorial art before America had produced any sculptor who could read his title clear to fame. It is to Hiram Powers (born in Vermont in 1805) that America must look as her first sculptor, chronologically considered, closely followed by Thomas Crawford, who was but eight years his junior, and by Horatio Greenough, who was also born in the same year as Powers, and who preceded him in Italy, but whose work has less artistic value. Mr. Greenough has left a colossal (if not an artistic) monument to his gifts in stately shaft marking Bunker Hill which he designed. Problematic in their claim to artistic excellence as are his "Washington" — a seated figure in the grounds of the Capitol in Washington — and his group in relief called

"The Rescue" in the portico of the Capitol, his name lives by his personality as a man of liberal culture and noble character, if not by his actual rank in art. First of the American group in Italy, he was followed by Powers, who sought the ineffable beauty and enchantment of Florence in 1837. Horatio Greenough died in comparatively early life, leaving perhaps the most interesting of his works in a relief (purchased by Professor George Ticknor, the distinguished historian of Spain) "representing in touching beauty and expression a sculptor in an attitude of dejection and discouragement before his work, while a hand from above pours oil into his dying lamp, an allegory illustrative of the struggles of genius and the relief which timely patronage may extend to it."

Mr. Powers passed his entire life in Florence. His work attracted great attention and inspired ardent appreciation. In portrait busts Powers was especially successful; and his "Greek Slave," his "Fisher Boy," "Il Penseroso," and "Proserpine" impressed the art-loving public of the time as marked by strong artistic power and as entitled to permanent rank in sculpture.

ITALY, THE MAGIC LAND

Mr. Crawford died young; but his name lives in the majestic bronze statue of "Beethoven" which is in the beautiful white and gold interior of Symphony Hall, in Boston; and his "Orpheus." and some other works claim high appreciation. Writing of Crawford, Mr. Hillard said:—

"Crawford's career was distinguished by energy, resolution, and self-reliance. While yet a youth, he formed the determination to make himself an artist; and with this view went to Rome — alone, unfriended, and unknown — and there began a life of toil and renunciation; resisting the approaches alike of indolence and despondency. His strength of character and force of will would have earned distinction for powers inferior to his. Nothing was given to self-indulgence; nothing to vague dreams; nothing to unmanly despair. He did not wait for the work that he would have, but labored cheerfully upon that which he could have. Success came gradually, but surely; and his powers as surely proved themselves to be more than equal to the demand made upon them."

ITALY, THE MAGIC LAND

On the death of Mr. Crawford, Thomas William Parsons wrote a memorial poem in which this stanza occurs:—

"O Rome! what memories awake,
   When Crawford's name is said,
 Of days and friends for whose dear sake
 That path of Hades unto me
   Will have no more of dread
 Than his own Orpheus felt, seeking Eurydice!
   O Crawford! husband, father, brother
   Are in that name, that little word!
 Let me no more my sorrow smother;
   Grief stirs me, and I must be stirred."

Thomas Ball, who went in early manhood to Florence, where he remained until when nearly at the age of fourscore he returned to his native land, still continues, at the age of eighty-five, to pursue the art he loves. He has created works, as his equestrian statue of "Washington" in the Public Gardens and his "Lincoln Freeing the Slave" in Park Square, both in Boston; his great Washington Memorial group in Methuen, Massachusetts; his "Christ Blessing Little Children," and many other historic and ideal sculptures, that seem endowed with his beautiful and winning spirit as well as with his rare gifts. Larkin G. Mead chose Florence rather than Rome for his home and work. His noble "River God," placed at the head of the Mississippi near St. Paul, as well as other interesting creations, link his name with that of his native land. Randolph Rogers, a man of genius; Rinehart, Paul Akers, and Thompson all died before the full maturity of their powers; Akers at the early age of thirty-six, leaving, as his bride of a year, the poet, Elizabeth Akers Allen, who, under the *nom de plume* of "Florence Percy," has endeared herself to all lovers of lyric art. In a monograph on Paul Akers, written after his death, the writer says of his studio in Rome:—

"Linked with this studio is Hawthorne's tale of 'The Marble Faun,' as Kenyon's studio was none other than Paul Akers's. Though Hawthorne in his romance saw fit to lay the scene in the rooms once occupied by Canova, it was in the Via del Crecie that he wove the thread of his Italian romance.

"Paul Akers's growing reputation and increase of work ere long made it necessary for him to seek a more commodious studio, and he took rooms once occupied by the famous

Canova. Here he had made under his supervision copies in marble of many of the famous works of the Vatican and the Capitol. The largest collection of these was a commission from Mr. Edward King of Newport, and among them were busts of Ariadne, Demosthenes, and Cicero, and a facsimile of the 'Dying Gladiator' which Mr. King presented to the Redwood Library of Newport.

    .   .   .   .   .

"During his first winter in Rome he was permitted by the authorities to make a cast of a mutilated bust of Cicero which had long lain in the Vatican. A critic writing from Rome in 1857 says of this bust of Cicero: 'Mr. Akers obtained permission to take a cast from it; he then restored the eye, brow, and ears, and modelled a neck and bust for it in accordance with the temperament shown by the nervous and rather thin face. He has succeeded admirably. It is the very head of the Vatican, yet without the scars of envious time, and sits gracefully on human shoulders, instead of being rolled awkwardly back upon a shelf.' This bust is unlike the portrait which so long passed for Cicero's, but has been identified by means of a medal which was struck by the Magnesians in honor of the great orator during his consulate, and is now the authorized portrait of Cicero. The finest of Paul Akers's creations executed during hs stay in Rome are 'St. Elizabeth of Hungary,' which represents the princess at the moment the roses have fallen to the ground; 'Una and the Lion,' an illustration of the line in Spenser's 'Faerie Queene,' —

'Still while she slept he kept both watch and ward;'

the head of Milton and the 'Pearl Diver.' The 'Pearl Diver,' now owned by the city of Portland, represents a youth stretched upon a sea-worn rock and wrapped in eternal sleep. The arms are thrown above the head, and about the waist is a net containing pearl-bearing shells for which he has risked his life. There is no trace of suffering; all is subdued to beauty. It is death represented as the ancients conceived it, the act of the torch-reverting god. This youth, who has lost his life at the moment when all that for which he had dared was within his grasp, suggests Paul Akers's own untimely death on the eve of his triumph."

ITALY, THE MAGIC LAND

It was from his Roman studio that Mr. Akers wrote to a friend: —

"Yesterday Browning called. He looked a long time at my Milton, and said it was Milton, the man-angel. He praised the wealth of hair which I had given the head, and then said that Mrs. Browning had a lock of Milton's hair, the only one now in existence. This was given her by Leigh Hunt, just before his death, who had the records proving it to be genuine. The hair was, he said, like mine. He invited me to visit him in Florence, where he would show me the first edition of Milton's poems, marked to indicate the peculiar accent which the poet sometimes adopted, a knowledge of which makes clear somewhat that otherwise seems discordant. Milton was so great a musician that there could have been no fault in sound in his compositions. He looked over my books; said my edition of Shelley was one which he had corrected for the press, not from a knowledge of the original MS., but from his internal evidence that so it must have been; said Poe was a wonderful man; spoke of Tennyson in the warmest terms. Took up a copy of his own poems published in the United States, and remarked that it was better than the English edition, yet had some awful blunders, and wished me to allow him to correct a copy for me. My head of the 'Drowned Girl' caught his eye and interested him. I told him that I had thought of Hood's 'Bridge of Sighs.' He then said that Hood wrote that on his deathbed, and read it to him before any one else had seen it. Hood was doubtful whether it was worth publishing. To-morrow Mrs. Browning is to come; she has been quite ill since she came to Rome, and I have seen her but once. I derive much comfort from the friendship of Charlotte Cushman. She has just gone from here. She has frequent breakfast parties; I have attended but one. Mr. and Mrs. James T. Fields, Wild, the painter, and myself were the guests. Fields I like much."

The first works of Mr. Akers were two portrait busts, of Longfellow and of Samuel Appleton. Of his bust of Milton, Hawthorne in the "Marble Faun" has said: —

"In another style, there was the grand, calm head of Milton, not copied from any one bust or picture, yet more authentic than any of them, because all known representations of the poet had been profoundly studied and solved in the artist's mind. The bust over the tomb in Greyfriar's Church, the original miniatures and pictures wherever to be found, had mingled each its special truth in this one work — wherein likewise by long perusal and deep love of 'Paradise Lost,' the 'Comus,' the 'Lycidas,' and 'L'Allegro,' the sculptor had succeeded even better than he knew in spiritualizing his marble with the poet's mighty genius. And this was a great thing to have achieved, such a length of time after the dry bones and dust of Milton were like those of any other dead man."

Richard Greenough and the painter, Mr. Haseltine, were prominent figures among the early American group of the nineteenth-century artists in Rome. There came Emma Stebbins, who modelled a fine portrait bust of Charlotte Cushman; and Anne Whitney, whose statues of Samuel Adams and of Leif Ericson adorn public grounds in Boston; whose life-size statue of Harriet Martineau is the possession of Wellesley College; and whose "Chaldean Astronomer,"

"Lotus-Eater," and "Roma" — a figure personifying the Rome of Pio Nono — reveal her power in ideal creation.

The name of Harriet Hosmer stands out in brilliant pre-eminence among those of all women who have followed the plastic art. Her infinite charm of personality seems to impart itself to her work, and she has the gift to make friends as well as to call forms out of clay — the success of friendship being one even more permanently satisfying. In her early life as a girl hardly more than twenty, she sought Rome, living with art as her chaperon. Her versatility, her picturesque individuality, and her imaginative power all combined to win sympathetic recognition. Gibson, whose guidance was particularly well adapted to develop her gifts, received her into his own studio and took a deep interest in her work. It was during the period of her early efforts that Hawthorne was in Rome, and she is graphically depicted in his notebooks in her boyish cap at work in the clay. Gibson was an artist, *con amore*, and Miss Hosmer's joyous abandon to her art captivated his sympathy. "In my art what do I find?" he questioned; "happiness; love which

does not depress me; difficulties which I do
not fear; resolution which never abates; flights
which carry me above the ground; ambition
which tramples no one down." Master and
pupil were akin in their unwearied devotion to
art. Of Gibson, whose absence of mind regarding all the details of life made him almost
helpless in travel and affairs, Miss Hosmer
used gleefully to say that he "was a god in
his studio, but God help him out of it!" This
glancing sprite of a girl, frightening her friends
by her daring and venturous horseback riding;
gravitating by instinct to offer some generous,
tender aid to the sick, the destitute, or the helpless; the life and light of gay dinners and of
social evenings; working from six in the morning till night in her studio, "with an absence of
pretension," says Mrs. Browning, "and simplicity of manners which accord rather with
the childish dimples in her rosy cheeks than
with her broad forehead and high aims," had
the magic gift that merged her visitors and
patrons into enthusiastic friends; and Mrs.
Browning has chronicled the pretty scene when
Lady Marion Alford, the daughter of the Earl
of Northumberland, knelt before the girl artist

and slipped on her finger a ring — a precious
ruby set with diamonds — as a token of her
devotion. Reading Miss Hosmer's life still
further backward, the reader is transported, as
if on some magic carpet, to St. Louis, in the
United States, where a noble and lofty man,
Hon. Wayman Crow, — a generous friend, a
liberal patron of the arts, a man of the most
refined tastes and culture, whose great qualities
were always used in high service, — first aided
Miss Hosmer to the preliminary studies in her
art, and whose accomplished and lovely daughters (now Mrs. Lucien Carr of Boston, Mrs.
Edwin Cushman of Newport and Rome, and
Mrs. Emmons of Leamington, England) were
as a trio of sisters to the young artist. And
"the flowing conditions of life" bear on this
lifelong friendship until a fair young girl,
Élise (the daughter of Mrs. Emmons), catches
up this sweet tie and as an accomplished and
lovely young woman in Roman society, when
these "flowing conditions" had come down even
into the season of 1906–7, Miss Emmons cherished the fame of Harriet Hosmer and enjoyed
the privilege of a constant correspondence with
the distinguished artist. So the past links itself

again with the present; and who can tell where any story in life begins or ends in the constant evolutionary progress?

Miss Hosmer's work attracted wide attention. Her majestic statue of "Zenobia;" the winsome "Puck;" the impressive statue of "Beatrice Cenci," representing her as she lay in her cell in Castel San Angelo the night before her execution, — these and other works of hers are of an interesting character and will hold their permanent rank in sculpture.

Were all the muses present at the christening of William Wetmore Story — sculptor, musician, poet and painter, jurist and man of letters, and the friend whose social relationships made life a thing of beauty —

> "To winds and waterfalls,
> And autumn's sunlit festivals,
> To music and to music's thoughts
> Inextricably bound"?

Mr. Story made his first visit to Italy in 1847; not at that time with any fixed purpose of exchanging his profession of the law for art. He loved literature, and his grace and ease in expression had already manifested his literary talent; he had an inclination toward modelling — it could hardly, at this time, have been called by a stronger name — and curiously enough with him the usual conditions were reversed and he received a commission for a statue of his father, Judge Story, before he had made any definite turning toward the art of sculpture. A young man of versatile gifts and accomplished scholarship, sculpture was to him one among the many attractive forms of art rather than the supreme attraction; and it was the stimulus of the given work that determined him as a sculptor, rather than his determination to be a sculptor that determined the work. Among the goddesses of life Destiny must, perhaps, be allowed a place. At all events, after Mr. Story's initial glance at Italy, he sought Rome again a year later, and this time it was his choice for life, however unrevealed to his eye were the resplendent years that lay before him. He had fallen under the spell of the Magic Land. In a letter to Lowell, Mr. Story had questioned how he should ever endure again "the restraint and bondage of Boston." It was the picturesque Rome of the Popes that he first knew. The years of 1848–49 were those of revolutionary activities in Italy. Pio Nono, one of the most saintly and beloved of the Popes, — whose mortal form now rests in that richly decorated chapel in old San Lorenzo, *fuori le mura*, on the site of the church that Constantine founded on the burial place of St. Lawrence, — made his flight to Gaeta and the Roman republic was established. It was a dramatic scene when Pio Nono returned (April 12, 1850), entering Rome by the Porta San Giovanni. The scene from this gate was then, as now, one of the most impressive in the Eternal City.

It was in this vast Basilica of San Giovanni Laterano that Pio Nono entered that April day, leaving his carriage and walking alone to the altar, where he knelt in devotion. A splendid procession awaited without to accompany the Holy Father to the Papal Palace. The superb state carriages conveyed princes and foreign ambassadors and great nobles. From the Piazza San Giovanni to St. Peter's every house was illuminated, and the populace cheered and waved until the very air vibrated with sound and color. These were the days when the methods of government were a visible spectacle,

a drama, making the life in Rome a daily illuminated missal.

The Storys, on their return to Italy, located
themselves for a time in Florence, where they
met the Brownings, and that lifelong friendship
between the poet and the sculptor was initiated.
In these happy Florentine days Mr. Story
worked in his studio while his wife read to him
the life of Keats, then just issued, written by
Monckton Milnes, later Lord Houghton. But
the "flowing conditions" soon bore them onward to Rome, where they settled themselves
in the Via Porta Pinciana, and met the Craw-
fords, who were domiciled in the Villa Negroni.
In these Roman days, too, appeared Mr. Crop-
sey, of poetic landscape fame, and here, too, was
Margaret Fuller. Mazzini was then a leading
figure in the Chamber of Deputies, — "the
prophet not only of modern Italy, but of the
modern world." He found Italy "utilitarian and
materialistic, permeated by French ideas, and
weakened by her reliance on French initiative.
He was filled with hope that Italy might not only
achieve her own unity, but might once more
accomplish, as she had in the Rome of the
Cæsars and the Rome of the Church, the unity

of the Western world. 'On my side I believe,' he says, 'that the great problem of the day was a religious problem, to which all other questions were but secondary.'" He was asserting that "we cannot relate ourselves to the Divine, but through collective humanity. It is not by isolated duty (which indeed the conditions of modern life render more and more impossible), nor by contemplation of mere Power as displayed in the material world, that we can develop our nature. It is rather by mingling with the universal life, and by carrying on the evolution of the never-ending work."

The studios of Mr. Crawford in those days were in the Piazza delle Terme, near the Baths of Diocletian. William Page, the painter, was domiciled on the slope of the Quirinal where he painted a portrait of Charlotte Cushman which Mrs. Browning described as "a miracle"; one of Mrs. Crawford; the head of Mrs. Story, which he insisted upon presenting to her husband; and a magnificent portrait of Browning which the artist presented to Mrs. Browning. "Both of us," wrote Robert Browning of this gift, "would have fain escaped being the subjects of such princely generosity; but there was no

withstanding his delicacy and noble-minded-
ness." Mrs. Jameson was much in Rome in
the early years of the 1850-60 decade, living
in the old port by the Tiber nearly opposite
to the new and splendid building of the law
courts. Near the Tarpeian Rock Frederika
Bremer had perched, in a tiny room of which
she took all the frugal care, even to washing
the blue cups and plates when she invited
the Hawthornes to a tea of a simplicity that
suggested, indeed, the utmost degree of "light"
housekeeping. Thomas Buchanan Read was
one of the hosts and guests of this social
group, and it was at a dinner he gave that
Hawthorne met Gibson, whose conversational
talents were evidently (upon that occasion)
chiefly employed in contemning the pre-Raphaelite school of painters and emphasizing the need
of sculptors to discover and to follow the prin-
ciples of the Greeks, — "a fair doctrine, but
one which Mr. Gibson fails to practise,"
observes Hawthorne. The Brownings were
variously bestowed in Rome through succeeding winters, — in the Bocca di Leone, in the
Via del Tritone and elsewhere. Mrs. Browning,
as her "Casa Guida Windows" and many other

poems attest, took always the deepest interest in Italian politics. American and English friends come and go, but the little group of residents and the more permanent sojourners, as the Hawthornes and the Brownings, continue their daily variations on life in the social dinners and teas, the excursions and the sightseeing of the wonderful city.

Only the magician could "call up the vanished past again" and summon into an undeniable materialization those charming figures to come forth out of the shadowy air of the rich, historic past, and stand before us in the full light of contemporary attention. Not alone this group of choice persons, but the environment of their time, the very atmosphere, are demanded of this necromancy. The figure of Adelaide Kemble (Mrs. Sartoris) is one of these, and the tradition still survives of a concert given in the splendid, spacious hall of the Palazzo Colonna where she was the prima donna of the occasion. There were also musicals at the house of Mrs. Sartoris, where the guests met her famous sister, Fanny Kemble. Mrs. Browning was fond of both the sisters, and said of them that their social brilliancy was their least distinction. She found them both "noble and sympathetic," and her "dear Mr. Page" and "Hatty" (Miss Hosmer) "an immense favorite with us both," she said of her husband and herself; these and the Storys made up the special circle for the Brownings in Rome. "The Sartoris house has the best society in Rome," writes Mrs. Browning to Miss Mitford, "and exquisite music, of course. We met Lockhart there and my husband sees a good deal of him. . . . A little society," she says, "is good for soul and body, and on the Continent it is easy to get a handful of society without paying too dear for it. This is an advantage of Continental life."

Mrs. Browning greatly admired the work of Mr. Page, whose portraits she found "like Titian's." But the tinted statues of Gibson seemed to her inartistic. His famous painted Venus she called "pretty," but only as a wax doll might be, not as a work of genuine art. Then Thackeray and his two daughters came; Miss Anne (now known to the world of literature as Anne Thackeray Ritchie) was a special favorite with Mrs. Browning.

Coming to Rome at one time from Florence

in midwinter, the Brownings found that the
Storys had taken an apartment for them (in
the Via Bocca di Leone), and they arrived to
find lighted fires and lamps. Their journey
had included a week's visit at Assisi, studying
the rich art of Cimabue and Giotto in the
church of the great Franciscan monastery.
Mrs. Browning visited studios in Rome and
found that of Mr. Crawford more interesting
to her than Mr. Gibson's, but no artist is "as
near" to her, as she herself says, as Mr. Page.
The Storys left the Porta Pinciana to live at
No. 93 in the Piazza di Spagna, and in the
same house with the Brownings, in the Bocca
di Leone, Mr. Page had his apartment. To
Lowell, Mr. Story wrote of the Brownings:—

"The Brownings and we became great
friends in Florence, and, of course, we could
not become friends without liking each other.
He, Emelyn says, is like you. He is of my
size, but slighter, with straight black hair,
small eyes, a smooth face, and manner nervous and rapid. He has great vivacity, but
not the least humor; some sarcasm, considerable critical faculty, and very great frankness

and friendliness of manner and mind. Mrs.
Browning will sit buried up in a large easy-
chair listening and talking very quietly and
pleasantly. Very unaffected is she. . . . I
have hundreds of statues in my head, but they
are in the future tense. Powers I knew very
well in Florence. He is a man of great mechanical talent and natural strength of perception, but with no poetry in his composition,
and I think no creative power. . . . I have
been to hear Allegri's 'Miserere' in the Sistine
Chapel, with the awful and mighty figures of
Michael Angelo looking down from the ceiling; to
hear Guglielmi's 'Miserere' in St. Peter's, while
the gloom of evening was gathering in the lofty
aisles and shrouding the frescoed domes, was
a deeply affecting and solemnly beautiful experience. Never can one forget the plaintive
wailing of the voices that seemed to implore
pity and pardon."

It was in 1856 that the Storys located
themselves in Palazzo Barberini, which Bernini
designed and which was built "out of the
quarry of the Coliseum" by Urban VIII. It
is one of the wonderful old palaces of Rome, —

this mass of Barberini courts, gardens, terraces, and vast apartments, with the interminable winding stairs, where on one landing Thorwaldsen's lion lies before the great doors decorated with the arms of Popes and princes. Here the old Cardinal Barberini lived his stormy life; here are the gallery and the library, — the latter stored with infinite treasures of ancient documents, old maps whose portrayal of the earth bears little resemblance to the present, and famous manuscripts and volumes in old vellum, some fifty thousand in all. In the Barberini gallery are a few noted works, — Raphael's "Fornarina," Guido's "Beatrice Cenci," a "Holy Family" by Andrea del Sarto, and others.

The Via delle Quatre Fontane, on which the Palazzo Barberini stands, might well be known as the street of the wonderful vista. One strolls down it to the Via Sistina and to Piazza Trinità de' Monti at the head of the Spanish steps (the Scala di Spagna), pausing for the loveliness of the view. Across the city rises the opposite height of Monte Mario, and to the left the Janiculum, now crowned with the magnificent equestrian statue of Garibaldi, which is in evidence from almost every part of Rome.

SPANISH STEPS, PIAZZA TRINITÀ DEI MONTI, ROME

Page 72

ITALY, THE MAGIC LAND

As far as the eye can see the Campagna stretches
away, infinite as the sea — a very Campagna
Mystica. The luminous air, the faint, misty
blue of the distance, the deep purple shadows
on the hills, make up a landscape of color. At
the foot of the Spanish steps the flower venders
spread out their wares, — great bunches of the
flame-colored roses peculiar to Italy, the fragrant white hyacinths, golden jonquils, baskets
of violets, and masses of lilies of the valley.

On many a night of brilliant moonlit glory
the artistic sojourners in Rome lingered on the
parapet of the Pincian Hill watching the moonlight flood the Eternal City until churches and
palaces seemed to swim in a sea of silver. Or
in the morning, when the rose-red of dawn
was aglow, there seemed to hover over the
city that wraith of mist whose secret Claude
Lorraine surprises in his landscapes. These
dawn visions of mysterious, incredible beauty
are a part of the very identity of Rome.

There were mornings when the Hawthornes
with Mrs. Jameson or some other friend would
drive out to the old San Lorenzo (*fuori le mura*),
the church founded by Constantine in 330 on
the site where the body of St. Lawrence was

buried. At various periods the church was enlarged and finally, as recently as in 1864, Pio Nono had great improvements made under the architect Vespignani. In the piazza in front was placed an immense column of red granite, some sixty feet high, with the statue of St. Lawrence, a standing figure, at the top. It is most impressive. The colonnade at the entrance of the church is decorated with frescoes and contains two immense sarcophagi, whose sides are beautifully sculptured with reliefs. The roof is supported by six Ionic columns. Entering the church one finds an interior of three aisles divided by colossal columns of Oriental granite. In the middle aisle, on both sides the galleries, are fresco paintings illustrating the martyrdom of St. Lawrence and of St. Stephen, one series on the right and the other on the left. One of these paintings, especially, of the life of St. Lawrence, is strangely haunting to the imagination. It represents the youthful, slender figure, nude, save for slight drapery, laid on the gridiron while the fire is being kindled under it and the fagots shovelled in. The physical shrinking of the flesh — of every nerve — from the torture, the spiritual strength

TOMB OF PIO NONO, SAN LORENZO (FUORI LE MURA), ROME

Page 75

and invincible energy of the countenance, are wonderfully depicted. The great aisle was painted by order of Pius IX by Cesare Fracassini; in it are two pulpits of marble. A double staircase of marble conducts to that part of the Basilica of Constantine which by Honorius III was converted into the presbytery. It is decorated at the upper end by twelve columns of violet marble which rise from the level of the primitive basilica beneath. At the end is the ancient pontifical seat, adorned with mosaic and precious marbles. The papal altar is under a canopy in the Byzantine style. The pavement of this presbytery is worthy of particular attention. Descending to the confessional which is under the high altar the tomb of the martyred saints, Lawrence, Stephen, and Justin, is found.

It was the request of Pio Nono that his mortal body should rest here, where it is placed in a simple tomb, according to his own instructions; but the chapel is very rich in decoration which was paid for by money sent from all parts of the world.

The chapel walls are entirely encrusted in mother-of-pearl, gilt bronze, and beautiful marbles. The mosaic paintings are formed of gold and precious stones of fabulous value. This interior is perhaps the richest in the world in its decoration. San Lorenzo is a patriarchal church, and one of the seven pilgrimage churches of Rome. Near San Lorenzo is the Campo Verano, a cemetery containing many beautiful memorial sculptures.

In those days, half a century ago, the entrance most often used by visitors to Rome was through the Via Flaminia and the Porta del Popolo, opening on the Piazza del Popolo, rather the most picturesque and impressive place in all Rome. On the left is the Pincian Hill (Monte Pincio), with its rich terraces, balustrades, its beautiful porticos filled with statuary, its groves of cypress and ilex trees; a classic vision rising on the sight and enchanting the imagination. On the side opposite the Porta three roads diverge in fan shape — the Via Babuino, the Corso, and the Ripetta, with the "twin churches" side by side; one between the Babuino and the Corso, the other between the Corso and the Ripetta.

The Corso (which was the ancient Flaminian Way) runs straight to the Piazza Venezia at the foot of the Capitoline Hill. This Piazza del

Popolo was widened and decorated by Pius VII.
It is formed by two semicircles, adorned with
fountains and statues, and terminated by four
symmetrical edifices. In the semicircles are
colossal groups in marble, and a road opposite
the Pincio leads to the Ponte Margherita and
the Prati di Castello.

The obelisk in the centre of the piazza was
brought to Rome from Heliopolis by Cæsar
Augustus and originally stood in the Circus
Maximus. It was erected here by Pope Sixtus
V, and it is nearly a hundred feet in height.
It is formed of red granite, and while it has
been broken in three places, the hieroglyphics
are still legible. This obelisk was first erected
in Egypt as a part of the Temple of the Sun
at Heliopolis, in a period preceding that of
Rameses II. After the battle of Actium, Augustus transported it to Rome, and it was first
placed in the Circus Maximus, but during the
reign of Valentinian it fell from its pedestal
and lay buried in the earth, until in the sixteenth century Pope Sixtus V had it placed in
the centre of the Piazza del Popolo, and consecrated it to the cross. The two inscriptions
are on opposite sides. One thus reads: —-

"The Emperor Cæsar, son of the divine Cæsar Augustus, Sovereign Pontiff, twelve times Emperor, eleven times Consul, fourteen times Tribune, having conquered Egypt, consecrated this gift to the Sun."

The other inscription is as follows: —

"Sixtus V, Sovereign Pontiff, excavated, transported, and restored this obelisk, sacrilegiously consecrated to the Sun by the great Augustus, in the great Circus, where it lay in ruins, and dedicated it to the cross triumphant in the fourth year of his pontificate."

The Church of Santa Maria del Popolo is built into the very wall of Monte Pincio on the site of Nero's tomb. It dates back to 1099, and consists of three naves and several chapels. In the first chapel is a "Nativity" by Pinturicchio, who also painted the lunettes. Another chapel belongs to the Cibo family, and is rich in marbles and adorned with sixteen columns of Sicilian jasper. The "Conception" is by Maratta, the "Martyrdom of St. Lawrence" by Morandi, and the "St. Catherine" by Volterra. The "Visitation" was sculptured by Bernini in 1679. The third chapel is painted by Pinturicchio (1513), and the fourth has an interesting bas-relief of the fifteenth century. The picture of the Virgin, on the ·high altar, is one of those attributed to St. Luke; the paintings on the vault of the choir are by Pinturicchio. The two marble monuments are, from their perfection of design and execution, reckoned among the best modern works. They are by Cantucci da S. Savino. In the chapel following is an "Assumption" by Annibale Carracci; the side pictures are by Caravaggio. The last chapel but one in the small nave is the Chigi chapel, and is one of the most celebrated in Rome.

Raphael gave the designs for the dome, the paintings of the frieze, and the altar picture. This latter was begun by Del Piombo and finished by Salviati. The statue of Daniel is by Bernini. The front of the altar and the statues of Jonah and Elijah were done by Lorenzetto (1541), from designs by Raphael. Outside this chapel is the monument of Princess Odescalchi Chigi (1771), by Paolo Posi. The stained windows of the choir belong to the fourteenth century, and in the sacristy and the vestibule are monuments also of the fourteenth century and of the fifteenth. Luther resided in the convent attached to this church when he was in Rome.

There is a legend that a large walnut tree grew on the site of Nero's tomb in whose branches innumerable crows had their home, and that they devastated all that part of Rome. An appeal was made to the Virgin, who declared that the crows were demons who kept watch over the ashes of Nero, and ordered the tree to be cut down and burned, the ashes being scattered to the air, and that, on the spot, a church should be built to her honor. This was accomplished, and the crows no more troubled the Eternal City.

The gardens of Lucullus were on the Monte Pincio. The view of the terraced hillside from the Piazza del Popolo is one of the most impressive in Rome.

The Hawthornes left Rome in 1859; and the death of Mrs. Browning in June of 1861 left the little circle of the Roman winters irreparably broken. "Returning to Rome," wrote Story to Charles Eliot Norton, "I have not one single intimate . . . no one with whom I can walk

any of the higher ranges of art and philosophy."
Mr. Story had modelled the busts of both Mr.
and Mrs. Browning during their sojourns in
Rome; in 1853 Harriet Hosmer had made the cast
of the "clasped hands" of the poets, the model
having since been cast in bronze; Mr. Page had,
as already noted, painted a portrait of Robert
Browning; and Mr. Leighton (afterward Sir
Frederick) had made a beautiful portrait sketch
of Mrs. Browning. In later years all these
memorials, with other paintings or plastic
sketches of the wedded poets, were grouped in
Mr. Barrett Browning's palace in Venice.

At this time Mr. Story had completed his
"Cleopatra," which Hawthorne had embalmed
in literary mention in "The Marble Faun;"
and beside his "Judith," "Sappho," and other
lesser works, he had achieved one of his finest
successes in the "Libyan Sibyl." Both the
"Cleopatra" and the "Sibyl" became famous.
Whether they would produce so strong an effect
at the present stage of twentieth-century life is
a problem, but one that need not press for
solution. Mr. Story was singularly fortunate
in certain conditions that grouped themselves
about his life and combined to establish his

fame. These conditions, of course, were largely
the outer reflection of inner qualities, as our
conditions are apt to be; still, the "lack of
favoring gales" not infrequently foredooms some
gallant bark to a disastrous course.

> "Man is his own star. . . .
>
> .   .   .   .   .
>
> Our acts, our angels, are, for good or ill,
> Our fatal shadows that walk by us still,"

it is true; yet has not Edith Thomas embodied
something of that overruling destiny that every
thoughtful observer must discern in life in these
lines? —

> "You may blame the wind or no,
> But it ever hath been so —
> Something bravest of its kind
> Leads a frustrate life and blind,
> For the lack of favoring gales
> Blowing blithe on other sails."

Only occasionally have we

> " . . . the time, and the place,
> And the loved one all together."

Mr. Story's nature was eminently sympathetic
with the other arts; he was himself almost as
much a literary man as he was a sculptor; he

was the friend and companion of literary men, and to the fact that art in the middle years of the nineteenth century was far more a literary topic than a matter of critical scrutiny, Mr. Story owed an incalculable degree of his fame. He was an extremely interesting figure with his social grace, his liberal culture, and his versatile gifts. His life was centred in choice and refined associations. If not dowered with lofty and immortal original genius, he had a singular combination of talent, of fastidious taste, and of the intellectual appreciation that enabled him to select interesting ideal subjects to portray in the plastic art. These appealed to the special interest of his literary friends and were widely discussed in the press and periodicals of the day. It is a *bonmot* of contemporary studio life that Hawthorne rather than Story created the "Cleopatra," and one ingenious spirit suggests that as Mr. Story put nothing of expression or significance into his statues, the beholder could read into them anything he pleased; finding an empty mould, so to speak, into which to pour whatever image or embodiment he might conjure up from the infinite realm of imagination. One of the latest of these contemporary critics declares that "Story declined appreciably, year by year, falling away from his own standard; haunted to the point of obsession by visions of mournful female figures, generally seated, wrapped in gloom. It seems strange," this critic continues, "that so active a mind should dream of nothing but brooding, sinister souls, of bodies bowed in grief, or tense with rage. Never once, apparently, did there come to him a vision of buoyancy and grace; of a beauty that one could love; of good cheer and joy of very living; always these unwholesome creatures born of that belated Byronic romanticism."

This criticism, while it has as little appreciation of Mr. Story's exquisite culture and of the taste and refinement of his art as the general rush of the motor car and telephonic conversational life of the first decade of the twentieth century has of the thoughtful, the poetic, the leisurely atmosphere of Mr. Story's time, is yet not without a keen flashlight of truth. Painting had its reactionary crisis from the pre-Raphaelite ideals and the *intransigeants* have had their own conflicts in which they survived, or disappeared, according to the degree

of artistic vitality within. Sculpture and literature must also meet the series of tests to which
the onward progress of life persists in subject-
ing them, and those who are submerged and
perish can only encourage the survivors as did
the Greeks, as sung by Theocritus: —

> "A shipwrecked sailor, buried on this coast,
>   Bids you set sail.
> Full many a gallant ship, when we were lost,
>   Weathered the gale."

"As we refine, our checks grow finer," said
Emerson. As life becomes more elaborate and
ambitious, the critical tests increase. Contemporary fame can be created for the artist by
favorable contemporary comment; but it rests
with himself, after all; it rests in the abiding
significance of his work — or the lack of it —
as to whether this fame is perpetuated. That
of Mr. Story does not hold within itself all the
qualities that insure the appreciation of the
present day. It is, as the critic of the hour
expresses himself, "too literary," — too largely
a question of classic titles which appealed to
the mid-nineteenth-century authors whose judgment of art the twentieth century finds particu-

larly amusing. Henry James has somewhere
held up to ridicule the early Beacon Hill Boston
for its impassioned devotion to the "atten-
uated outlines" of Flaxman's art. But the
work of Story will survive all transient variations of opinion, even of the present realistic
age; for is not true realism, after all, to be
found in the eternal ideals of truth, grace,
dignity, refinement, significance, and beauty?
These qualities have a message to convey; and
no one can study with sympathetic appreciation any sculpture of William Wetmore Story
without feeling that the work has something to
say; that it is not a mere reproduction of some
form, but is, rather, an idea impersonated, and
therefore it has life, it has significance. The
criticism of the immediate hour is not neces-
sarily infallible because it is contemporary.
What does William Watson say?

> "A deft musician does the breeze become
> Whenever an Æolian harp it finds;
> Hornpipe and hurdy-gurdy both are dumb
> Unto the most musicianly of winds."

It is an irretrievable loss if, in the passion
for the *vita nuova*, a generation, or a century,

shall substitute for the Æolian harp the mere
hornpipe and hurdy-gurdy of the hour. In
another of his keenly critical quatrains William
Watson embodies this signal truth:—

"His rhymes the poet flings at all men's feet,
  And whoso will may trample on his rhymes.
Should Time let die a song that's pure and sweet,
  The singer's loss were more than matched by Time's."

Art is progressive, and the present is always
the "heir of all the ages" preceding; but it
cannot be affirmed that it invariably makes the
best use of its rich inheritance.

There are latter-day sculptors who excel in
certain excellences that Story lacked; still, it
would not be his loss, but our own, if we fail
in a due recognition of that in his art which
may appeal to the imagination; for, whatever
the enthusiasms of other cults may be, there are
qualities of beauty, strength, and profound significance in the art of Story that must insure
their permanent recognition. Still, it remains
true that Mr. Story owes his fame in an incalculable degree to the friendly pens of Hawthorne and others of his immediate circle, —
Lowell, Motley, Charles Eliot Norton, Thack-

eray, Browning, — friends who, according to
the latest standards of art criticism, were not
unqualified nor absolute judges of art, but
who were in sympathy with ideal expression
and recognized this as embodied in the statues
of Story.

Browning wrote to the London *Times* an
article on Mr. Story's work, in which he con-
jured up most of the superlative phrases of
commendation that the limits of the English
language allow to praise his work, none of
whose marshalled force was too poor to do him
reverence. The versatile gifts of Story's personality drew around him friends whose influence was potent and, indeed, authoritative in
their time.

Still, any analysis of these conditions brings
the searcher back to the primary truth that
without the gifts and grace to attract about him
an eminent circle of choice spirits he could not
have enjoyed this potent aid and inspiration;
and thus, that

"Man is his own star,"

is an assertion that life, as well as poetry, justi-
fies. In the full blaze of this fundamental

truth, it is, not unfrequently, the mysterious spiritual tragedy of life that many an one as fine of fibre and with lofty ideals

> "Leads a frustrate life and blind,
> For the lack of favoring gales
> Blowing blithe on other sails."

Mr. Story was himself of too fine an order not to divine this truth. With what unrivalled power and pathos has he expressed it in his poem — one far too little known — the "Io Victis": —

"I sing the song of the Conquered, who fell in the Battle of
  Life, —
The hymn of the wounded, the beaten, who died overwhelmed
  in the strife;
Not the jubilant song of the victors, for whom the resounding
  acclaim
Of nations was lifted in chorus, whose brows wore the chaplet
  of fame,
But the hymn of the low and the humble, the weary, the
  broken in heart,

  . . . .

Whose youth bore no flower on its branches, whose hopes
  burned in ashes away,
From whose hands slipped the prize they had grasped at, who
  stood at the dying of day
With the wreck of their life all around them. . . ."

ITALY, THE MAGIC LAND

In this poem Mr. Story touched the highest note of his life,— as poet, sculptor, painter, or writer of prose; in no other form of expression has he equalled the sublimity of sentiment in these lines:—

"... I stand on the field of defeat,
In the shadow, with those who are fallen, and wounded, and dying, and there

.   .   .   .

Hold the hand that is helpless, and whisper, 'They only the victory win
Who have fought the good fight, and have vanquished the demon that tempts us within;
Who have held to their faith unseduced by the prize that the world holds on high;
Who have dared for a high cause to suffer, resist, fight, — if need be, to die.'"

Such a poem must have its own immortality in lyric literature.

For a period of forty years the home of the Storys in Palazzo Barberini was a noted centre of the most charming social life. Mr. Story's literary work — in his contributions of essays and poems to the *Atlantic Monthly;* in his published works, the "Roba di Roma," "Conversations in a Studio," his collected "Poems," and others — gave him a not transitory rank in literature which rivals, if it does not exceed, his rank in art.

Meantime other artists were to take up their permanent abode in the Seven-hilled City, — Elihu Vedder in 1866; Franklin Simmons two years later; Waldo and Julian Story, the two sons of William Wetmore Story, though claiming Rome as their home, are American by parentage and ancestry; and Mr. Waldo Story succeeds his father in pursuing the art of sculpture in the beautiful studios in the Via San Martino built by the elder Story. In 1902 Charles Walter Stetson, with his gifted wife, known to the contemporary literary world by her maiden name, Grace Ellery Channing, set up their household gods and lighted their altar fires in the city by the Tiber, ready, it may be, to exclaim with Ovid: —

"Four times happy is he, and times without number is happy,
 Who the city of Rome uninterdicted enjoys."

If art is a corner of the universe seen through a temperament, the temperament of Mr. Vedder must offer an enthralling study, for it seems to be a lens whose power of refraction defies prophecy because it deals with the incalculable forces.

His art concerns itself little with the æsthetic, but is chiefly the art of the intellect and the imagination. All manner of symbols and analogies; the laws of the universe that prevail beyond the stars; the celestial figures; the undreamed significance in prophecy or in destiny; omens, signs, and wonders; the world forces, advancing stealthily in the shadows of a dusky twilight; the Fates, under brilliant skies, gathering in the stars; oracles and supernatural coincidences that lurk in undreamed-of days; the Pleiades dancing in a light that never was on sea or land; unknown Shapes that meet outside space and time and question each other's identity; the dead that come forth from their graves and glide, silent and spectral, through a crowd, unseen by any one; the prayer of the celestial powers poured forth in the utter solitude of the vast desert, — it is these that are the realm of Vedder's art, and what has the normal world of portrait and landscape to do with such art as this? Can it only be relegated to a class, an order, of its own, and considered as being — Vedderesque? It seems to stand alone and unparalleled. In his work lies the transfiguration of all mystery. Vedder

THE DANCE OF THE PLEIADES
Elihu Vedder
Page 92

never paints nature, in the sense of landscapes, and yet one often feels that he has the key to the very creation of nature; that he has supped with gods and surprised the secrets of the stars. Do the winds whisper to him? —

> "The Muse can knit
> What is past, what is done,
> With the web that's just begun."

How can he find the design to phrase his thought — this painter of ideas?

> "Can blaze be done in cochineal,
> Or noon in mazarin?"

Whatever the Roman environment may have done for Allston, Page, and Story, there is no question but that to Vedder it has been as his soul's native air. For him the sirens sing again on the coast; the sorceress works her spell; the Cumæan Sibyl again flies, wraithlike, over the plain, clasping her rejected leaves of destiny which Tarquin in his blindness has refused to buy. The Rome that lies buried under the ages rises for Vedder. His art cannot be catalogued under any known division of portrait,

landscape, marine, or genre, but it is simply —
the art of Vedder. It stands alone and absolutely unrivalled. The pictorial creations of
Vedder are as wholly without precedent or
comparison as if they were the sole pictorial
treasures of the world. The visitor may care
for them, or not care, according to his own
ability to comprehend and to recognize the
inscrutable genius there manifested; but in
either case he will find nowhere else, in either
ancient or contemporary art, any parallel to
these works.

One could well fancy that to any interroga-
tion of his conceptions the artist might reply: —

> "I am seeker of the stone,
> Living gem of Solomon.
> But what is land, or what is wave,
> To me, who only jewels crave?
>
> .   .   .   .   .
>
> I'm all-knowing, yet unknowing;
> Stand not, pause not in my going."

In the rich, weird realm of Omar Khayyam's
Persian poem, the Rubaiyat, Mr. Vedder found
the opportunity of his life for translating its
thought into strange, mystic symbolism. **Never**

were artist and poet so blended in one as in Vedder's wonderful illustrations for this poem. It has nothing in common with what we ordinarily call an illustrated work. It is a great treasure of art for all the ages. It is a very fount of inspiration for painter and poet. An exquisite sonnet suggested by "The Angel of the Darker Cup" is the following by Louise Chandler Moulton: —

> "She bends her lovely head to taste thy draught,
>   O thou stern Angel of the Darker Cup!
>   With thee to-night in the dim shades to sup,
> Where all they be who from that cup have quaffed.
> She had been glad in her own loveliness, and laughed
>   At Life's strong enemies who lie in wait;
>   Had kept with golden youth her queenly state,
> All unafraid of Sorrow's threat'ning shaft.

> "Then human Grief found out her human heart,
>   And she was fain to go where pain is dumb;
>   So Thou wert welcome, Angel dread to see,
>   And she fares onward with thee, willingly,
>   To dwell where no man loves, no lovers part, —
>   Thus Grief that is, makes welcome Death to come."

The sonnet, the stanza, and the pictorial interpretation all form one beautiful trio in poetic and graphic art.

ITALY, THE MAGIC LAND

Writing of Mr. Vedder, Mr. W. C. Brownell speaks of the personal force in a picture and says that with Vedder this personal force is imagination, — "the imagination of a man whose natural expression is pictorial, but who is a man as well as a painter; who has lived as well as painted, who has speculated, pondered, and felt much. . . . It is this," he continues, "that places Vedder in the front rank of the imaginative painters of the day." Of Mr. Vedder's painting called "The Enemy Sowing Tares," Mr. Brownell writes: —

". . . Here you note a dozen phases of significance. The theme is unconventional; the man has become the archenemy; the night is weird and awe-inspiring; the tares represent the foe of the church — money; they are sown at the foot of the cross — the symbol of the church. . . . Mr. Vedder has not passed his life in Rome for nothing. His attitude is in harmony with the spirit of the Sistine and the Stanze."

One of the interesting and mystical works of Vedder is "The Soul between Doubt and

Faith," — three heads, that of the Soul hooded and draped, looking before her with eyes that seem to discern things not seen by mortals; the sinister face of Doubt at the left, the serene, inspiring countenance of Faith at the right. It is a magical picture to have before one with its profoundly significant message. The works of Mr. Vedder will grow more priceless as the years pass by. They are pictures for the ages.

In Mr. Ezekiel, another American artist whose almost lifelong home has been in Rome, is a sculptor whose touch and technique have won recognition. In a recumbent figure of Christ is seen one of the best examples of his art. It is pervaded by the classic influences in which he has lived. The studios of Mr. Ezekiel, in the ruins of the old Baths of Caracalla, are very picturesque and his salon, with its music, its wealth of books including many rare and beautiful copies, and its old pictures and bric-a-brac, is one of the fascinating interiors of the Eternal City.

The visitor who is privileged to see the Story studios in the Via San Martino finds Mr. Waldo Story occupying these spacious rooms where the flash of a fountain in the court, a view of the garden, green-walled by vines, with flowers and shrubs and broken statues, make the place alluring to dreamer and poet. In these rooms may be seen many of the elder Story's finest statues in cast or marble, the "Libyan Sibyl," "Nemesis," "Sappho," the "Christ," "Into the Silent Land," and others, with many portrait busts, among which are those of Browning, Shelley, Keats, Theodore Parker, Mrs. Browning, Marchesa Peruzzi de Medici (Edith Story), John Lothrop Motley, one of Story's nearer friends, and Lord Houghton.

In the work of Mr. Waldo Story one admirable portrait bust is of Cecil Rhodes. A decorative work, a fountain for the Rothschild country estate in England, is charmingly designed as a Galatea (in bronze), standing in a marble shell that is drawn by Nereids and attended by Cupids. The happy blending of marble and bronze gives to this work a pleasing variety of color. Another decorative design is that of "Nymphs Drinking at the Fountain of Love." These studios are among the most interesting in Rome.

It was in 1868 that Franklin Simmons, then a young artist from Maine, turned to Rome as his artistic Mecca. Since then the Eternal City has always been his home, but his frequent and prolonged sojourns in America have kept him closely in touch with its national life. Mr. Simmons is the idealist who translates his vision into the actuality of the hour and who also exalts this actuality of the hour to the universality of the vision. In the creation of portrait busts and of the statues and monumental memorials of great men he infuses into them the indefinable quality of extended relation which relegates his work to the realm of the universal and, therefore, to the immortality of art, rather than restricting it to the temporal locality. Louis Gorse observes that it is not the absence of faults that constitutes a masterpiece, but that it is flame, it is life, it is emotion, it is sincerity. Under the touch of Mr. Simmons the personal accent speaks; to his creative power flame and life respond, and to no sculptor is the truth so admirably stated by M. Gorse more applicable.

Mr. Simmons has been singularly fortunate in a wide American recognition, having received a liberal share of the more important commissions for great public works of sculpture. The

splendid statue, *al fresco*, of the poet Longfellow for his native city, Portland, was appropriately the work of Mr. Simmons as a native of
the same state; the portrait statues of General
Grant, Gov. William King, Roger Williams, and
Francis H. Pierrepont, all in Statuary Hall in
the Capitol in Washington; the portrait busts of
Grant, Sheridan, Porter, Hooker, Thomas, and
other heroes of the Civil War; the colossal
group of the Naval Monument at the head of
Pennsylvania Avenue in Washington, — are all
among the works of Mr. Simmons.

Like all artists who, like the poet, are
born and not made, Mr. Simmons gave evidence of his artistic bent in his early childhood.
After graduating from Bates College he modelled a bust of its president, and a little
later, going to Washington (in the winter of
1865–66), many of the noted men of the time
gave him sittings, and in a series of portrait
busts his genius impressed itself by its dignity
of conception and an unusual power of sympathetic interpretation. He modelled the bust of
Grant while he was the General's guest in
camp, taking advantage of whatever spare
minutes General Grant could give for sittings

in the midst of his pressing responsibilities; and it is perhaps due to this unusually intimate intercourse with the great hero, and the *rapport*, not difficult of establishment, between two men whose natures were akin in a certain noble sincerity and lofty devotion to the purest ideals, that Mr. Simmons owes the power with which he has absolutely interpreted the essential characteristics of General Grant in that immortal portrait statue in the Capitol.

Washington is, indeed, the place to especially study the earlier work of Franklin Simmons. An important one is the Logan memorial, — an equestrian statue which is considered the finest work in sculpture in the capital, and which is the only statue in the United States in which both the group and the pedestal are of bronze. The visitor in Washington who should be ignorant of the relative rank of the great men commemorated by the equestrian memorial monuments of the city might be justified in believing that General Logan was the most important man of his time, if he judged from the relative greatness of his statue. When Congress decided upon this group, Mr. Simmons was requested to prepare a model. This proving eminently acceptable, Mr. Simmons found himself, quite to his own surprise, fairly launched on this arduous work, involving years of intense concentration and labor. For this monumental work was to be not merely that of the brave and gallant military leader, — a single idea embodied, as in those of Generals Scott, Sheridan, Thomas, and others, — but it was to be a permanent interpretation of the soldier-statesman, mounted on his battle-horse; it was to be, in the comprehensive grasp of Mr. Simmons, the vital representation of the complex life and individuality of General Logan and, even more, it must reflect and suggest the complex spirit of his age. In this martial figure was thus embodied a manifold and mysterious relation, as one of the potent leaders and directive powers in an age of tumultuous activities; an age of strife and carnage, whose goal was peace; of adverse conditions and reactions, whose manifest outcome was yet prosperity and national greatness and splendid moral triumph. All these must be suggested in the atmosphere, so to speak, of the artist's work; and no sculptor who was not also an American — not merely by ancestry and activity, but one in mind and heart only; one who was an intense patriot and identified with national ideas — could ever have produced such a work as that of the Logan monument. So unrivalled does it stand, unique among all the equestrian art of this country, that it enchants the art student and lover with its indefinable spell. When this colossal work was cast in bronze, in Rome, the event was considered important. The king and the Royal family visited the studio of Mr. Simmons to see the great group, and so powerfully did its excellence appeal to King Umberto that he knighted Mr. Simmons, making him Cavaliere of the Crown of Italy. Nor was Mr. Simmons the prophet who was not without honor save in his own country, for his *alma mater* gave him the degree of M.A. in 1867; Colby College honored him with the Master's degree in 1885, and in 1888 Bowdoin bestowed upon this eminent Maine artist the same degree. In 1892 Mr. Simmons married the Baroness von Jeinsen, a brilliant and beautiful woman who, though a lady of foreign title, was an American by birth. An accomplished musician, a critical lover of art, and the most delightful of hostesses and friends, Mrs. Simmons drew around her a

remarkable circle of charming people and made
their home in the Palazzo Tamagno a notable
centre of social life. No woman in the American colony of the Seven-hilled City was ever
more beloved; and it was frequently noted by
guests at her weekly receptions that Mrs. Simmons was as solicitous for the enjoyment of
the most unknown stranger as for those of
rank and title who frequented her house. Her
grace and loveliness were fully equalled by her
graciousness and that charm of personality
peculiarly her own. Her death in Rome, on
Christmas of 1905, left a vacant place, indeed,
in many a home which had been gladdened by
her radiant presence. One of the most beautiful works of Mr. Simmons is a portrait of his
wife in bas-relief, representing her standing just
at the opening of parted curtains, as if she
were about to step behind and vanish. It is
a very poetic conception. A bust of Mrs. Simmons, also, in his studio, is fairly a speaking
likeness of this beautiful and distinguished
woman. It is over her grave in the Protestant
cemetery that Mr. Simmons has placed one of
his noblest ideal statues, "The Angel of the
Resurrection," — a memorial monument that is

"GRIEF AND HISTORY," DETAIL FROM NAVAL MONUMENT, WASHINGTON
Franklin Simmons

one of the art features of Rome to the visitor in the Eternal City.

The brilliant and impressive Naval Monument, or Monument of Peace, as it is known in Washington, placed at the foot of Capitol Hill on Pennsylvania Avenue, is eloquent with the power of heroic suggestion that Mr. Simmons has imparted to it. The work breathes that exaltation of final triumph that follows temporary defeat. Those who died that the nation might live, are seen in the perpetual illumination of immortality. Not only has Mr. Simmons here perpetuated the suffering, the sacrifices of the Civil War, but that sublime and eternal truth of victory after defeat, of peace and serene exaltation after conflict, and the triumph of life after death, are all immortally embodied in this group crowned with those impressive and haunting figures, "Grief" and "History," which are considered as among the most classically beautiful and significant in the range of modern sculpture.

In the early winter of 1907 Mr. Simmons was invited by the American Ambassador to the Court of St. James, Hon. Whitelaw Reid, to send for Dorchester House, London, three busts of distinguished Americans, — those of Alexander Hamilton, Chief Justice Chase, and Hon. James G. Blaine, which Mr. Reid, in visiting the Roman studios of Mr. Simmons, had seen and greatly admired. The Ambassador observed that he "would like a few Americans, as well as so many Roman Emperors," about him.

These portrait busts all reveal an amazing force and mastery of work. The fine sculptural effect of the Hamilton and the wonderful blending of subtle delicacy of touch and vigor of treatment with which the nobility of character is expressed, mark this bust as something exceptional in portrait art. It has a matchless dignity and serene poise. The bust of Chief Justice Chase is a faithful and speaking reproduction of the very presence of its subject, instinct with vitality; and the fire and force and brilliancy of the bust of Hon. James G. Blaine fairly sweeps the visitor off his feet. The modelling is done with an apparent instantaneousness of power that is the highest realization of creative art. It is the magnetic Blaine, the impassioned and eloquent statesman, that rises before the gazer.

Mr. Simmons has long been a commanding

figure in plastic art. No American sculptor abroad has, perhaps, received so many important public commissions as have been given to him. He has created nearly a score of memorial . groups; he has modelled over one hundred portrait busts and statues. His industry has kept step with his genius. The latest success of Mr. Simmons in the line of monumental art is the statue (in bronze) of Alexander Hamilton, which was unveiled at Paterson, N. J., in May of 1907. The splendidly poised figure, the dignity, the serene strength and yet the intense energy of the expression and of the entire pose are a revelation in the art of the portrait statue.

It is not, however, true that Mr. Simmons has ever resigned himself to the necessity of producing portrait and memorial sculpture exclusively. In the realm of the purely ideal Mr. Simmons finds his most felicitous field for creative work. A bas-relief entitled "The Genius of Progress Leading the Nations," with all its splendid fire and action, the *motif* being that of the spirits Life and Light beating down and driving out the spirits of darkness and evil; "The Angel of the Resurrection," with its glad, triumphant assertion of the power of the immortal life; the poetry and sacredness of maternity as typified in the "Mother of Moses;" the statues of the "Galatea" and the "Medusa," and other ideal creations, indicate "the vision and the faculty divine" of Mr. Simmons. To a very great degree his art is that which the French describe as the grand manner, and to this is added a spiritual quality, a power of radiating the intellectual purpose, the profounder thought and the aspiration of the subject represented.

One of the most charming of these ideal works is a statue of "Penelope," represented seated in the chair, her rich robe falling in graceful folds, and the little Greek fillet binding her hair. The face bears a meditative expression, into which has entered a hint of pathos and wistfulness in the dawning wonder as to whether, after all, Ulysses will return. The classic beauty of the pose; the exquisite modelling of the bust and arms and hands, every curve and contour so ideally lovely; the distinction of the figure in its noble and refined patrician elegance, are combined to render this work one that well deserves immortality in art, and to rank as a masterpiece in modern sculpture.

"THE GENIUS OF PROGRESS LEADING THE NATIONS"

Franklin Simmons

Page 107

ITALY, THE MAGIC LAND

Another of his ideal figures, "The Promised Land," is a work of great spiritual exaltation and beauty. An Israelite woman has just arrived at the point when before her vision gleams the "Promised Land"; the face tells its own story of all she has passed through, — the trials, the sadness, the obstacles to be overcome; but now she sees the fulfilment of her hopes and dreams. It is a most interesting creation, and one in which is portrayed the artist's spiritual insight and susceptibility to poetic exaltation. To one visitor to Mr. Simmons's studio this statue suggested the following lines: —

Fair on her sight it gleams, — the Promised Land!
  The rose of dawn sifts through the azure air,
  And all her weariness and toil and care
Vanish, as if from her some tender hand
  Lifted the burden, and transformed the hour
  To this undreamed-of sense of joy and power!
The rapture and the ecstasy divine
  Are deep realities that only wait
  Their hour to dawn, nor ever rise too late
To draw the soul to its immortal shrine.

O Sculptor! thy great gift has shaped this clay,
  To image the profoundest truth, and stand
As witness of the spirit power that may
  Achieve the vision of the Promised Land!

ITALY, THE MAGIC LAND

In a statuette in bronze called "Valley Forge," Mr. Simmons has fairly incarnated the entire spirit of the Revolutionary period in that mysterious way recognized only in its result; all that unparalleled epoch of tragic intensity and sublime triumph lives again in this work. The fidelity to a lofty ideal which essentially characterizes Mr. Simmons is as unswerving as that of Merlin, who followed "The Gleam."

> "Great the Master
> And sweet the Magic
> When over the valley
> In early summers,
> Over the mountain,
> On human faces,
> And all around me
> Moving to melody,
> Floated the Gleam."

This American sculptor who, in his early youth, sought the artistic atmosphere of Rome as the environment most stimulating to his dawning power, who accepted with unfailing courage the incidental privations of art life in a foreign land more renowned for beauty than for comfort, who

> ". . . never turned his back, but marched breast forward,
> Never doubted clouds would break,"

has expressed his message in many purely ideal works, — the message that the true artist must always give to the world and that leads humanity to the crowning truth of life, that of the ceaseless progress of the soul in its immortality.

For the brief and significant assertion of the apostle condenses the most profound truth of life when he says: —

"To be carnally minded is death; but to be spiritually minded is life and peace."

In these words are imaged the supreme purpose of all the experiences of the life on earth; and to the artist whose works bear this lofty message of the triumph of spirituality, his reward shall appear, not in the praise of men, but in the effect on character that his efforts have aided to exalt; in the train of nobler influences that his work shall perpetually inspire and create.

Mr. Simmons has always found Rome potent in fascination. One may not want to go to St. Peter's every day, but one knows it is there, and there is some inexplicable satisfaction in being where it is possible to easily enter this impressive interior. One may not go near the

Forum for a month, or even a season, but the knowledge that one may find it and the wonderful Palatine Hill any hour of any day is a perpetual delight. The Vatican galleries, with their great masterpieces; the Sistine Chapel, the stately, splendid impressiveness of San Giovanni Laterano; the wanderings in Villa Borghese, and the picturesque climbing of the Spanish steps, even all the inconveniences and deprivations, become a part of the story of Rome which the artist absorbs and loves.

The studios of Mr. Simmons in the Via San Nicolo da Tolentino are a centre of artistic resort, and his personal life is one of distinction amid the picturesque beauty and enchantment of the Eternal City.

For many years (until the death of Mrs. Simmons in 1905) the sculptor and his wife had their home in the beautiful Palazzo Tamagno in the Via Agostino Depretis, where one of those spacious apartments of twenty to thirty rooms, only to be found in a Roman palace, was made by them a brilliant centre of social life. Mrs. Simmons was herself a musical artist, with impassioned devotion to music; and her rare personal charm and distinction of presence drew

"MOTHER OF MOSES"
Franklin Simmons
Page 108

around her a most interesting circle. Her receptions were for many years a noted feature of
Roman society. The social life in Rome is
very brilliant, interesting, and fascinating. The
sight-seeing is a kind of attendant atmosphere,
— the perpetual environment offering, but not
intruding itself. People come to Rome for reasons quite disconnected with the Golden House
of Nero or the latest archæological discoveries
in the Forum. The present, rather than the
past, calls to them, and the present, too, is
resplendent and alluring.

Of the foreign painters in Rome, Charles
Walter Stetson, whose work recalls the glory
of the old Italian masters, is especially distinguished for his genius as a colorist. No visitor
in Rome can afford to miss the studio of one of
the most imaginative of modern artists. A
wonderful picture still in process is a genre
work with several figures, called "Music." An
idyllic scene of a festa amid the ilex trees —
with the Italian sky and the golden sunshine
pervading a luminous atmosphere, while the joyous abandon of the dancers appeals to all who
love Italy — is one of the many beautiful pictorial scenes of Mr. Stetson which enchant the

eye and haunt the imagination. Another picture is called "Beggars," — a name that illy suggests its splendor. There is the façade of a church to which a long flight of steps leads up, a procession of cardinals and friars in their rich robes, while at one side the groups of beggars shrink into the darkness. It is an impressive commentary upon life.

For a long period, through the early and middle years of the nineteenth century, Rome held her place as the world centre of modern artistic activity. Great works of poetic and ideal sculpture elevated the general public taste to a high degree of appreciation. The standards were not ingeniously adjusted to mere spectacular methods whose sole appeal was to the crude fancy of possible patrons. Art held her absolute and inviolate ideals, and the spirit of her votaries might well have been interpreted in Mrs. Browning's words: —

> "I, who love my art,
> Would never wish it lower to suit my stature."

The tone of public appreciation is raised to a high quality only when the artist refuses to sell his soul for a mess of pottage. He may,

to be sure, need the pottage, but the price is
too great. Rather will he find his attitude expressed in these wonderful lines: —

> "I can live
> At least my soul's life without alms from men.
> And if it be in heaven instead of earth,
> Let heaven look to it — I am not afraid."

All art that has within itself true vitality must
ever be the leader and the creator of the popular taste; only when it falls into decadence does
it become the servile follower.

It is a serious question as to the degree in
which the art of to-day keeps faith with the
eternal ideals. The great expositions of the
past quarter of a century, while they have con-
tributed immeasurably to the popularization of
art and to the familiarization of the public with
the work of individual painters and sculptors,
have yet, in many ways, been a demoralizing
influence in their insidious temptation to produce pictures or plastic art calculated to arrest
immediate attention, thus putting a premium
on the spectacular, the sensational, on that
which makes the most immediate and direct
appeal to the senses. The work becomes fairly

a personal document wrought with perhaps an almost amazing finesse, but utterly failing in power to inspire joyous sensibility to beauty or to impart to the gazer that glow of radiant energy which lofty art invariably communicates to all who respond to its infinite exaltation.

All great art is inspired by religious ideals. Painting and sculpture give to these a presence. Under their creative power are these ideals manifested. To embody them in living form becomes the absolute responsibility of the artist. In Greece all the fortunate conditions to produce great art were curiously combined and preeminently supported by the conjunction of events and by the prevailing sentiment of the time. The artist drew his inspiration from the most exalted conception of life embodied in gods rather than in men. Art, too, was an affair of the state. It was the supreme interest and held national importance. The temple was erected to form an inclosure for the statue, rather than that the statue was created as an adornment for the temple. The greatest gifts were consecrated to the service of art, and under these stimulating influences it is little wonder that artistic creation achieved that vital potency

"VALLEY FORGE"
Franklin Simmons
Page 110

which has thrilled all succeeding centuries and has communicated to them something of the divine air of that remote period. With the Renaissance in Italy art culminated in the immortal work of Raphael and Michael Angelo. In the Sistine Chapel, where that sublime grouping of prophets and sibyls speaks of the very miracle of art in their impassioned fire and glow; where the figures, the pose, the draperies are so grandly noble and infused with dignity and presence, — the very atmosphere is vocal with the language of the spirit and the expressions of religious reverence. These marvellous shapes of grandeur and sublime intimations carry the soul into a conscious communion with the divine. In these stupendous works Michael Angelo has given to all the ages the message of the highest exaltation of art. In the technique, in the marvellous dignity of the sentiment, in the depth of the feeling involved, in the grace and power of the composition, these works embody the artistic possibilities of painting.

Are such works as those of Canova and Thorwaldsen no longer created?

Can it be that art is no longer of national importance? In our own country vast appropriations are made for internal improvements of all kinds, while art that kindles and re-enforces life is almost ignored. Our government — the government of the richest country in the world — appropriated $200,000 for a memorial monument to General Grant to be placed in Washington, while Italy—whose resources are so slender in comparison — appropriates seven million dollars — thirty-five times the amount — for her great monument to Victor Emmanuel which is now being erected in Rome to stand near the Capitol and the Palace of the Quirinale. Great art has always been closely associated with great devotion to religious ideals. The artist was the servant of the Lord, and it was his supreme purpose to embody the aspirations of the age and render his works a full and complete symbol of those true realities of life which have their being in the spiritual universe rather than in the changing temporal world of the outer universe. The so-called realism of the day is based on a false interpretation. "The things that are seen are temporal, while the things that are not seen are eternal." True realism is in spiritual qualities, not in physical attributes. True realism is found in such works as Canova's

sublime group, where the figures of Religion
and of Death forever impress all who stand
before this magnificent monument; it is found
in Thorwaldsen's "Christ;" in Franklin Simmons's "Angel of the Resurrection," — in such
works as those that have a language for the
soul, rather than in a "Saturnalia."

Again, another fatal rock on which art must
inevitably make shipwreck is the theory that it
is good to perpetuate ugliness, in either painting or in sculpture. The permanent reality of
life is beauty. So far as any person or object
departs from this enduring reality, so far it is
the result of distortion and deformity, and these,
being the temporary, the accidental, the deficient,
should not be perpetuated in ideal creation.
It is an Apollo who embodies the permanent
ideal of manhood — not a cripple or a hunch-
back. Still further: art should not only refuse
to embody the defective, which is a mere nega-
tive; it should not only give form to the utmost
perfection it beholds in nature or in humanity,
but beyond this the responsibility is upon the
artist to penetrate into loftier realms, to catch
the vision not revealed to mortals. The artist
is, by virtue of his high calling, a co-worker

with God. An English wit has declared that life copies art rather than that art copies life. In this he expresses a truth rather than a merely clever epigram. It is the artist's business to lead, not to follow. Only as he leads does he fulfil his divinely appointed destiny. "I maintain that life is not a form of energy," writes Sir Oliver Lodge; "that it is not included in our present physical categories; that its explanation is still to be sought. And it appears to me to belong to a separate order of existence, which interacts with this material frame of things, and while here exerts guidance and control on the energy which already here exists; for although they alter the quantity of energy no whit, and though they merely utilize available energy like any other machine, live things are able to direct inorganic terrestrial energy along new and special paths, so as to achieve results without which such living agency could not have occurred." Does it for an instant seem that a great scientist's theoretical speculations of the laws of the universe and of organic life have no connection with the province of art? On the contrary. Truly does Balzac exclaim: "Is not God the whole of science, the all of love,

"LA PIETA," ST. PETER'S, ROME
Michael Angelo
Page 117

the source of poetry?" The artist is he who enters into the divine realm; who discerns the divine creations as the true ideals of humanity, and who interprets to the world the sublime significance of the divine thought. Shall such an artist degrade his power by portraying ugliness — the mere defects of negations and distortions? Shall he degrade life by calling these the realities?

The painter or sculptor who holds that it is as truly art to represent distortion and repulsiveness as it is to represent beauty is as false to his high calling as would be the poet who should insist that doggerel and mere commonplace truisms expressed in rhyme are poetry. Compare, for example, two statues, Cecioni's "*La Madre*," in which a woman's utter lack of personal attraction is so complete as to make her fairly repulsive to the gazer, and the "Mother of Moses," by Franklin Simmons, in which the mystic beauty, the very ideal of maternity, is embodied. Which of these statues is calculated to uplift and to exalt all who come near? This marvellously beautiful creation of Mr. Simmons shows a woman of exquisite delicacy and loveliness sitting, slightly bending forward, holding her baby to her breast. The modelling of the draped figure with the bare arms and neck revealing the tender curves, the yielding delicacy of the flesh and that inscrutable light upon the beautiful countenance, whose expression suggests that she is looking far into the future of the infant whom she holds in her arms, are a wonderful portrayal of the mystery and the sacredness of motherhood. The one statue degrades maternity; the other ennobles and exalts. The one embodies a pernicious and a false ideal; the other embodies the ideal that must appeal to all that is noble and divine in human life, and it thus ministers to moral progress by its contribution to the elevation of the social tone. For indeed, life follows art. It is art that exerts this powerful influence upon life which it may lead to loftier heights or drag down to the moral abyss. The artist is not merely the portrayer of existing types; he is the inspirer of those ideal types which human life should recognize as its pattern, its model to be followed and ultimately achieved. The world needs ideal and poetic art to minister to the attainment of the true social life and to the full and complete expression of man himself.

ITALY, THE MAGIC LAND

Do not the visions of Fra Angelico and Botticelli still inspire the artist of to-day with the absolute realization of all the deep significance of the past?

> "Is there never a retroscope mirror,
> In the realms and corners of space,
> That can give us a glimpse of the battle,
> And the soldiers face to face?"

Religion and art are inseparably united. In its true significance religion takes precedence of all else in that its influence is felt in every department and in every direction and expression of man's activity. It is the inexhaustible fountain of that lofty energy which communicates itself to every channel that carries inspiration to life and to art. Religion is the influence that redeems the mere shallow, surface presentation, — the petty trick to capture popularity, and holds art true to its real purpose. The glory of the mediæval art of Italy owed its greatness to religion. Cimabue and Giotto were directly inspired by that spring of a diviner life given to Italy and later to the world of that "sweet saint," Francis of Assisi. In an age of cruelty and terror he brought the

new message that man is dear to God; that
the soul is ceaselessly joyful; that man, created in the divine image, is a part of the
divine life, and that only when he lives in
this response and recognition does he truly
live at all. In this restatement of the truth
that Jesus came to proclaim, St. Francis
opened the way for a revival of art, and
opened the gates of that infinite and divine
energy which has immortally recorded itself for
all ages in the "Divina Comedia" of Dante.
The irresistible wave of power which resulted
from that liberating of thought, feeling, and
emotion by the work of St. Francis expressed
itself in the sublimest poem of all the ages, and
in that glorious triumph of art that is still the
treasure and the source of artistic inspiration.

It is only when the world is lifted out of the
limitations of the material by a period of great
art that humanity. is brought into close and
inspiring relation with the living Christ.

Men and women make the world,
As head and heart make human life.

MRS. BROWNING.

Alas, our memories may retrace
Each circumstance of time and place;
Season and scene come back again,
And outward things unchanged remain;
The rest we cannot reinstate,
Ourselves we cannot re-create,
Nor set our souls to the same key
Of the remembered harmony.

LONGFELLOW.

And as, after the lapse of a thousand years, you stand upon that hallowed spot, the yellow Tiber flowing sluggishly beneath you, the ruins of the Eternal City all around you speaking of fallen greatness, the mighty Basilica of St. Peter rising before you like some modern tower of Babel that would monopolize the road to heaven, the eye rests upon the figure of the Archangel sheathing his glittering sword upon the summit of the Castle of St. Angelo, and the heart asks, Why should that be a legend? Why should that be a projection of a morbid and devout imagination? Why should it not have been the clairvoyance of supernatural ecstasy opening the world of spirits? It was no unreality when the angel of God, with his sword drawn in his hand, withstood the prophet Balaam. It was no morbid imagination when the angel of God smote with the edge of the sword the first-born of the land of Egypt. It was no imposture when the shining hosts of the army of the Almighty smote the Assyrians. It was no deception when Gabriel, the King's messenger from the court of heaven, was sent to comfort Daniel by the river Hiddekel; or when he announced to the maiden, whom all generations have called blessed, that she was to be the mother of the Divine Redeemer. . . . The written Word from first to last is full of the holy angels. It begins with angels, it ends with angels.

THE VENERABLE ARCHDEACON WILBERFORCE,
Westminster Abbey.

II

SOCIAL LIFE IN THE ETERNAL CITY

And others came, — Desires and Adorations,
Winged Persuasions and Veiled Destinies!
SHELLEY.

In what ethereal dances! ·
By what eternal streams!
POE.

SOCIAL life in Rome is no misnomer. From the
most stately and beautiful ceremonials of balls
at the court of the Quirinale, in ducal palaces,
or at the embassies; of dinners whose every
detail suggests stage pictures in their magnificence, to the simple afternoon tea, where conversation and music enchant the hours; the
morning call *en tête-à-tête*, and the morning
stroll, or the late afternoon drive, — a season in
Rome prefigures itself, by the necromancy of
retrospective vision, as a resplendent panorama
of pictorial scenes. There rise before one those
mornings, all gold and azure, of loitering over
the stone parapet on Monte Pincio, gazing down

on the city in her most alluring mood. The new bridge that is to connect the Pincio with the Villa Borghese is a picturesque feature in its unfinished state; but the vision traverses the deep ravine and revels in the scene of the Borghese grounds carpeted with flowers. Its picturesque slopes under the great trees, with a view of Michael Angelo's dome in the near distance, are the resort of morning strollers, who find that lovely picture of Charles Walter Stetson's — a stretch of landscape under the ilex trees, the scarlet gowns of the divinity students giving vivid accents of color here and there — fairly reproduced in nature before their vision. One should never be in haste as the bewildering beauty of the Roman spring weaves its emerald fantasies on grass and trees, and touches into magical bloom the scarlet poppies that flame over all the meadows, and caress roses and hyacinths and lilies of the valley into delicate bloom and floating fragrance until the Eternal City is no more Rome, but Arcady, instead — one should never be in haste to toss his penny into the *Fontane de Trevi*. Yet in another way it may work for him an immediate spell that defies all other necromancy. Judiciously thrown in, on the very eve of departure, it is the conjurer that insures his return; but at any time prior to this it may even weave the irresistible enchantment that falls upon him and may prevent his leaving at all. Nor can he summon up the moral courage to regret even the missing of all other engagements, and the failure to keep faith with his plans. For in the May days Rome falls upon him anew, like a revelation, and he is ready to confess that he has never seen her who sees her not in her springtime loveliness. The Italian winter by no means lives up to its reputation. It is not the chill of any one special day that discourages one from any further effort to continue in this vale of tears, but the cold that has, apparently, the chill and dampness and cold of all those two thousand and two hundred and sixty winters that have gone before which concentrate themselves in the atmosphere. One could presumably endure with some degree of courage, if not equanimity, the chill in the air of any *one* winter; but when all the chill and cold that has ever existed in more than the two thousand winters of the past concentrates itself in the winter, say, of 1906–7, why, patience ceases to be a virtue although one that the sojourner in Rome is particularly called upon to practise if he fares forth to visit churches and galleries in the winter.

Torrents of rain pour down, rivalling the cloud-bursts of Arizona. Virgil's cave of the winds apparently lets loose its sharpest blasts. Tramontana and sirocco alternate, and each is more unendurable than the other.

The encircling mountains are white with snow. The streets are a sea of mud, for they are paved with small stones, and except in the new Villa Ludovisi quarter and along the Via Nazionale and a few other of the newer thoroughfares there are no sidewalks, the foot passengers (in all old Rome) pressing close to the wall to avoid the dangerously near proximity of carts and cabs. This rough pavement makes all driving hard and walking difficult. The Roman lady, indeed, does not walk; and the visitors who cannot forego the joy of daily promenades enter into the feelings of that nation which is said to take its pleasures sadly. But spring works a transformation scene. The air is filled with the most transparent shining haze; the sky lacks little of that intense, melting

blue that characterizes the ineffable beauty of
the skies in Arizona; and ruins and fragments
and strange relics — ghosts of the historic past
— are all enshrined in trailing green and riotous
blossoms. To drive on the terraced roads of
Monte Mario with all Rome and the emerald-
green Campagna before one; through the
romantic "Lovers' Lane," walled in by roses
and myrtle; to enjoy the local life, full of gayety
and brilliancy, is to know Rome in her most
gracious aspects. One goes for strolls in the
old Colonna Gardens, where still remain the
ruins of the Temple of the Sun and of the
Baths of Constantine. The terraces offer lovely
views over the city. The old palace is occupied by the present Prince Colonna, and it is
not unfrequently the scene of most elaborate
and gorgeous receptions where the traditional
Roman splendor is to be found. A series of
arched bridges over the narrow street of the
Via della Pilotta connect the Gardens with the
Colonna Palace in the Piazza San Apostoli.
Very fine old sarcophagi are half buried in
trailing vines on the slope of the hill, dark with
magnificent cypress trees. The Colonna Gardens are a very dream of the past, in their ruins

of old temples, their shattered statues, their strange old tablets and inscriptions, and their grand view of the Capitol.

In one's retrospective vision of a Roman season all the inconveniences and discomforts of the winter disappear, leaving only the beauty and the enjoyment to be "developed," as the photographer would say, on the sensitive plate of memory.

No one really knows Rome until he has watched the transcendent loveliness of spring investing every nook and corner of the Eternal City. The picturesque Spanish steps are a very garden of fragrance, the lower steps of the terraced flight being taken possession of by the flower venders who display their wares, — masses of white lilac, flame-colored roses, rose and purple hyacinths and baskets of violets and carnations. Did all this fragrance and beauty send up its incense to Keats as he lay in the house adjoining, with the musical plash of Bernini's fountain under his window? It is pleasant to know that by the appreciation of American and English authors, the movement effectively directed by Robert Underwood Johnson, this house consecrated to a poet's memory has been purchased to be a permanent memorial to Keats and to Shelley. A library of their works will be arranged in it; and portraits, busts, and all mementos that can be collected of these poets will render this memorial one of the beautiful features of Rome.

From the flower venders and the circulating libraries in the Piazza di Spagna that allure one in the morning, from the fascinating glitter of the little Via Condotti which is, in its way, the rue de la Paix of Rome, one leisurely climbs the steps to where the great obelisk looms up in front of the Convent Church of the Trinità di Monti and on, across the Piazza di Trinità, toward the Pincian, one wanders along the brow of the hill surmounted by the low stone parapet. The view is a dream of beauty. Over the valley lies Monte Mario, crowned with the Villa Madama, silhouetted against the blue Roman sky; and the commanding dome of St. Peter's, the splendid new white marble buildings of the Law Courts, the domes of other churches, all make up a picturesque panorama, while on the Janiculum the great equestrian statue of Garibaldi can be descried. Strolling on, one turns into the gardens of the Villa

Medici, the French Academy of Art, in which
the present director, the great Carolus Duran,
is domiciled and in which twenty-four students
— of painting, sculpture, music, and architecture — are maintained at the expense of the
French government for several years, the twenty-
four being chosen from those who have given
signal proof of their ability. The Villa Medici
has, perhaps, a more beautiful site than any
other building in Rome. Facing the west, with
the Janiculum and Monte Mario forever before
it, while below lies the Piazza di Spagna and
the Piazza del Popolo, and all the changing
splendors of the sunset sky as a perpetual picture gallery, the situation is, indeed, magnificent. It is still conceivable, however, that Mon-
sieur Carolus Duran must have many quarters
of an hour when he longs for the brilliancy and
the movement and the stimulus of his Paris.
The gardens of the Villa Medici are large, but
they are laid out with narrow paths bordered
with box, forming a wall as impervious as if
of stone, and dark and damp by the shade
of foliage. These walks are paved with gravel,
and are always damp. These formal rectangles
and alleys are utterly shut in, so that in any one

VILLA MEDICI, ROME

Page 184

part one can see only the two dense green walls
of box that inclose him and the glimpse of sky
overhead, — not precisely a cheering promenade.
This is the Italian idea of a garden. Much
broken sculpture, weather-stained and defective, is placed all along the way, and the
perpetual Roman fountain is always gushing
somewhere.

Another phase of the Roman season may rise
before one in the stately beauty of any old historic palace, where the hostess, all grace and
sweetness, receives her guests in the apartment
in which Galileo had been confined when imprisoned in Rome. The approach to this *piano
nobile* was up a flight of easily graded marble
stairs, where in frequent niches stood old
statues. The large windows in the corridor on
the landing were curtained with pale yellow,
thus creating a golden light to fall on the old
sculptured marbles. One salon was decorated
with Flaxman's drawings on the wall, in their
classical outlines. From a steep, dark stone
stairway, down which one descended (at the
imminent risk of a broken neck in the darkness and from the irregular stairs rudely carved
in the stone), one emerged on a landing, where a

little door opened into the balcony of the chapel,
a curious, gloomy place, with tombs and altar
and shrine, and some very poor old paintings.
One's progress to it recalled the lines from
Poe's "Ulalume": —

> "By a route, obscure and lonely,
> Haunted by ill angels only."

Then, sitting in one of the richly decorated
salons at afternoon tea in this same old palace
one day, while an accomplished harpist was
discoursing delicate music from its vibrating
chords, flights of birds kept passing a window,
making a scene like that of a Wagner opera.
The groups present, largely of the Roman
nobility, the titled aristocracy, resembling so
closely some of the old portraits in the palazzo
that it was easy to recognize that they were all
one people, descendants of the same race.

Many of the guests looked, indeed, as if they
had stepped from out the sumptuously carved
frames on the wall. At these pretty festas one
meets much of the resident Roman world. The
guests assembled seem to be speaking in all the
romance languages. There are Russian and
Spanish as well as Italian, French, German,

and English at these alluring teas. All the salons of the spacious apartments are thrown open, and the men in their picturesque court dress or military costume, and the women and girls in dainty gowns, make up an alluring scene. The salons are richly furnished and abound in works of art, old pictures, inlaid cabinets, carvings, rich vases, busts, and statuettes. The library, with its wealth of books; the music room; the salon for dancing; the supper room, and the quiet rooms where groups gather before the blazing open fires, grateful in these lofty rooms whose temperature suggests the frozen circles of Dante, — all make up a delightful picture. One meets the most varying individualities. A Russian lady of title may confide her conviction that her country is ruined, and that she never desires to return to it. Italy is the country that attracts not only political refugees from other European countries, but many who are out of sympathy with conditions elsewhere and who find the cosmopolitan society and the varied interests of this land of sunshine their most enjoyable environment.

One pleasant feature of a Roman winter is that of the usual course of lectures given by

Professor Lanciani. The celebrated archæologist is a man of special personal charm, and his conversation, as well as his public lectures, is full of interest and value. The lectures are given under the auspices of the Societa Archeologica, and a special subject recently discussed was the celebration to be held in 1911 in Rome. One project for this celebration includes the plan to lay out a carriage road around the Forum and the Palatine, and also around the Baths of Titus and of Caracalla, extending the drive to all those places included between the Appian and the Latin Way, the Villa Celimontana and the Circus Maximus.

Professor Lanciani discussed the artistic history of Rome and the different appearances the city took on in different periods; the regulation plan drawn up by Julius Cæsar and accepted and carried out by Augustus, by which one-fifth of the total area of the city was reserved for public parks. In the third century of the empire the city was inclosed by parks and crossed from end to end by delightful portico gardens, where valuable works of art were collected. During the period of the Renaissance there were the famous villas and the Cesarini

Park on the slopes of the Esquiline, and after regretting the many unnecessary acts of vandalism committed since 1870 in Rome, Professor Lanciani suggested that a complete reconstruction of the Baths of Caracalla should be made, to serve in 1911 as the Exhibition Building. He believed no artistic difficulties would present themselves, as in the fifteenth century different architects took plaster casts of the decorations of the statues and of every detail of the Baths. The archæological exhibition would be arranged in the two large halls, another hall would be for concerts, another for lectures, the others for different congresses to be held.

In this way Rome would inaugurate for 1911 the Mediæval Museum in Castel Sant' Angelo, the mediæval collections in the Torre degli Anguillara, and the grand archæological exhibition in the reconstructed Baths of Caracalla.

Italian women are by no means behind the age in their organizations to aid in social progress. The most important one in Italy is that of the leading women of the nobility and aristocracy, called "The Society for Women's

Work," which holds annual meetings, over which Lady Aberdeen, the president of the International Council, and the Contessa Spalletti, the president of the National Council of Italy, preside. Many of the prominent women of the Italian nobility are taking active part in the larger outlook for women; and in this movement Margherita, *la Regina Madre*, leads the way, supported by a large following of the titled nobility.

"Margherita holds the hearts of the people," remarked Cora, Contessa di Brazzá Savorgnan, at a brilliant little dinner one night, and no expression could more admirably represent the feeling of the nation toward the Queen Mother.

Queen Elena as the reigning sovereign has, of course, her exclusive royal prerogatives, and she has youth and initiative and precedence; but Margherita is a most attractive woman, with learning and accomplishments galore, and she has an art of conversation that allures and fascinates visiting foreigners of learning and wit, as well as of rank. Roman society is not large numerically, and the same people are constantly meeting and consolidating their many points of contact and interest. Social life in

these Italian cities is the supreme occupation of
the residents, and one must concede that in
proportion as one meets the same people constantly does society gain in dramatic interest.
With each person who is in any sense an individual the play of life begins. It gains in
dramatic sequence as it proceeds. The Eternal
City is a wonderful scenic setting for the human
drama.

Local gossip suggests perceptible rivalry between the stately palace of the King and the
pink palace on the hill, in which Margherita
holds her state with not less ceremony than
that observed at the Court of the Quirinale. It
is a beautiful thing for a country to have in it a
woman of high position, of leisure and of culture, who is so admirably fitted to be the friend
of the people as is Margherita. She is a con-
noisseur in art; she has a most intelligent interest in science; she is a critical lover of literature;
she is a wise and judicious and deeply sympathetic leader in all philanthropic work and purposes. One can hardly visit painter or poet or
artist in any line, or school, institute, or association, but that he hears of the personal
sympathy and encouragement bestowed by this

noble and beautiful Italian Queen, — the *Regina Madre*.

Practically there are, indeed, two courts in Rome; that of the Palazzo Margherita seeming to quite rival that held at the Palazzo Quirinale. The palace of the Queen Mother is an imposing three-story structure of pink-hued marble, with beautiful gardens and terraces, and adjoining it, in the palace grounds, is a marble villa, used for the entertainment of royal guests. This palace has been the residence of Margherita when in Rome since the tragic death of King Umberto, in 1900. It is in the Ludovisi quarter, and stands on the very site of the Gardens of Sallust. The Queen Mother receives noted visitors constantly, and entertains visiting royalties and members of the aristocracy. No great man of science, literature, and art visits Rome without seeking a presentation to the liberal-minded and accomplished *Regina Madre*, who is one of the most winning and attractive of all the royal women of Europe.

It has become quite a feature in introducing young girls to present them first in private audience to Margherita, and then later to Queen Elena at the Court of the Quirinale. Surely no

girl could be given a lovelier idea of woman-
hood than that embodied in the Dowager Queen.
When the poet Carducci died in the early
months of 1907, Margherita sent beautiful messages of consolation to his family, and, later,
to his home city of Bologna she sent the following letter: —

"I announce that I make a free gift to the
city of Bologna of the house where Giosuè Carducci passed the last years of his life, and the
library he collected there.

"Bologna, that showed such affectionate hospitality for Giosuè Carducci for so many years,
and surrounded him with so much devotion,
will know, I feel sure, how to carefully preserve
this remembrance of the greatest poet of modern
Italy.   MARGHERITA."

The Syndic replied in a letter hardly less fine
in its expression of Bologna's appreciation, and
with assurances that the name of the first Queen
of Italy will in future be forever associated with
Italy's greatest modern poet.

The Regio Palazzo del Quirinale is near the
Capitol, in the older part of the city, and only

a small part of this is shown to visitors when the King and Queen are in residence. The Sala Regia may be seen, the chapel in which are preserved a large number of the wreaths and the addresses sent from all parts of the civilized world on the occasion of the death of Victor Emmanuel II, and a suite of reception rooms, the throne room with many historic portraits, the Sala des Ambassadeurs, and the audience chamber, containing Thorwaldsen's "Triumphal Procession of Alexander the Great," a gift from Napoleon I. In the small chapel of the Annunciation is an altar piece by Guido Reni.

To artists the Queen Mother is most generously kind. One of the younger Italian sculptors, Turillo Sindoni, Cavaliere of the Crown of Italy, whose latest creation is a very beautiful statue of St. Agnes, has his studios in the Via del Babuino, and to especially favored visitors he sometimes exhibits a beautiful letter that he received from Margherita, who purchased two of his statues. With the letter expressing her warm appreciation of his art was an exquisite gift of jewelled sleeve-links.

Notwithstanding the fascinating lectures of

Professor Lanciani and the valuable and interesting work in the Forum that is being accomplished under the efficient directorship of
Commendatore Boni, yet all the roads that tra-
ditionally lead to Rome do not converge to the
palace on the Palatine. Modern Rome is only
mildly archæological, and while it takes occasional recognition of the ancient monuments,
and drives to the crypt of old St. Agnes, to
the tomb of Cecilia Metella, and may manage
a descent into the catacomb of St. Calixtus, it
is far more actively interested in its dancing
and dining and driving. As a scenic background for festivities Rome is a success, and as
one comes into social touch with the titled
nobility, and the resident life, by birth or adop-
tion, one finds a city of infinite human interest
and picturesque possibilities.

Between the "Whites" (the loyal followers of
the Palazzo Quirinale and the King) and the
"Blacks" (the devoted followers of the Palazzo
Vaticano and the Pope) a great gulf is fixed
over which no one may cross.

Pope Pius X is wonderfully accessible, con-
sidering the great responsibilities and duties he
has on him, and his generous goodness, his

gracious tact and the beauty of his spirit endear him to all, Catholic or Protestant alike, for every one recognizes in him the Christian gentleman, whose ideals of gentleness and inspiring helpfulness impress themselves on all who are so fortunate as to meet him.

The most impressive ceremonial receptions of the "Blacks" are those given at the Spanish Embassy in the Piazza di Spagna. At the Embassy or in the private palace of any Roman noble which a Cardinal honors by accepting an invitation, he is received according to a most picturesque old Roman custom. At the foot of the stairs two servants bearing lighted torches meet his Eminence, and, making a profound obeisance, escort him to the portals of the grand reception salon and await, in the corridor, his return. On his departure they escort him in the same way down the staircase.

In the College of Cardinals and among the many interesting individualities of the Vatican, the most marked figure is that of the Cardinal Secretary of State, Merry del Val. He occupies the Borgia apartments, which are hung with tapestry and ornamented with the most unique and valuable articles *de vertu,* — wonderful vases, inlaid cabinets, old tapestries, paintings, statues, busts, and ivories. These Borgia apartments are one of the most interesting features of the Palazzo Vaticano, and may be seen now and then by special permission when the Cardinal secretary is out, or when he may be pleased to retire into his more private salons in the apartment while the others are shown. Cardinal Rafael Merry del Val is an impressive personality, whose life seems strangely determined by destiny. His father was an *attaché* of the Spanish embassy to the Court of St. James when the future Cardinal was born in 1865. In 1904, at the early age of thirty-nine, he was advanced from the soutane violet of the bishop to the mantelletta scarlet of the cardinal, and after the accession of the present Pope, Pius X, he was appointed to the highest office in the Vatican, that of Secretary of State, the Pope paying him the high tribute because of his "devotion to work, his capability and absolute self-negation."

Cardinal Merry del Val has had a wonderful training of experience and circumstances. At the early age of twenty-two he was a member of the papal embassy commissioned to the jubilee of Queen Victoria in 1887. He was also appointed a member of the embassy from the Vatican to attend the funeral of Emperor William I; and at the jubilee of Francis Joseph, Emperor of Austria, Cardinal (then Bishop) Merry del Val was the sole and accredited representative of the Holy See, as he was also at the coronation of King Edward. The Spanish Cardinal is the special trusted counsellor of the royal family of Spain.

In Rome, Cardinal Merry del Val is an impressive figure. He is always attended by his *gentilinomo*, who is gorgeously arrayed in knee breeches, military hat and sword. This gentleman in waiting walks behind him on a promenade, sits in his carriage and stands near him in all religious ceremonies. His equipage is well known in the Eternal City, — a stately black carriage drawn by two massive black horses with luxurious flowing manes.

It is freely prophesied in Rome that the Cardinal secretary is destined to yet exchange the mantelletta scarlet for the zucchetta white, when Pius X shall have gone the way of all his predecessors in the papal chair. He is the Cardinal especially favored by Austria and Spain.

ITALY, THE MAGIC LAND

Although the conflict with France was at first ascribed to Cardinal Merry del Val, he has of late been completely exonerated from blame, even by the French prelates and clergy.

Cardinal Merry del Val represents the most advanced and progressive thought of the day. He is an enthusiastic admirer of Marconi and the marvels of wireless telegraphy; he is an advocate of telephonic service, electric motors, electric lights, and of phonographs and type-writers for the Vatican service. He is a great linguist, speaking English, French, and German as well as Spanish, which is his native tongue, and Italian, which has become second nature. He is a good Greek scholar and a profound Latin scholar, and he speaks the ancient Latin with the fluency and the force of the modern languages. He is, indeed, a remarkable twentieth-century personality and one who has apparently a very interesting life yet to come in his future.

At the Villa Pamphilia Doria, built by a former Prince Doria, the largest villa in the Roman environs and the finest now remaining, the Cardinal enjoys his game of golf, of which he is very fond. The Doria family rendered the villa magnificent in every respect. Besides the spacious avenues, woods, fountains, a lake, and cascades, are various edifices, among which is one in the form of a triumphal arch, decorated with ancient statues; the casino of the villa in which are preserved some ancient marbles and several pictures; the beautiful circular chapel, adorned with eight columns of marble and other stately ornaments. There is a monument erected by the present Prince Doria, to the memory of the French soldiers who were killed there during the siege of 1849. From the terrace of the palace there is a magnificent view of the environs of Rome, as far as the sea. In consequence of excavations, some columbaria, sepulchres, inscriptions, and other relics have been found, which have attracted much attention from archæologists.

It is near these grounds that the "Arcadians" still hold their *al fresco* meetings. The society dates back to 1690, and the first *custos* (whose duty was to open and close the meetings) was Crescimbeni. The "Arcadians" organized themselves to protest against the degeneracy of Italian poetry that marked the seventeenth century. To keep their meetings a secret from the populace the "Arcadians" held their meetings in an open garden on the slope below San Pietro in Montorio, — a terrace still known as "Bosco Parrasio degli Arcadi."

One of the enchanting views in Rome is from the Piazza San Giovanni. One looks far away past the Coliseum in its ruined grandeur and the *casa* where Lucrezia Borgia lived, and in the near distance is the colossal pile of San Giovanni di Laterano, its beautiful and impressive façade crowned with the statues of the apostles silhouetted against the western sky. In the piazza formed by the church, the museums, and the Baptistery of San Giovanni and the Scala Santa is one of the most remarkable obelisks in Rome, ninety-nine feet in height, formed, of red granite and carved with hieroglyphics. This shaft is placed on a pedestal which makes it in all some 115 feet in height. It was placed in 1568 by Sixtus V. The museums of the San Giovanni are the "Museo Sacro" and the "Museo Profano," — the latter founded by Pope Gregory XVI, and very rich in sculptures and mosaics. The "Museo Sacro" was founded by Pio Nono, and is rich in the antiquities of the Christian era. Within

San Giovanni the visitor finds himself in a vast interior divided by columns of verd-antique into three aisles, each of which is as wide as, and far longer than, the interior of an ordinary church. Statues fill the niches, and the chapels and confessionals are all beautifully decorated. The Corsini Chapel is the richest and was executed by order of Clement XII, in honor of St. Andrew Corsini, who is represented in a rich mosaic painting copied from Guido. Two sculptured figures, "Innocence" and "Penitence," stand before the altar, and above is a relief depicting St. Andrew protecting the Florentine army at the battle of Anghiari.

The tomb of Pope Clement XII (who himself belonged to the Corsini family and who was an uncle of Cardinal Corsini) is in a niche between two columns of porphyry, and there is a bronze statue of the Pope. On the opposite side is a statue of Cardinal Corsini, and in the crypt below are tombs of the Corsini family. On the altar — always lighted — is a "Pieta" by Bernini, of which the face of the Christ is very beautiful.

Near the centre of the Basilica is a rich tabernacle of precious stones, defined by four columns of *verde antico*, and it is said that the heads of St. Peter and St. Paul are preserved here. The table upon which Christ celebrated the Last Supper is placed here, above the altar of the Holy Sacrament, a sacred relic that thrills the visitors. In one chapel is a curious and grotesque group of sculpture, — a skeleton holding up a medallion portrait, while an angel with outstretched wings hovers over it.

San Giovanni has the reputation of being absolutely the coldest church in all Rome, which — it is needless to remark — means a great deal, for they all in winter have the temperature of the arctic regions. In all these great churches there is never any heat; no apparatus for heating has ever been introduced, and the twentieth century finds them just as cold as they were in the centuries of a thousand years ago. This colossal Basilica is considered the most important church in the world, as it is the cathedral of the Pontiff. It was founded in the third century by Constantine, destroyed by fire in 1308, and rebuilt by Pope Clement V, and every succeeding Pope has added to it. The façade is of travertine, with four gigantic columns and six pilasters, and the cornice is decorated with colossal figures of Jesus and a number of the saints. There are five balconies, the middle one being always used for papal benedictions. In the portico is the colossal statue of Constantine the Great. Within the columns are of *verde antico;* the ceiling was designed by Michael Angelo; the interior is very rich in sculpture, and there are some fine paintings and the chapels are most beautiful, one of them containing a tabernacle comprised wholly of precious stones. Above the altar of the Holy Sacrament the table upon which Christ celebrated the Last Supper with the disciples is preserved. It is wonderful to look upon this most sacred and significant relic.

It is in this church that the tomb of Leo XIII has been constructed by the eminent Italian sculptor, Tadolini, opposite the tomb of Innocent III. The work was completed in the spring of 1907, the design being a life-size portrait statue of the Pope with two figures, one on either side, representing the church and the workman-pilgrim, forming part of the group. This is one of the most memorable monu-

ments of all Rome, and the tomb of the great
Leo XIII will form a new shrine for Christian
pilgrimage.

Included in the group of structures that form
the great Basilica of San Giovanni is the Scala
Santa, which offers a strange picture whenever
one approaches it. These twenty-eight marble
steps that belonged to Pilate's house in Jerusalem are said to have been once trodden by
Jesus and may be ascended only on one's knees.
At no hour of the day can one visit the Scala
Santa without finding the most motley and
incongruous throng thus ascending, pausing on
each step for meditation and prayer. These
stairs were transported from Jerusalem to
Rome under the auspices of St. Helena, the
Empress, about 326 A.D., and in 1589 they were
placed by Pope Sixtus V in this portico built
for them with a chapel at the top of the stairs
called the "Sancta Sanctorum," formerly the
private chapel of the Popes. In this sanctuary
is preserved a wonderful portrait of the Saviour,
painted on wood, which is said to have been
partly the work of St. Luke but finished by
unseen hands. The legend runs that St. Luke
prepared to undertake the work by three days'

fasting and prayer, and that, having drawn it in outline, the painting was done by angelic ministry, the colors being filled in by invisible hands. In ancient times — the custom being abolished by Pius V in 1566 — this picture was borne through Rome on the Feast of the Assumption and the bearer halted with it in the Forum, when the "Kyrie Eleison" would be chanted by hundreds of voices.

Myth and legend invest every turn and foot-fall of the Eternal City, and there are few that are not founded on what the church has always called supernatural manifestations, but which the new age is learning to recognize as occurrences under natural law.

The story of Luther's ascent of the Scala Santa is thus told: —

"Brother Martin Luther went to accomplish the ascent of the Scala Santa — the Holy Staircase — which once, they say, formed part of Pilate's house. He slowly mounted step after step of the hard stone, worn into hollows by the knees of penitents and pilgrims. Patiently he crept halfway up the staircase, when he suddenly stood erect, lifted his face heavenward, and in another moment turned and walked slowly down again.

"He said that as he was toiling up a voice as if from heaven spoke to him and said, 'The just shall live by faith.' He awoke as if from a nightmare, restored to himself. He dared not creep up another step; but rising from his knees he stood upright like a man suddenly loosed from bonds and fetters, and with the firm step of a free man he descended the staircase and walked from the place."

The entire legendary as well as sacred history is almost made up of instances of the interpenetration of the two worlds; the response of those in the spiritual world to the needs of those in the natural world. Pope Paschal recorded that he fell asleep in his chair at St. Peter's (somewhere about 8.20 A.M.) with a prayer on his lips that he might find the burial place of St. Cecilia, and in his dream she appeared to him and showed him the spot where her body lay, in the catacombs of Calixtus. The next day he went to the spot and found all as had been revealed to him. The miraculous preservation of St. Agnes is familiar to all students of legendary art. Throughout all Rome, shrine and niche and sculpture, picture, monument, arch and column, speak perpetually of some interposition of unseen forces with events and circumstances in this part of life. The Eternal City in its rich and poetic symbolism is one great object lesson of the interblending of the two worlds, the natural and the spiritual. The first stage regarding all this marvellous panorama was entire and unquestioning acceptance; the succeeding stage was doubt, disbelief; the third, into which we are now entering, is that of an enlightened understanding and a growing knowledge and grasp of the laws under which these special interpositions and interventions occur.

For that "according to thy faith be it unto thee," is as true now in the twentieth century as it was in the first. The one central truth that is the very foundation of all religious philosophy is the continuity of life and the persistence of intercourse and communion, spirit to spirit, across the gulf we call death. The evidences of this truth have been always in the world. The earliest records of the Bible are replete with them. The gospels of the New

ENTRANCE TO VILLA PAMPHILIA-DORIA, ROME

Page 159

Testament record an unbroken succession of occurrences and of testimony to this interpenetration of life in the Unseen with that in the Seen. Secular history is full of its narrations of instances of clairvoyance, clairaudience, and of communications in a variety of ways; and the sacred and legendary art of Rome, largely founded on story and myth and legend, when seen in the light of latter-day science is judged anew, and the literal truth of much that has before been considered purely legendary is revealed and realized. One reads new meanings into Rome when testing it by this consciousness. It is a city of spiritual symbolism. It is a great object lesson extending over all the centuries. Making due allowance for the distortion and exaggeration of ages of testimony, there yet remains a residuum indisputable. The Past and the Present both teem with record and incident and experience proving that life is twofold, even now and here; that all the motives and acts of the life which we see are variously incited, modified, strengthened, or annulled by those in the realm of the Unseen.

The intelligent recognition of this truth changes the entire conduct of life. It entirely alters the point of view. It extends the horizon line infinitely. Instead of conceiving of life as a whole, as comprised between the cradle and the grave, it will be regarded in its larger and truer scope as a series of experiences and achievements, infinite in length and in their possibilities and unbroken by the change we call death. This will impart to humanity a new motor spring in that greater hope which puts man in a working mood, which makes him believe in the value of that which he undertakes, which encourages him to press on amid all difficulties and against all obstacles. Increasing hope, all activity is proportionately increased. It was an event of incalculable importance to the progress of humanity when the swift communication by cable was established between America and Europe. It is one of infinitely greater importance to establish the truth and enlarge the possibility of direct communication with the world of higher forces and larger attainment and scope than our own. This communication exists and has always existed, but it has been regarded as myth and legend and phenomenon rather than as a fact of nature whose laws were to be ascertained and understood. It must be made clear as an absolute scientific demonstration that the change of form by the process we call death does not put an end to intelligent and rational intercourse, but that, indeed, instead of setting up a barrier, it removes barriers and renders mutual comprehension far clearer and more direct than before. This realization alters the entire perspective of life, and is the new Glad Tidings of great joy.

It is something of all this that the Eternal City suggests to one as he makes his pilgrimages to shrine and cloister and chapel and Basilica. The mighty Past is eloquent with a thousand voices, and they blend into a choral harmony of promise and prophecy for the nobler future of humanity.

At the foot of the Scala Santa, on either side, are statues of Christ and Judas, and of Christ and Pilate, very interesting groups by Jacomletti, and there is also a kneeling statue of Pio Nono.

The statue of Judas is considered one of the most notable of the late modern Italian sculpture.

The Rome of to-day is in strange contrast even to the city that Page and Hawthorne

knew, in the comparatively recent past; and
the Rome of the ancients is traced only in the
churches and the ruins. It is a *mot* that one
hears every language spoken in Rome, except
the Italian! So largely has the Seven-hilled
City become the pleasure ground of foreign
residents. The contrast between the ordinary
breakfast-table talk in Rome and in — Boston,
for instance, or Washington, is amusing. In
the Puritan capital it usually includes the topic
of weather predictions and the news in the
morning paper, with whatever other of local or
personal matters of interest. In Washington,
where the very actors and the events that make
the nation's history are fairly before one's
eyes, the breakfast-table conversation is apt to
turn on matters that have not yet got into the
papers, — the evening session of the previous
night, perhaps, when too long prolonged under
the vast dome to admit of its having been noted
in the morning press. But in Rome the breakfast-table talk is apt to be of the new excavations just taken from the bed of the Tiber;
the question as to whether the head of St. Paul
could have touched (at the tragic scene of his
execution) at three places so far apart as the

tri-fontanes; or a discussion of the marvellous freshness of the mosaics in the interior of the Palace of the Cæsars; or, again, of the last night's balls or dinners, and matters most frankly *mondaine*, and of contemporary life.

The American Embassy, whose location depends on the individual choice of the Ambassador of the time, is now in the old Palazzo del Drago on the corner of the Via Venti Settembre and the Via dell Quattro Fontane. The street floor, like all the old palaces, is not used for living purposes. The portere, the guards, the corridors, and approaches to the staircases monopolize this space. The piano nobile is the residence of the beautiful and lovely Principessa d' Antuni, the youthful widow of the Principe who was himself a grandson of Marie Christine, the Queen of Spain. The young Princess who was married to him at the age of seventeen, ten years ago, is left with three little children, of whom the only daughter bears the name of her great-grandmother, the Spanish Queen. Perfectly at home in all the romance languages, an accomplished musician, a thinker, a scholar, a student, a lovely figure in life, a beautiful and sympathetic friend is the Princess

d'Antuni. She is "of a simplicity," as they
say in Italy, investing the dignity of her rank
with indescribable grace and sweetness. The
two long flights of stairs that lead up to the
secundo piano in the Palazzo del Drago — the
floor occupied by the American Embassy —
have at least a hundred steps to each staircase,
yet so broad and easy of ascent as hardly to
fatigue one. These flights are carpeted in
glowing red, while along the wall are niches in
each of which stands an old statue, making the
ascent of the guest seem a classic progress.

The Palazzo del Drago has an elevator, but
elevator service in Rome is a thing apart,
something considered quite too good for human
nature's daily food, and the slight power is
far too little to permit any number of people
to be accommodated, so on any ceremonial
occasion the elevator is closed and the guests
walk up the two long flights. The total lack
of any mastery of mechanical conditions in
Italy is very curious.

The grand ball given at the American Embassy just before Ash Wednesday in the winter
of 1907 was a very pretty affair. Up the rose-
red carpeted stairs the guests walked, the

statues looking silently on, but apparently there was no Galatea to step down from her niche and join the happy throng. In the antechamber each guest was asked to write his name in the large autograph books kept for that purpose, and then, passing on, was received by the Ambassador and Ambassadress in the first of the splendid series of salons thrown open for the occasion. At this time it was Mr. and Mrs. Henry White who represented the United States, and won the hearts of all Rome as well, and assisted by their charming daughter, Miss Muriel White, they made this ball an affair to leave its lovely pictures in memory. The scenic setting of an old Roman palace captivates the stranger. It may not impress him as especially comfortable, but it is certainly picturesque, and who would not prefer — at least for the "one night only" of the traditional *prima donna* announcements — the pictorially picturesque and magnificent to the merely comfortable? The lofty ceilings, painted by artists who have long since vanished from mortal sight, make it impossible to attain the temperature that the American regards as essential to his terrestrial well-being, and as the only sources of heat were the open fireplaces the guests hovered around these and their radii of comfortable warmth were limited. In one salon there was one especially beautiful effect of a great jar of white lilacs placed before a vast mirror at sufficient distance to give the mirror reflection an individuality as a thing apart, and the effect was that of a very garden of paradise. The music was fascinating, the decorations all in good taste, and the occasion was most brilliant, — *très charmante* indeed. The American ambassadress was ablaze with her famous diamonds, her corsage being literally covered with them, and her coiffure adorned with a coronet, but the temperature soon forced the ambassadress to partially eclipse her splendor with the little ermine shoulder cape that is an indispensable article for evening dress in Rome. The temperature does not admit the possibility of *décolleté* gowns without some protection, when these resplendent glittering robes that seem woven of the stars are worn. Among the more distinguished guests, aside from the *corps diplomatique* and the titled nobility of Rome and visiting foreigners, were M. Carolus Duran, the celebrated portrait artist of Paris, and among other

interesting people were Miss Elise Emmons of
Leamington, England, a grand-niece of Charlotte
Cushman. M. Carolus Duran was very magnificent, his breast covered with jewelled orders
and decorations from the various societies,
academies, and governments that have honored
him. He is a short man and has grown quite
stout, but he carries himself with inimitable
grace and dignity, and in his luminous eyes one
still surprises that far-away look which Sargent
so wonderfully caught in his portrait of the
great French artist, painted in his earlier life.

The number of spacious salons with their
easy-chairs and sofas enabled all guests who
desired to ensconce themselves luxuriously to
do so, and watch the glittering scene. The
supper room and the salon for dancing were
not more alluring than the salons wherein one
could study this brilliant throng of diplomates,
titled nobility, distinguished artists, social ce-
lebrities, and those who were, in various ways,
each *persona grata* in Rome. Among those at
this particular festivity were the American novelist, Frank Hamilton Spearman, with Mrs. Spearman. In late American fiction Mr. Spearman
has made for himself a distinctive place as the

novelist whose artistic eye has discerned the romance in the new phases of life created by the extensive systems of mountain railroading, and the great irrigation schemes of the far West, which have not only opened up new territory, but have called into evidence new combinations of the qualities most potent in human life, — love, sacrifice, heroism, devotion to duty, and tragedy and comedy as well. In his novels, "The Daughter of a Magnate" and "Whispering Smith," in such vivid and delightful short stories as "The Ghost at Point of Rocks," which appeared in *Scribner's Magazine* for August of 1907, Mr. Spearman has dramatized the pathos, the wit, the vast and marvellous spirit of enterprise, the desolation of isolated regions, the all-pervading potency and one may almost say intimacy of modern life made possible by the Arabian Nights' dream of wireless telegraphy, "soaring" cars, long-distance telephoning, and lightning express train service in cars that climb the mountains beyond the clouds, or dash through tunnels with ten thousand feet of mountains above them. Mr. Spearman is the novelist *par excellence* of this intense *vie modernité*.

ITALY, THE MAGIC LAND

On Washington's Birthday, again, the stately salons of the American Embassy in the old Palazzo del Drago were well filled from four to six with an assemblage which expressed its patriotism and devotion to Washington by appearing in its most faultless raiment and in an apparent appreciation of the refreshment tables, from which cake and ices, tea and various other delicacies, were served.

The informal weekly receptions at the Embassy are always delightful, and the dinners and ceremonial entertainments are given with that faultless grace which characterizes the American ambassadress.

The American consulate is always a charming centre in Rome, and in the present residence of Consul-General and Mrs. De Castro, who have domiciled themselves on a lofty floor of a palace in the Via Venti Settembre, commanding beautiful views that make a picture of every window, the consulate is one of the favorite social centres for Americans and other nationalities as well, who enjoy the charming welcome of Mrs. De Castro.

Professor and Mrs. Jesse Benedict Carter, in their lovely home in the Via Gregoriana, add another to the pleasant American centres in the Eternal City, Professor Carter having succeeded Professor Norton as the principal of the American Classical School.

Mrs. Elihu Vedder, assisted by her accomplished daughter, Miss Anita Vedder, has a pretty fashion of receiving weekly in Mr. Vedder's studio in the Via Flaminia, and these Saturday receptions at the Vedders' are a feature of social life in Rome which are greatly sought. The distinguished artist reserves these afternoons for leisurely conversation, and pictures and sketches are enjoyed the more that they may be enjoyed in the presence of their creator. Miss Vedder has called to life again the almost lost art of tapestry, and her productions of wonderful beauty are considered as among the most desirable in modern decorative art. Among these tapestries are "The Lover's Song," "Salome Dancing before Herod," "The Annunciation," "The Legend of the Unicorn," "The Lovers' Picnic," and "The Lovers." The tapestries were painted in Rome and in the Vedder villa, *Torre Quatro Venti* on Capri, where the artist and his wife and daughter pass their summers. The established

English Church has two chapels in Rome, one the Holy Trinity, of which Rev. Dr. Baldwin is the rector, and the other English chapel in Via del Babuino has for its chaplain Rev. Dr. Nutcombe Oxenham, whose ministry is one of the most helpful factors in Rome. Dr. and Mrs. Oxenham occupy a charming apartment in the Piazza del Popolo, the most picturesque piazza in Rome, with the terraced Pincion hillside crowned by the Villa di Medici on one side, and the "twin churches" on another; and the beautiful salon of Mrs. Oxenham, with its wealth of books and classic engravings and gems of pictures, is one of the homelike interiors in Rome. Mr. and Mrs. Oxenham receive on Wednesdays, and an hour with them and their guests is always a privileged one.

The work of this church, largely through the active co-operation of Mrs. Oxenham, extends into wide charities which are without discrimination as to sect or race, — the only consideration being the human need to be met in the name of Him whose care and love are for each and all.

Among the delightful hostesses of Rome is the American wife of Caviliere Cortesi, an

Italian man of letters, and in their apartment, in one of the notable palaces in the Corso, some of the most brilliant musicals and receptions are given, the "All' Illustrissima Signora" being assisted in the informal serving of tea by the two little fairy daughters, Annunziata and Elizabetta, whose childish loveliness lingers with the *habitués* of this pleasant home.

In the Palazzo Senni, in the old part of Rome, looking out on Castel San Angelo and the Ponte d' Angelo, across to the dome of St. Peter's, the Listers had their home; and though Mrs. Lister, one of the most distinguished English ladies of Rome, has gone on into the fairer world beyond, her daughter, Miss Roma Lister, sustains the charming hospitalities for which her mother was famous. Her salons on the piano nobile of the palace are rich in souvenirs and rare objects of art. Mrs. Lister, who was of a noted English house, was evidently a favorite with Queen Victoria and the royal family; and her marriage gifts included two drawings by the Queen, both autographed, and a crayon portrait of the Empress Frederick with autographic inscription to Mrs. Lister. Another personal gift was a portrait of Cardinal

Newman, with his autograph. A bust of Lady Paget of Florence, the widow of Sir Augustus Paget, formerly the English Ambassador to Italy, is another of the interesting treasures which include, indeed, gifts and offerings from a large number of those eminent in state, in art, in literature, or in the church. The gracious hospitality of Miss Lister is dispensed to groups of cosmopolitan guests, and her dinners and other entertainments are among the most brilliant in Rome.

The Eternal City is not as hospitable to various phases of modern thought as is Florence, in which Theosophy, Christian Science, and psychic investigation flourish with rapidly increasing ardor; but Rome has a Theosophical Society, among whose leaders is the Baroness Rosenkrans, the mother of the distinguished young Danish novelist, and the aunt of Miss Roma Lister. The society has its rooms in the very heart of old Rome, and holds weekly meetings, often with an English lecturer as the speaker of the hour. A Theosophical library, in both English and Italian, is easily accessible, and the meetings are conducted in either language as it chances at the time. The accession of Annie

Besant to the presidency of the Theosophical
Society, succeeding Colonel Olcott, whose death
occurred early in 1907, was most satisfactory
to the Roman members. Mrs. Besant is one
of the most remarkable women of the day. She
is in no sense allied with any fads or freaks;
she is essentially a woman of scholarship and
poise, of genuine grasp of significant thought
and of brilliant eloquence. Theosophy, rightly
interpreted, is in no sense antagonistic, but,
rather, supplemental to Christianity. It offers
the intellectual explanation — the details, so
to speak — of the great spiritual truths of the
Bible.

Rome seems fairly on its way to become an
English-speaking city, so numerous are the
Americans and English who throng to Rome
in the winter.

There are now at least a dozen large new
hotels on the scale of the best modern hotels in
New York and Paris, beside the multitude of
the older ones which are comfortable and retain
all their popularity; yet this increase in accommodation does not equal the increase in demand.
In February the tide of travel sets in toward
Rome, and from that date until after Easter

every nook and niche are filled to overflow-
ing. The demand for apartments in Rome is
greater than the supply, although the city is
being constantly extended and new buildings
are rapidly being erected. It would seem as if,
with the present increasingly large number of
Americans and English, it might be an admirable
financial enterprise for capitalists to come and
build comfortable modern apartment hotels.
There seems to be no adequate reason why, in
this age, people should be compelled to live in
these gloomy, dreary, cold, old stone palaces,
without elevator service and with no adequate
heating, lighting, and running-water facilities.
There would seem to be no conceivable reason
why these conveniences should not be at hand
in Rome as well as in New York. As for the
climate, with warm houses to live in, it would
be charmingly comfortable, for the deadly cold
is not in the temperature out of doors, but only
in the interiors. One is warm in the sunshine
in the streets, when he is fairly frozen in the
house. Mentioning this, however, with wonder
that some enterprising American did not begin
such building operations, a friend who has lived
for sixteen years in Rome replied that the

Italians would never permit it; that no foreigner is allowed to come in here and initiate business operations. And the Italians continue building after the old and clumsy fashion of five hundred years ago.

Italy has a curiously pervasive and general suspicion of any latter-day comfort. The new apartment houses of from four to seven stories are largely without any elevator; if there is one it usually only ascends about halfway, and it is so clumsy and slow in its methods, so poorly supported by power, that half the time it does not run at all. The streets of Rome are paved with rough stones; the sidewalks are very narrow; the lighting is inadequate. Bathrooms are rare and insufficient in number, and all interior lighting and heating arrangements lack much that is desirable according to American ideas of comfort.

Still the Eternal City is so impressive in and of itself that sunshine or storm, comfort or the reverse, can hardly affect one's intensity of joy and wonder and mysterious, unanalyzable rapture in it. The twentieth-century Rome is a very different affair from the Rome on which Hawthorne entered one dark, cold, stormy winter night more than half a century ago. In the best modern hotels one may be as comfortable as he likes, with all the fascinations of life added besides. No wonder that Rome is one of the great winter centres, with some of the most interesting people in the world always to be found under the spell of its enchantment.

The Rome of to-day is a curious mixture of ruins and of modern buildings which are neither modern nor mediæval in their structure, but many of which combine the most picturesque features of the latter with the latest beauty of French and American architectural art. The classic buildings are now largely in unpleasant surroundings; as, for instance, the Pantheon, which is surrounded by a fish market, with unspeakable odors and other repulsive features. "But the portico, with its sixteen Corinthian columns, is forever majestic; the interior, a vast circular cell surmounted by a dome through which alone it is lighted, there being no windows in the walls, is massive and grim, but the magical illumination, the eye constantly revealing the sky above, gives it wonderful beauty. Over the outer portals is the inscription of its erection by Agrippa twenty-seven years before

Christ, so it has stood for nearly two thousand years. Colossal statues of Augustus and Agrippa fill niches. In diameter the interior of the Pantheon is one hundred and thirty-two feet, and it is the same in height, which insures the singularly harmonious proportions. The tribune of the High-Altar is cut in the thickness of the wall in the form of a semicircle, and is ornamented, like the door, with four pilasters and two columns of violet marble. The six chapels are also cut in the wall and ornamented by two columns and two pilasters. The columns and the pilasters support the beautiful cornice of white marble; the frieze is of porphyry, and goes round the whole temple. Above this order there is a species of attic with fourteen niches, and the great cornice from which rises the majestic dome. Eight other niches are between the chapels, and these are also with a pediment supported by two Corinthian columns. They are now converted into altars. In this temple are buried several artists, among whom are Raphael, Giovanni da Udine, Baldassare Peruzzi, and Annibale Caracci. Raphael is buried beneath the base of the statue called la Madonna del Sasso, sculptured by Lorenzetti.

This church is, however, without paintings or sculptures of much interest. Victor Emmanuel was entombed here on the 20th of January, 1878, and King Umberto on the 9th of August, 1900." One of the imposing ceremonies of Rome is that always celebrated in the Pantheon on March 14, in memory of King Umberto Primo.

A grand catafalque, surmounted by the royal crown, and surrounded by tall candelabra with wax candles, is erected in the centre of the temple, draped with black velvet and gold lace, and lighted with electric lamps. The mass is for a chorus of voices only. All the civil and military authorities, the state dignitaries, and the *corps diplomatique* to the court of Italy are present. The troops, in full dress uniform, file in the Piazza of the Collegio Romano, Via Piè di Marmo, and the Piazza della Minerva, enclosing thus a large square in the Piazza del Pantheon. The spectacle is one of the most imposing of all Roman ceremonies.

The King, and Queen Elena, and the Dowager Queen Margherita, accompanied by their respective civil and military households, assist at the requiem mass celebrated in the Pantheon, and at a commemoration service, on the same day, in the Royal Chapel of the Sudario, where also assemble the ladies and gentlemen of the Order of the Annunziata.

On the same morning the feast of St. Gregory, Pope and Doctor of the church, is celebrated at his church on the Cælian Hill. He was born of a noble family, and was Prefect of Rome in 573. Pope Pelagius II made him regionary deacon of Rome, and sent him as legate to Constantinople in 578, where he remained till the death of Pelagius, when he was elected Pope (590). He introduced the Gregorian chant. His first great act was to send St. Augustine to convert the Saxons of England to the Christian faith. An inscription in the Church of San Gregorio Magno states that St. Augustine was educated in the abbey which was erected on the site of the present church by Gregory, and that many early archbishops of York and Canterbury were also educated there. It was on the steps of this church that Augustine and his forty monks took leave of Gregory, when setting out for England. He died in 604, after a pontificate of thirteen years and six months. He was buried in the portico of the Vatican Basilica, and his body lies under the altar dedicated to him in this same church. His church, on the Cælian Hill, was built on the site of the monastery founded by him. In the chapel of the triclinium, near the church, the table on which he served the poor is shown. Near the church also is seen his cell, where his marble chair and one of his arms are exhibited.

During the Lenten season of 1907 one of the privileges of Rome was to hear the sermons of Monsignor Vaughn, in the English Catholic Church of San Silvestre. Monsignor Vaughn is the private chaplain of the Pope. His discourses attracted increasing throngs of both Catholic and Protestant hearers. This celebrated prelate is a brother of the late English Cardinal. He is a man of great distinction of presence, of beautiful voice and fascination of manner. One discourse had for its theme the joys of the life that is to come. The spiritual body, he said, has many qualities not pertaining to the physical body. It is immured from all disease and accidents; it is subtle and can pass through any substance which is (apparently) solid to us, as, for instance, when Jesus appeared in the midst of his disciples, "the doors being

shut." It is not a clog on the soul, continued
Monsignor Vaughn; the spiritual body is the
vehicle of the soul and can waft its way through
the air; it can walk the air as the physical body
walks the earth. It is not — as is the physical
body — the prison of the soul, but the companion of the soul. This is all a very enlightened
presentation of spiritual truth, and it is little
wonder that such preaching attracts large con-
gregations. Holy Week in Rome bears little
resemblance now to that of the past. The
Pope is not visible in any of the ceremonials
in any of the churches; and the impressiveness
of former Catholic ceremonials is greatly les-
sened. Indeed, with the passing of the temporal
power of the Pope, the picturesqueness of Rome
largely vanished.

Not, assuredly, from any lack of reverence
for the colossal cathedral of St. Peter's is that
Basilica a resort for Sunday afternoons; it
suggests a social reunion, where every one
goes, listens as he will to the music of the
Papal choir in the Chapel of the Sacrament,
and strolls about the vast interior where the
promenade of the multitude does not yet dis-
turb in the least the vesper service in the chapel.

ITALY, THE MAGIC LAND

Here one meets everybody; the general news of the day is exchanged; greeting and salutation and pleasant little conversational interludes mark the afternoon, while the sun sinks behind the splendid pile of the Palazzo Vaticano, and the golden light through the window of the tribune fades into dusk. Can one ever lose out of memory the indescribable charm of this leisurely sauntering, in social enjoyment, in the wonderful interior of St. Peter's?

In the way of the regulation sight-seeing the visitor to Rome compasses most of his duty in this respect on his initial sojourn and goes the rounds that no one ever need dream of repeating. Once for all the visitor to Rome goes down into the Catacombs; makes his appallingly hard journey over Castel San Angelo, into its cells and dungeons, and to the colossal salon in which is Hadrian's tomb; once for a lifetime he climbs St. Peter's dome; drives out to old St. Agnes and descends into the crypt; visits the Church of the Capucines and beholds the ghastly spectacle of the monks' skulls; drives in the Appian Way; visits the Palace of the Cæsars, the Baths of Caracalla — a mass of ruins; the Forum; the Temples of Vesta and

Isis; the Coliseum, and the classic old Pantheon. These form a kind of skeleton for the regulation sight-seeing of the Eternal City; things which, once done, are checked off with the feeling that the entire duty of the tourist has been fulfilled, and that, henceforth in Rome, there is laid up for him the crown of enjoyment, if not re-joicing; that he may go again and again to study the marvellous treasures of the Vatican galleries, the masterpieces of art in the Raphael stanze in the Vatican, the interesting pictures and sculpture in the many rich churches and galleries. The deadly chill of most of these galleries and churches in the winter is beyond words to describe. It is as if the gloom and chill and darkness of a thousand centuries were there concentrated.

One of the regulation places for the devout sight-seer, who feels responsible to his conscience for improving his privileges, is the Museo Nazionale, or the Tiberine Museum, a large proportion of whose treasures have been ex-cavated in making the new embankments of the Tiber. It is located on the site of the Baths of Diocletian, the great ruins of which surround it in the most uncanny way. Built around a large court, the salons of the museum are entered from the inner cloisters. In the centre of the court is a fountain, and around it are antique fragments of statues, columns, and statuettes found in many places. The famous Ludovisi collection of antique statuary is now permanently placed in this museum, — a collection that includes the "Ludovisi Mars;" Hercules," with a cornucopia; the "Hermes of Theseus," the "Discobolus Hermes;" the "Venus of Gnidus" as copied by Praxiteles; the "Dying Medusa;" the "Ludovisi Juno," which Winckelmann declares to be the finest head of Juno extant, a Greek work of the fourth century; a "Cupid and Psyche;" the two "Muses of Astronomy" and of "Epic Poetry," "Urania and Calliope;" "an Antoninus;" the largest sarcophagus known; a "Tragic Mask" (colossal) in rosso antico; a bust of "Marcus Aurelius" in bronze, and many other priceless works.

The splendor of scenic setting for art in the magnificent salons of the Casino Borghese has never been surpassed. They are, perhaps, the most impressive of any Roman interior, with lofty, splendidly decorated ceilings and walls, where recess and niche hold priceless sculptures. The splendor of these salons, indeed, quite exceeds description. In the principal one is a group on one wall — a colossal relief — representing Marcus Curtius plunging into the gulf in the Forum. There are busts of the twelve Cæsars; there are busts of all the Roman Emperors, with alabaster draperies, placed on pedestals of red granite. There are Bernini's "Apollo and Daphne;" Canova's celebrated statue of Princess Pauline Borghese (the sister of Napoleon I); Bernini's "David" and "Æneas and Anchises;" Thorwaldsen's "Faun;" "Diana," "Isis," "Juno," and many other celebrated classic statues. All the great paintings which were formerly in the Palazzo Borghese — over six hundred in all — are now in this casino. The great work in this collection is Raphael's "Entombment of Christ," painted in his twenty-fourth year. Titian's "Divine and Human Love;" Raphael's portrait of "Cæsar Borgia;" Correggio's "Danaë;" Domenichino's "Cumæan Sibyl" and "Diana;" Peruzzi's "Venus Leaving the Bath;" Van Dyck's "Crucifixion;" Titian's "Venus and Cupid;" and "Annunciation," by Paul Veronese;

ITALY, THE MAGIC LAND

Vasari's "Lucrezia Borgia;" Botticelli's "Holy Family and Angels;" Van Dyck's "Entombment;" Carlo Dolce's "Mater Dolorosa," and Sassoferrato's "Three Ages of Man" are among the great masterpieces in this museum.

The Villa Borghese (by which is meant the park) is some three miles in extent, and was laid out some two hundred years ago by Cardinal Borghese. As recently as 1902 it was purchased by the government for three million francs, and its official name is now "Villa Comunale Umberto Primo." These grounds contain fountains, antique statues, tablets, small temples and many inscriptions, with statues of Æsculapius and Apollo, and an Egyptian gateway. They are open all day to every one freely and are one of the great attractions of Rome.

The great palaces of Rome are of later date than those of Florence. There are some eighty principal ones, of which the Palazzos Veneziano, Farnese, Doria, Barberini, Colonna, and the Rospigliosi (containing Guido's famous "Aurora") are the most important. The Farnesina Palace contains some of the most interesting pictures in Rome, and the traditions of the residence of Agostino Chigi, during the pontificate of Leo X, are still found in Rome,— traditions of the lavish magnificence of the entertainments given here to the Pope and the Cardinals.

The Monte Pincio is the famous drive of Roman society, and the promenade around the brow of the hill offers one of the most enchanting views of the world. Near the Trinità di Monti stands the historic Villa Medici, the French Academy of which the great Carolus Duran is now the director. The view across the valley in which lies the Piazza di Spagna, the river to St. Peter's, from the Villa Medici, is one of the finest in Rome.

The architecture of the garden façade is attributed to Michael Angelo. These gardens have a circuit of more than a mile, laid out in the formal rectangles and densely bordered walks of the Italian custom. All manner of old fragments of sculpture are scattered through them, — a torso, a broken bust, a ruined statue, an old and partly broken fountain, — and entablatures and reliefs are seen in the walls on every hand. No sound of the city ever penetrates into this dense foliage which secludes the gardens of the famous Villa Medici.

ITALY, THE MAGIC LAND

One of the features of Roman life is the fashionable drive on Monte Pincio in the late afternoons. An hour or two before sunset the terrace of the Piazza Trinità di Monti begins to be thronged with pedestrians, who lean over the marble balustrade, gazing at the incomparable pictured panorama where the vast dome of St. Peter's, the dense pines of the Villa Pamphilia-Doria on the Janiculum, and the dark cypress groves on Monte Mario loom up against the golden western sky.

Compared with the extensive parks of modern cities the Monte Pincio would prefigure itself as a drive for fairies alone. It comprises a few acres only, thickly decorated with trees and shrubbery, with a casino for the orchestra that plays every afternoon, and a circular carriage drive so limited in extent that the same carriage comes in view every few minutes.

The Eternal City has had so many birthdays that one would fancy them to have become negligible; but it was announced on April 21 of 1907 that the date was a special anniversary, and she took on aspects of festivity. The municipal palaces and museums were hung with tapestries, flags were flying from the Capitol, the municipal guards were all in full dress uniform and the municipal orchestra played in the Piazza Colonna. The historic bell began ringing at eight in the morning in peals that were well calculated to call the Cæsars from their tombs and which might, indeed, have been mistaken for the final trumpet calls of Gabriel. But the Romans take their pleasures rather sadly and sternly,—not like the light-hearted Florentines in song and laughter, or with the joyous abandon of the Neapolitans,—so there was no special manifestation on the part of the populace, and the day, cold, gloomy, and cheerless, did not inspire gayety.

When the Republic of Rome was established (on Feb. 9, 1849) a provisional government was appointed. In March of that year Mazzini proposed that the assembly should appoint a Committee of War, and it was decided to send troops to Piedmont. Later a triumvirate, consisting of Mazzini, Saffi, and Armellini, was formed, but disaster was near. In April the French troops landed at Città Vecchia, and the Italians prepared to defend their country from the control of Louis Napoleon. Mazzini is said to have been "the life and the soul" of this defence. But the Republic was doomed, and when it had fallen the Pope returned, only under the protection of the French. But the French Empire, too, was doomed to fall; and when Garibaldi transferred his successes to Victor Emmanuel, the monarchy was consolidated by the union of Rome with Italy, and the present "Via Venti Settembre" in Rome — the street named to commemorate that 20th of September, 1870, on which the Italian troops entered the city and the Papal reign ended — perpetuates the story of those eventful days. "Victor Emmanuel, Cavour, and Garibaldi have been designated, along with Mazzini, as the founders of the modern Italy," said Dr. William Clarke, "but a broad line divides Mazzini from the others." Dr. Clarke sees between Cavour and Mazzini "the everlasting conflict between the idealist and the man of the world. The former," he continues, "stands by the intellect and the conscience; the latter by the limitations of actual fact and the practical difficulties of the case," and Dr. Clarke notes further: —

"It was pre-eminently Mazzini who gave to Italy the breath of a new life, who taught her people constancy in devotion to an ideal good. Prophets are rarely successful in their own day, and so it has been with the prophet of modern Italy. The making of Italy has not proceeded in the way he hoped it would; for the Italians, who are an eminently subtle and diplomatic people, have apparently thought it best to bend to the hard facts by which they have been surrounded. But if, as Emerson teaches, facts are fluid to thought, we may believe that the ideas of Mazzini will yet prevail in the nation of his birth, and that he may yet be regarded as the spiritual father of the future Italian commonwealth. For of him, if of any modern man, we may say that he

'Saw distant gates of Eden gleam,
And did not dream it was a dream.' "

Between the period of the establishment of the Roman Republic in 1849 and the consummation of United Italy in 1870 the years were rich to the artist, whatever they may have been to philosopher and patriot. The way for the painter and the sculptor seems to have been a flowery and a pictorial one,— a very *via buona*

STATUE OF CHRIST, ANCIENT CHURCH OF SAN MARTINA, ROME
From the Artist's Original Cast
Albert Bertel Thorwaldsen
Page 193

fortuna, through a golden, artistic atmosphere. The perpetual excursions may lead the serious spectator to wonder where working hours come in, but, at all events, those days are rich in color. Friends grouped together by the unerring law of elective affinities loitered in galleries and churches. San Martina, near the Mamertine prisons, was a point of interest because of Thorwaldsen's bequest to it of the original cast of his beautiful statue of "Christ" which is in Copenhagen. This is, perhaps, the finest work ever conceived by the Danish sculptor, and is one that no visitor of to-day can behold unmoved. Both Canova and Bernini are also represented in this church,— the former by a statue of "Religion" and the latter by a bust of Pietro da Cortona. Beneath the present Church of San Martina is the ancient one containing the shrine of the martyr, under a superb bronze altar. Of this church, Mrs. Jameson says in her "Sacred and Legendary Art ": —

"At the foot of the Capitoline Hill, on the left hand as we descend from the Ara Cœli into the Forum, there stood in very ancient times a small chapel, dedicated to St. Martina, a Roman virgin. The veneration paid to her was of very early date, and the Roman people were accustomed to assemble there on the first day of the year. This observance was, however, confined to the people, and was not very general till 1634, an era which connects her in rather an interesting manner with the history of art. In this year, as they were about to repair her chapel, they discovered, walled into the foundations, a sarcophagus of terra cotta, in which was the body of a young female, whose severed head reposed in a separate casket. These remains were very naturally supposed to be those of the saint who had been so long venerated on that spot. The discovery was hailed with the utmost exultation, not by the people only, but by those who led the minds and consciences of the people. The Pope himself, Urban VIII, composed hymns in her praise; and Cardinal Francesco Barberini undertook to rebuild her church."

The painter, Pietro da Cortona, entered into this feeling and at his own expense built the chapel and painted for its altar piece the pic-

ture representing the saint in triumph, while
the temple in which she has gone to sacrifice
falls in ruins from a raging tempest.

In any stray ramble in Rome the sojourner
might chance, at any moment, upon obelisk, a
pedestal or inscription linked with the great
names of the historic past. Hawthorne has recorded how, by mere chance, he turned from
the Via delle Quattro Fontane into the Via Quirinale and was thus lured on to an obelisk and
a fountain on the pedestal of which on one side
was the inscription, "Opus Phidias," and on
the other, "Opus Praxiteles," and he exclaims:—

"What a city is this, when one may stumble, by
mere chance — at a street corner as it were — on
the works of two such sculptors! I do not know
the authority," he continues, "on which these
statues (Castor and Pollux I presume) are attributed to Phidias and Praxiteles; but they impressed me as noble and godlike, and I feel inclined to take them for what they purport to be."

While the Papal ceremonies are neither so
frequent nor so magnificent as in former days,
still any hotel guest in Rome is liable, any

morning, on coming down to the *salle-à-manger*
for coffee, to find every woman (who is taking
her Rome seriously) arrayed in a black robe
with a black lace veil on her head. One would
fancy they were all a procession of nuns, about
to retire from the world into the strict seclusion
of the cloister. But it is nothing so momen-
tous. It is only that every lady, with the
devotion to spectacles which every visitor in
Rome feels, as a matter of course, has secured
the pink ticket entitling her to admission to
the Vatican Palace to see the "passage" of the
Pope, as he makes his way, attended by the
Cardinals of the Sacred College, to the Sistine
Chapel where his Holiness "creates" new
Cardinals. Although rumored that the spectacle will be a gorgeous one, that the Pope
will be carried aloft preceded by the silver
trumpeters and attended by the Cardinals and
the ambassadors and other dignitaries in the
full dress of their ceremonial costumes and their
orders, the reality is less impressive. Some
feminine enthusiasts fare forth at the heroic
hour of eight, although the procession is not
announced to pass until a quarter after ten
(which in Italy should be translated as a quarter

after eleven, at the earliest, if not after twelve, which would be the more probable), in order to secure good standing room. For everybody is to stand — of course, comfort being a thing conspicuous only by its absence in Italy! Those of us too well aware by the experiences of previous visits to Italy that no Italian function was ever on time, from the starting of a railway train to the crowning of a king, only betake ourselves to the glories of the Palazzo Vaticano at the hour named, and we have then — as one's prophetic soul or his commonplace memory warned him — to wait more than an hour wedged into a dense crowd of all nationalities, none of whom seem at this particular juncture, at least, to be at all overburdened with good manners. And what went they out for to seek? Instead of an impressive spectacle — a thing to remember for a lifetime — one merely sees Pius X walking, surrounded by his Cardinals in a group, — not a procession, — he alone in the centre with his mitre on his head, — the whole scene hardly lasting over a minute, and as his Holiness is not as tall as most of his Cardinals, he is almost hidden from view. It had been rumored that the Pope was to be borne aloft in the Papal chair, preceded by the traditional white fan and the silver trumpets; but the present Pope is temperamentally inclined to minimize all the ceremonials investing his sacred office.

Yet there is always a thrill in entering the Vatican. To ascend that splendid *Scala Regia* designed by Bernini, with one of the most ingeniously treated perspective effects to be found, it may be, in the entire world; to cross this *Scala* with its interesting frescoes by Salviati and others; to see at near range the picturesque Swiss Guard, — surely any pretext to enjoy such a morning is easily accepted of whatever occurrence one may grasp in order to obtain the hour.

One curious feature of the past is to-day equally in evidence in Rome. Strolling at any time into the Church of San Agostino one beholds a curious spectacle. It is in this church that is placed the beautiful bronze statue of the Virgin and Child by Sansovino. It is approached by a platform on which is placed a stool that enables one to mount and thus reach the foot of the statue, which is kissed and the wish of the devotee is offered. This Madonna is believed to have the power to grant each wish and prayer; to heal the sick; restore the blind, the deaf, and the lame; to grant immunity from loss or illness; to grant success and prosperity. The poor Madonna must have her hands full with these avalanches of petitions, but she sits calmly in state and, if the striking testimony of votive offerings can be credited, she is most amiable in granting the prayers of her devotees. For she is hung with priceless jewels; necklaces, brooches, bracelets, diamond and ruby and sapphire rings on her fingers, she is a blaze of splendor. Around this statue there is a perpetual crowd, whatever hour of day one chances to wander in, and from prince to beggar the bronze foot is kissed, as each waits his turn to mount the stool and prefer his secret wish. The walls of the church are covered with the votive offerings to the Madonna for her aid, — rich jewels, orders, tablets, — offerings of all kinds. In this church is entombed the body of Santa Monica, the mother of St. Augustine, placed in an urn of verd-antique, in a special chapel beautifully decorated. After preferring one's secret wish to the Virgin one must wander on to the Fontane de Trevi and throw his penny into the water to insure his return to Rome, and then he may rest, *mens conscia recta!*

Although Holy Week in Rome has less ceremonial observance in these latter days than those of the impressive scenes so vividly portrayed by Mme. de Staël in "Corinne," it still attracts a multitude of visitors and offers much to touch and thrill the life of the spirit, quite irrespective as to whether the visitor be of the Catholic or Protestant faith. In the great essentials of Christianity, all followers of Christ unite. The Pope does not now take part in public services on Easter, and that scene of the Pontifical blessing from the balcony of St. Peter's given to the multitude below who throng the piazza remains only in memory and in record. But the stately and solemn services of Good Friday in the vast and grand interior of St. Peter's are an experience to linger forever in memory. The three hours' service — the chanting of the Miserere — was a scene to impress the imagination. This service is held in the late afternoon of Good Friday, in the tribune of St. Peter's, the extreme end of the church where the vast window of yellow glass gives a perpetually golden light. The chair believed to have been that of St. Peter's is here placed, enclosed in ivory and supported by statues of four Fathers of the church, St. Augustine, St. Ambrose, St. Chrysostom, and St. Athanasius, from a design of Bernini.

In the tribune is the tomb of Urban VIII (who was Matteo Barberini), of which the redundant decoration tells the story that it is also Bernini's work. Opposite this tomb is that of Paul III, by della Porta, under the supervision of Michael Angelo, it is said, and the beauty and dignity of the bronze figure of the aged Pope, in the act of giving the benediction, quite confirm this tradition. On a tablet in the wall of the tribune are engraved the names of all the bishops and prelates who, in 1854, accepted the belief of the Immaculate Conception, — this tablet being placed by the order of Pio Nono.

In this tribune on the late afternoon of the Good Friday of 1907 the seats were filled with worshippers to listen to the three hours' chant of the Miserere. Princes and peasants sat side by side, and an immense throng who could not find seats stood, often wandering away in the dim distances of the cathedral and ever and again returning. The high altar, where Canova's beautiful figure of the kneeling Pope always enchains the visitor, was, as usual, surrounded. The lights burned — these perpetual lamps — and the moving throng went and came. The scene grew mystic, dream-like, as the solemn music floated on the air.

The Chapel of the Holy Sacrament, on the left of the cathedral, was made into the sepulchre that day, and anything more beautiful than the myriad altar lights and the flowers could not be imagined. At the altar black-robed nuns were kneeling, and all over the chapel, kneeling on the floor, were people of all grades and ranks of life, from the duchess and princess to the beggar woman with a ragged shawl on her shoulders and her baby in her arms. St. Peter's was nearly filled all that day with people, not crowded, but apparently thronged in almost every part.

The altar in the Chapel of the Holy Sacrament was one mass of deep red roses. The chapel was completely darkened, but the blaze of myriads of tall candles illuminated the roses and the black-robed nuns and the black-robed devotees. It was a scene never to be forgotten.

Even in the latter-day Rome, historic names are not wanting. One of these, the Princess Christina Bonaparte, *née* Ruspoli, died in 1907 in her Roman villa in Via Venti Settembre. She was the widow of Prince Napoleon Charles Bonaparte and a cousin of the Empress Eugénie. With her husband in Paris until 1870, she fled (whilst her husband was fighting at Metz) as soon as the Commune was proclaimed. The princess was considered a beautiful woman and her portrait had been painted by Ernest Hébert, but it was lost when the Palace of the Tuileries was destroyed in 1870.

With this princess dies the name of the Bonaparte family. Her daughters, Donna Maria Gotti-Bonaparte and Princess Maria della Moskowa, were often with her in Rome.

. The Palazzo Bonaparte is very near Porta Pia. Although called a palace, it is simply a plain house of some five stories, with narrow halls and stone staircases, no elevator, no electric lights. The princess occupied the first floor, while the apartments above were let to various families.

With the exception of the royal palaces there are few in which suites are not obtainable for residence by any one who desires them.

It was at a pleasant *déjeûner* one spring day in Rome that the project was launched, that we should go motoring that afternoon to Frascati, Albano, Castel Gandolfo, Lago di Nemi, and all that wonderful region. We were lunching with a friend who had a charming apartment in one of the sumptuous old palaces of Rome, where, in a niche on the marble staircase, the statue of Cæsar Augustus stood, — a copy of the famous statue in the Capitoline, — where lofty, decorated ceilings, old paintings and sculptures adorned the rooms, and where from the windows we looked out on the tragedy-haunted Castel San Angelo, with the dome of San Pietro in the background. Our friend who invited us to fly in his motor had brought his touring car over from America. The one note of new luxury now is for travellers to journey with their touring cars. In a year or two more it will be airships or soaring machines. On this wonderful May afternoon, all azure and gold, we started off in the great, luxurious touring car which was arranged even

CASTEL SAN ANGELO AND ST. PETER'S, ROME

Page 204

to carry two trunks, with a safe in it for the deposit of valuables, a hamper for refreshments, and, indeed, almost every conceivable convenience. On we flew through Rome, past the great Basilica of San Maria Maggiore; past the wonderful pile of San Giovanni Laterano, with the colossal statues of the apostles surmounting the façade; through the Porta San Giovanni into the narrow, walled lane leading out on the Campagna; on, on, to the Alban hills. We flew past olive orchards and vineyards, and the vast green pasture lands of the Campagna whose vivid green was ablaze with scarlet poppies. Far away to the west there was a white shining line — the line of the sea.

At Frascati we stopped at the Villa Torlonia, the country place of the ducal family, whose grand Roman palazzo is in the Boca di Leone in the old part of Rome. The Torlonia have an only daughter, Donna Teresa, whose *débutante* ball a year ago is said to have been the most magnificent entertainment in Rome for fifty years. A writer, in a recent article on the nobility of Rome, said of this family: —

"The Torlonia figure repeatedly in the novels

of Thackeray, who was never tired of portraying them. They have been most useful citizens, and since the days of the old army contractor, who founded the house, have augmented the family wealth by judicious investments, especially in connection with the draining and reclaiming of the marsh lands that abound in the former Papal States. They have contracted matrimonial alliances with the Colonna, with the Borghese, the Belmonte, the Doria, and the Sforza."

The Villa Torlonia at Frascati is a very large estate with extensive gardens, terraces, and a cascade of three falls on the hillside, which is turned on (the water) at pleasure. The house, however, is a shabby-looking affair, a two or three story, rambling, yellow structure, which, at Newport, would not be considered too good for the gardener.

After the usual fashion of the Italians who seldom travel, the Torlonia, wealthy as they are, simply remove from their palace in Rome to their villa at Frascati instead of travelling to Switzerland, Germany, or elsewhere in the summer.

ITALY, THE MAGIC LAND

The Duke and Duchess of Cumberland were the guests of the Torlonia that day, the entire party enjoying themselves *al fresco*, and the beautiful cascade pouring down within the near distance.

These outlying towns, Frascati, Albano, Castel Gandolfo, and Lago di Nemi, the picturesque group in the Alban Mountains, are some sixteen to eighteen miles from Rome. These Alban hills rise like an island from the vast plain of the Campagna, the highest point being some three thousand feet above sea level. They are covered with villages and castles and villas, and have in all a population of some fifty thousand. The region is volcanic, and the beautiful Lago di Nemi and Lago di Albano were the craters of extinct volcanoes. All this region was the haunt of Cicero, Virgil, and Livy. At Tusculum, near Frascati, are the remains of Cicero's villa, and also of an ancient theatre hewn out of solid rock. The view to the west toward Rome is most beautiful. The dome of St. Peter's crowns the Eternal City; and the Campagna — a sea of green — is as infinite in sight as is the Mediterranean. There are splendid villas and estates in these Alban hills

that belong to the Roman nobility, and here
the Pope has his summer palace. "The Alban
Mount is also full of historical and legendary
interest," says a writer on the country around
Rome. "The Latin tribe, one of the constitu-
ent elements of the Roman people, had here
its seat. Upon the highest peak of the range
was the temple of Jupiter Latiaris, where all
the tribes of Latin blood, the Romans included,
met every year to worship; and where the vic-
torious generals of the Republic repaired to
offer praises and acknowledgments. In these
mountain glens undoubtedly most of that
ballad literature of Rome, the loss of which
Macaulay so eloquently laments and so suc-
cessfully restores, had its origin. Nor need the
scholar be reminded that this is the scene of
the most original and vigorous portions of the
Æneid of Virgil; nor how the genius of the
poet, which rather languidly recounts the traditions borrowed from Greece, wakes to new life,
when he feels his feet upon his own soil and
deals with Latin names and Latin legends."

The Villa Aldobrandini at Frascati is celebrated for its fantastic waterworks in elaborate fountains and cascades. In the gardens a

statue of Pan with a pipe of reeds and one of a satyr with a trumpet are made to play (both the pipe and the trumpet) by water. The hydraulic engineer must have found in Frascati his earthly paradise, for he commanded the water to leap into foam and spray in the air, to rush down marble terraces, and to form itself into obelisks of liquid silver.

At Grotto Ferrata is a vast monastery of monks of the Order of Basilio (Greek), a monastery so colossal as to be mistaken for a fortress. The chapel has frescoes by Domenichino. At Castel Gandolfo is the summer Papal palace, that has not been occupied by a Pope since the overthrowing of the temporal power in 1870. It has a beautiful and commanding view toward Rome. It was built by Urban VIII.

All the magic of Italy is in this picturesque excursion. In the vast grounds of the Villa Barberini are the ruins of the ancient palace and gardens of Domitian. On one hillside is a broken wall; a long avenue of ilex trees reveals here and there fragments of mosaic pavement. Crumbling niches hold fragments of statues. The hill itself is still pierced with the long tunnels driven through it by Domitian that he might pass unseen, — presumably safe from his enemies, — from the palace to the gardens. From the parapet, Rome is seen across the shining Campagna and the dome of Michael Angelo gleams against the blue Italian sky.

"The wreck is beautiful," writes Mrs. Humphry Ward, in "Eleanor," of this romantic spot; "for it is masked in the gloom of the overhanging trees; or hidden behind dropping veils of ivy; or lit up by straggling patches of broom and cytisus that thrust themselves through the gaps in the Roman brickwork and shine golden in the dark. At the foot of the wall, along its whole length, runs a low marble conduit that held the sweetest, liveliest water. Lilies of the valley grow beside it, breathing scent into the shadowed air; while on the outer or garden side of the path the grass is purple with long-stalked violets, or pink with the sharp heads of the cyclamen. And a little farther, from the same grass, there shoots up, in happy neglect, tall camellia trees, ragged and laden, strewing the ground red and white beneath them. And above the camellias again the famous stone-pines of the villa climb into the high air, overlooking the plain and the sea, peering at Rome and Soracte."

One could wander all day in the strange ruins of the old Barberini grounds, and in the vast spaces of the gardens and through the Villa Doria.

The beauty of the avenue of ilex trees through which we flew from Castel Gandolfo to Lago di Nemi surpasses description. This lake, some four miles in circumference, lies in a crater hollow, with precipitous hills surrounding it, the water so clear that the ancients called it the "Mirror of Diana." In it was constructed an artificial island in the design of a Roman state barge.

Over the long viaduct at Ariccia we flew; everywhere in the little town people, donkeys — an almost indistinguishable mass — filled the narrow streets; and thus on to Genzano and the Lago di Nemi, with its fabled fleet at the bottom.

The Chigi woods, that fill the deep ravine under the great viaduct at Ariccia, were in the most brilliant emerald green. Past these forests lay the vast stretch of the Pontine Marshes; and turning toward Rome again, the splendor of the sunset flamed in the sky. One could but recall Mrs. Humphry Ward's vivid picture of a storm seen over this part of the Campagna: —

"The sunset was rushing to its height through every possible phase of violence and splendor. From the Mediterranean, storm clouds were rising fast to the assault and conquest of the upper sky, which still above the hills shone blue and tranquil. But the northwest wind and the sea were leagued against it. They sent out threatening fingers and long spinning veils of cloud across it — skirmishers that foretold the black and serried lines, the torn and monstrous masses behind. Below these wild tempest shapes again — in long spaces resting on the sea — the heaven was at peace, shining in delicate greens and yellows, infinitely translucent and serene, above the dazzling lines of water. Over Rome itself there was a strange massing and curving of the clouds. Between their blackness and the deep purple of the Campagna rose the city — pale phantom — upholding one great dome, and one only, to view of night and the

world. Round and above and behind, beneath
the long flat arch of the storm, glowed a furnace
of scarlet light. The buildings of the city were
faint specks within its fierce intensity, dimly
visible through a sea of fire. St. Peter's alone,
without visible foundation or support, had con-
sistence, form, identity; and between the city
and the hills, waves of blue and purple shade,
forerunners of the night, stole over the Campagna towards the higher ground. But the
hills themselves were still shining, still clad in
rose and amethyst, caught in gentler repetition
from the wildness of the west. Pale rose even
the olive gardens; rose the rich brown fallows,
the emerging farms; while drawn across the
Campagna from north to south, as though some
mighty brush had just laid it there for sheer
lust of color, sheer joy in the mating it with the
rose,— one long strip of sharpest, purest green."

The Villa Falconicri, in Frascati, which was
built by Cardinal Ruffini, with the old ilex tree
preserved in the portals, has recently been purchased by the Emperor of Germany, who pro-
poses to transform it into an Academy for the
accommodation of German students in Rome.

These national academies draw their corresponding numbers of students from the nations thus represented, and contribute to the cosmopolitan aspects of Rome. The American Academy in Rome is now being transferred from the Ludovisi quarter to a large and convenient building outside Porta Pia.

Perhaps the eminently social quality of Roman life may be indirectly due to the lack of library privileges which is a conspicuous defect in Rome. The Biblioteca Vittorio Emanuele, under the courteous administration of Commendatore Conte Guili, has, it is true, a collection of over half a million volumes and thousands of very rare and valuable manuscripts. It has a large public reading room, and books are loaned on the signature of any embassy or consulate; yet this library, while offering peculiar advantages to theological and other special students and readers, does not afford any extended privileges to the general reader of modern English and American publications. It is located in a grim and forbidding old stone palace, approached by an obscure lane from the Corso, where, as there is no sidewalk, the pedestrian shares the narrow, dark, cold, stone-paved little street with carts, donkeys, peasants, and beggars.

The great monument to King Victor Emmanuel, of mingled architecture and sculpture, a colossal structure of white marble with arches and pillars forming beautiful colonnades, the capital of each column heavily carved, and the sculpture, which is being done by a number of artists, will be of the most artistic and beautiful order. This memorial will occupy an entire block, and it is located very near the Capitol. All the old buildings in the vicinity will be torn down to give a fine vista for this transcendently noble and sumptuous memorial.

The directors of this work aim to have it completed and ready to be unveiled in 1911, the jubilee year of Italy's resurrection as a united country.

Encircled by the old Aurelian wall and near the great pyramid that marks the tomb of Caius Cestius, who died 12 B.C., lies the Protestant cemetery of Rome, full of bloom and fragrance and beauty, under the dark, solemn cypress trees that stand like ever-watchful sentinels. When Keats was buried here (in 1820), Shelley wrote of "the romantic and lovely cemetery . . . under the pyramid of Caius Cestius, and the mossy walls and towers now mouldering and desolate which formed the circuit of ancient Rome. The cemetery is an open space among the ruins, covered even in winter with violets and daisies. It might make one in love with death," he added, "to think of being buried in so sweet a place."

In the old cemetery (immediately adjoining the pyramid and separated from the new one by a wall) is the grave of Keats (who died in 1821) with its unique inscription, "Here lies one whose name was writ in water." Beside it is that of his friend, Joseph Severn, who died in 1829, and near these the grave of John Bell, the famous writer on surgery and anatomy. In the new or more modern cemetery the visitor lingers by the graves of Shelley and his friend, Trelawney; August Goethe (the son of the poet); of William and Mary Howitt, who died in 1879 and 1888. Not merely, however, do the names of Keats and Shelley allure the visitor to poetic meditations; but here lie the earthly forms of many a poet, painter, and sculptor of our own country, with their wives

PORTA SAN PAOLA, PYRAMID OF CAIUS CESTIUS, ROME

Page 216

and children, who have sought in the Eternal
City the atmosphere for art and who, enamoured
by the loveliness of Rome, continued there for
all their remaining years. These graves, these
sculptured memorials, are eloquent with the
joys, the sorrows, the achievements and the
failures, the success and the defeat, of the
artistic life in a foreign land. Many of these
memorial sculptures are the work of the husband or the father, into which is inseparably
joined the personal tenderness to the artist's
skill. Especially noticeable are the graves of
the wives of three American sculptors, — William Wetmore Story, Richard S. Greenough, and
Franklin Simmons. Each of these is marked
by a memorial sculpture created by the husband, and the three different conceptions of
these sculptors are interesting to contrast. That
of Mr. Story is of an angel with outspread
wings, kneeling, her head bowed in the utter
despair and desolation of hopeless sorrow.
The figure has the greatest delicacy of beauty
and refinement and tenderness; but it is the
grief that has no support of faith, the grief that
has no vision of divine consolation. On the
memorial monument is simply the name, Emelyn

Story, born in Boston, 1820, died in Rome in 1898, and the note that it is the last work of W. W. Story, in memory of his beloved wife. Here, also, is Mr. Story buried, his name and dates of birth and death (1819–1901) alone being inscribed.

At the tomb of Sarah B. Greenough, the wife of Richard S. Greenough, the monument is designed to represent Psyche escaping from the bondage of mortality. This Psyche is emerging from her garments and she holds in her hand a lamp. On this is the inscription: "Her loss was that as of a keystone to an arch."

Mrs. Greenough was a very accomplished musician, and she had the unique honor of having been made a member of the "Arcadians."

The memorial sculpture over the grave of Mrs. Franklin Simmons is, as elsewhere noted, the work of her husband, a figure called "The Angel of the Resurrection." The angel is represented as a male figure (Gabriel) holding in the left hand a golden trumpet while the right is outstretched. His wings are spread, his face partly turned to the right. The form is partially draped and in every detail is instinct with a complete harmony; every fold of the drapery, every curve of the body, and the lofty and triumphant expression of the face in its ineffable glory of achievement proclaim the triumph of immortality. It stands on a pedestal that gives it, from the base of the pedestal to the tip of the outstretched wings, a height of some twenty-one feet. This monument, seen against a background of dark cypress trees, speaks the word of positive and complete faith in the divine promise of eternal life.

> "Then life is — to wake, not sleep,
>   Rise and not rest, but press
> From earth's level where blindly creep
>   Things perfected, more or less,
> In the heaven's height — far and steep."

The visitor lingers over the grave of that interesting painter, J. Rollin Tilton, whose landscapes from Egypt and Italian scenes were so vivid and picturesque.

Richard Henry Dana, the elder, born in Boston in 1815, came to Rome to die in 1882.

Very near the tomb of William Wetmore and Emelyn Story is that of Constance Fenimore Woolson. Over the graves of William and

Mary Howitt is the inscription: "Let not your heart be troubled; believe in God, believe also in me."

On the wall just back of the new tomb erected over the ashes of Shelley by Onslow Ford in 1891 is a memorial tablet placed to Frederick W. H. Myers, bearing this inscription:—

"This tablet is placed to the memory of Frederick William Henry Myers, born at Keswick, Cumberland, Feb. 6, 1843; died in Rome, Jan. 17, 1901. 'He asked life of Thee, and Thou gavest him long life ever and forever.'"

Over the grave of John Addington Symonds, whose best monument is in his admirable History of the Renaissance in Italy, is a Latin inscription written by Professor Jowett of Oxford, and a stanza from the Greek of Cleanthes, translated by Mr. Symonds as follows:—

> "Lead thou, our God, law, reason, motion, life;
> All names for Thee alike are vain and hollow;
> Lead me, for I will follow without strife,
> Or, if I strive, still more I blindly follow."

John Addington Symonds, who certainly ranks as the most gifted interpreter of Italy, in her art, her legends and associations, and her landscape loveliness, died in the Rome he so loved in 1893. His wife was ill in Venice, but his daughter, Margaret, — his insepara- ble companion and his helper in his work, — was with him. It is Miss Symonds who pref- aced a memorial volume to her father with the exquisite lines: —

> "O Love; we two shall go no longer
> To lands of summer beyond the sea."

Near the graves of Keats and of his friend, Joseph Severn, are those of Augustus William Hare and John Gibson, the sculptor, who died in 1868. Some ten years before Hawthorne, meeting Gibson at a dinner given by T. Bu- chanan Read, wrote of him that it was whispered about the table that he had been in Rome for forty-two years and that he had a quiet, self-contained aspect as of one who had spent a calm life among his clay and marble.

Dwight Benton, an American painter and writer, who was for some time in the dip- lomatic service and whose home had been in Rome for more than a quarter of a century, lies buried here. For many years he was the editor of *The Roman World*, which still sustains the interesting character that marked it during his editorship. Of his work in art a friend wrote: —

"In painting, as in literature, Dwight Benton took his inspiration from nature. His paintings of Italian scenery are true and faithful representations of its character and atmospheric effects. His tramps on the Roman Campagna were long and often tiring, but he worked with all an artist's enthusiasm, unmindful of cold, rain, and even hunger. He would delight, as all true artists, in an old convent, a tree, a tower, a cross, which he would reproduce with a peculiar and striking perfection of tone and color. In his paintings of Keats's and Shelley's tombs, not only are the slabs and marble there, but there, also, in all their naturalness, are the stately pines and cypresses above, with the sunshine and shadows alternating between them, and in the background the turreted top of St. Paul's Gateway, the Pyramid of Caius Cestius, all lending effect and picturesqueness to the whole."

ITALY, THE MAGIC LAND

The present King of Italy purchased one of Mr. Benton's paintings, called "Giornata di tristezza."

While art abounds in Rome, less can be said for literature. There is a large and admirable selected Italian library in connection with the Collegio Romano; but while these books circulate, under certain conditions, to visitors, and the courtesy of the librarian and his staff is generously kind, the location and the Italian methods render it a matter of some difficulty to avail one's self of its resources. In the Piazza di Spagna there are two circulating libraries, but although one of these claims twenty-five thousand volumes, the majority are of mediocre fiction and almost none, if any, of the important modern works are to be found here. The visitor who is a subscriber to this library passes into a small, dark room, where one window looking on the street hardly does more than make the darkness visible, and he must take the catalogue to the window and stand in order to decipher the list, which is hardly, indeed, worth the trouble, as there are very few volumes of any pretension to importance in the collection, and of late years no additions, apparently, have ever been made. The other circulating library, while far preferable, is still in crowded rooms and the assortment is limited. The visitor in Rome who cares for reading matter looks forward with delight to Florence, with its noble circulating library, to which access is so easy and whose conduct in all ways is so convenient and grateful to the guest.

In Rome, however, one finds his romance embodied in life and his history written in the streets and in the marvellous structures. His poetry is in her art, her ruins, her magical loveliness of hillside vistas, her infinite views over the Campagna, her sapphire skies, and her luminous, golden atmosphere.

"Here Ischia smiles
  O'er liquid miles,
    And yonder, bluest of the isles,
  Calm Capri waits
  Her sapphire gates,
    Beguiling to her bright estates."

"Oh, Signor! thine the amber hand,
    And mine the distant sea
  Obedient to the least command
    Thine eyes impose on me."

III

DAY-DREAMS IN NAPLES, AMALFI, AND CAPRI

"With dreamful eyes
My spirit lies
Where summer sings but never dies."

NAPLES is the paradise of excursions. It is set
in the heart of incomparable loveliness. Over
its sapphire sea one sails away — to the Fortunate Isles, or some others equally alluring.
Its heights and adjacent mountains offer views
that one might well cross the ocean to enjoy.
Its atmosphere is full of classic interest; of song,
and story, and legend, and romance; of history,
too, which in its tragic and exciting episodes is
not less vivid in color and in strange studies
of human life than is any romance. Naples
is the city of fascination. Rome is stately and
impressive; Florence is all beauty and enchantment; Genoa is picturesque; Venice is a
dream city; but Naples is simply — fascinating.
There is the common life of the streets and the

populace continually *en scène;* the people who are at home on the sunny side in winter, or the shady side in summer; there is the social life of the nobility, which is brilliant and vivacious. The excursions, of which Naples is the centre, are the chief interest to travellers, and these, while possible in winter, are far more enjoyable in the early spring. Still even in midwinter the days are sunny, and while the air is crisp and cool, it is not cold. The grass is as green as in June; but the foliage and flowers are more or less withered. Naples has the high and the lower town, the former the more desirable, and the fine hotels perched on the terraces, with the view all over the Bay of Naples, Capri, Sorrento, and Vesuvius, offer a vista hardly to be duplicated in the entire world. The lower town has its fine hotels on the water's edge, with a beautiful view over the bay, less enchanting than when seen from above. The Bay of Naples is enclosed in two semicircular arms that extend far out at sea, the southern reaching nearly to Capri, while near the termination of the northern,

> "Fair Ischia smiles
> O'er liquid miles."

ITALY, THE MAGIC LAND

Far out at sea the sun shines dazzlingly on the blue Mediterranean. The landscape is full of those curious formations that are always inherent in volcanic regions. The region surrounding Naples is abrupt, picturesque, with the same irregular outline of hills that characterizes the elevations in the Tonto basin in Arizona. The vegetation is of the tropical type. The cactus is common, although it grows to no such monstrous heights as in Arizona. Orange and lemon groves prevail as far as the eye can see. On every height towns and villages crown the crests and sweep in winding terraces around the hillsides. Olive orchards abound. Castles and ruins gleam white in the sunshine on the ledge of rocky precipices. The curved shores shine like broken lines of silver, with deep indentations at Naples and at Castellammare. Between these two points rises Vesuvius, the thin blue smoke constantly curling from the summit that, since the eruption of 1906, has lost much of its elevation. In many places there is hardly the width of a roadway between the low mountains and the coast, but the cliffs are tropically luxurious in vegetation. Everywhere the habitations of the people crowd the space. From the monasteries and the castles that crown the heights, both distant and near to the clustered villages of the plain and those clinging to the hillsides, the scene is one unending panorama of human life. For Naples is only the focussing point of these densely populated regions of Southern Italy. The city stretches along the coast on both sides her semicircular bay; but the terraced hills, the stretches of land beyond, and every peak and valley are thickly sown with human habitations. Its commanding heights, two of which rise in the middle of the town, and its beautiful mirrored expanse of water give to it the most unparalleled variety and beauty of landscape loveliness.

"What words can analyze," says George S. Hillard, "the parts and details of this matchless panorama, or unravel that magic web of beauty into which palaces, villas, forests, gardens, vineyards, the mountains, and the sea are woven? What pen can paint the soft curves, the gentle undulations, the flowing outlines, the craggy steeps, and the far-seen heights, which, in their combination, are so full of grace and, at the same time, expression? Words here are imperfect instruments, and must yield their

CASTEL SANT' ELMO, NAPLES

Page 231

place to the pencil and the graver. But no canvas can reproduce the light and color which play round this enchanting region. No skill can catch the changing hues of the distant mountains, the star-points of the playing waves, the films of purple and green which spread themselves over the calm waters, the sunsets of gold and orange, and the aerial veils of rose and amethyst which drop upon the hills from the skies of morning and evening. The author of the book of Ecclesiasticus seems to have described Naples, when he speaks of 'the pride of the height, the clear firmament, the beauty of heaven, with his glorious show.' 'See Naples and then die,' is a well-known Italian saying; but it should read, 'See Naples and then live.' One glance at such a scene stamps upon the memory an image which, forever after, gives a new value to life."

Naples gives to the visitor the impression of being a city without a past. If she has a history, it is not written in her streets. She is poetic and picturesque, not historic. The heights of Capodimonte and Sant' Elmo divide her into unequal parts, and there is the old Naples which only the antiquarian or the political economist would wish to see, and the new and modern city which is such a miracle of beauty that one longs to stay forever, and fails to wonder that the siren sought these shores. Naples has either been very much misrepresented as to its prevailing manners and customs, or else it has changed within the past decade, for, as a rule, the gentle courtesy and kindness of the people are especially appealing. Augustus often sojourned in Naples, and it was an especially poetic haunt of Virgil, whose tomb is here. Although the poverty and the primitive life of the great masses of the people have been widely discussed, it is yet true that Naples has a very charming social life, and that the University is a centre of learning and culture. One of the oldest universities in Europe, it has a faculty of over one hundred and twenty professors and more than five thousand students. A large and valuable library, and a mineralogical collection which specialists from all over the world come to study, are among the treasures of this University, which was founded in the early part of the thirteenth century by Emperor Frederick William II. There is now in process of erection a new group of buildings which will embody the latest laboratory and library and other privileges. Archæology is, naturally, a special feature of the University of Naples, and the proximity to Pompeii, Herculaneum, and to the wonderful Pompeian collection in the Museum of Naples affords peculiar and unrivalled advantages to students. A bust of Thomas Aquinas, during his life a lecturer at this University, is one of the interesting treasures. The Archives of the Kingdom of Naples attract many a scholar and savant to this city. There are in this collection (which is kept in the monastery adjoining the Church of San Severino) over forty thousand Greek manuscripts, some of which date back to the year 700. The Naples Museum is the great repository of all Pompeian art, and it is rich in sculpture; but it is badly arranged and the vast series of galleries and the long flights of stairs make any study of its work so fatiguing that a visit to it might rank as one of the seven labors of Hercules.

In the royal museum of the Palazzo di Capodimonte, which is located on the beautiful height bearing that name, there are some pictures that are well worth visiting, not because they are particularly good art, but because of the interest attaching to the subjects. This gallery is largely the work of modern Neapolitan artists. Here is the celebrated picture of Michael Angelo bending over the dead body of Vittoria Colonna, kissing only her hand, and haunted by the after-regret that he did not kiss her forehead. Virginia Lebrun has here portraits of Maria Theresa and of the Duchess of Parma; there is one canvas (by Celentano) showing Benvenuto Cellini at the Castel Sant Angelo; a scene depicting the death of Cæsar and a few others of some degree of interest.

Curiously, Naples has never produced great art. Salvator Rosa was, to be sure, a Neapolitan, but his is almost the only name that has made itself immortal in the art of this city. Domenico Morelli, who has recently died, made himself felt as an original painter with certain claims that arrested attention. He is not a draughtsman, but he is a colorist of passionate intensity; he has original power and, more than all, he has a curious endowment of what may be called artistic clairvoyance. Transporting himself by the magic of thought to places on which his eye never rested, he yet sees as

in vision their special characteristics. In one
of his most important works, the motive of
which is the temptation of Jesus in the wilderness, he has painted the desert with a startling reality. Here is a great plain, the stony,
parched Judean plain, with the very feeling of
its desolation pervading the atmosphere. The
Royal Chapel in Naples was decorated by
Morelli, the ceiling painted with an "Assumption of the Virgin," which stands alone in all
the interpretations of this theme; not by virtue
of superior artistic excellence, — on the contrary its art does not make a strong appeal,
— but by its originality of treatment. The
"Salve Regina" and the "Da Scala d' Oro"
are among the more interesting works of this
artist, whose recent death has removed a figure
of exceptional character in modern art, one
who had, pre-eminently, the courage of his
convictions. Some few years ago Morelli's
"Temptation of St. Anthony" was exhibited
in both Paris and Florence, and was generally
condemned, perhaps because not wholly understood. The form of the temptation was supposed to be the shapes taken by a morbid and
diseased imagination; but while as a psycho-

logical conception it was not without value,
it was yet far from attractive as a work of art.
The finest conception, perhaps, ever depicted
of the temptation of St. Anthony — a subject
that has haunted many an artist — is that
painted by the late Carl Guthers of Washington,
a lofty and gifted spirit whose too brief stay
on earth ended in the early months of 1907.
In this picture the temptation of the saint
appears as a vision of all that is purest and
sweetest in life, — wife, children, home; it was
from all this peace and loveliness that St. Anthony turned, sacrificing personal happiness to
the duty of consecrated service to his Master,
in the exquisite conception of Mr. Guthers.
Edoardo Dalbano is the typical leader of the
Neapolitan school of painting of the present
day, and his fascinating picture, called the
"Isle of Sirens," representing the sirens singing in the sunlit Bay of Naples, might well be
held as the keynote to all this enchanting
region. Surely, if the sirens sing not in those
blue waters, it were useless to search elsewhere
for them. Buono is an artist of the Neapolitan
shores, who paints its fisher-folk; Brancaccio
catches the very spirit and animated atmosphere

of the street scenes of Naples; Camprani and
Pratello are landscapists of note; Esposito, too,
despite his Spanish name, is a Neapolitan
marine painter whose work is often most ar-
resting in its power to catch the flickering sunshine over blue water that bathes the rocks
rising out of the sea, — these isles of the
sirens from which float the melodies that enchanted Odysseus.

The traveller may be surprised to find that
in size Naples ranks fourth on the European
Continent, — Paris, Berlin, and St. Petersburg,
only, exceeding it. Naples should be, not
only a port, a pleasure haunt, and a paradise
for excursions, but one of the great cities
of the world in commercial and in social importance. It has one of the finest natural
harbors of the world; it has a beautiful and
attractive adjoining country in which to extend,
indefinitely, its residence and trade districts;
it has the most enchanting fairyland of views
that ever were seen this side the ethereal world;
it has an atmosphere of song and story and a
climate that is far from being objectionable.
Naples is seldom the possessor of a higher
temperature in summer than is New York or

Boston; the winters are mild, and they offer weeks of sunny loveliness when Rome is swept by the icy tramontana from the snow-clad Alban hills. Naples offers, too, exceedingly good facilities for living; the groups of excellent hotels, both on the terraces and on the water's edge in the lower town and along the Villa Nazionale, offer every comfort, and the politeness and courtesy of the Neapolitans, as a rule, are among the alluring features of this enchanting city.

What shall be said of one hotel, especially, perched on the cliffs, to which one ascends by an elevator, finding it the most luxurious fairyland that imagination can conjure? Leaving the street one walks through a marble tunnel lighted with electricity, wondering if he is, indeed, in the grotto of the Muses. Entering a "lift" truly American in its comfort and speed, he is wafted up the heights and steps out in — is it paradise? Here is a large salon entirely of glass with an incomparable view all over the gleaming bay, with Capri and Sorrento shining fair on the opposite sides and Vesuvius, a purple peak, in the near distance. The great city of Naples lies spread out below, with its interior heights of Capodimonte and others. It is a view for which alone one might well sail the four thousand miles of sea from the American shores. Through open French windows one may step out on the terrace. If it is cold he may still enjoy this sublimely wonderful view behind the glass walls that reveal all its beauty and protect him from wind or chill. Elsewhere adjoining salons stretch away, where sunshine, music, reading matter, and dainty writing-desks allure the guest and create for him, indeed, an earthly paradise.

Of the drive on the Strada Nuova di Posilipo, skirting the coast while following the winding rise of the hill, with the sumptuous villas and gardens on one side and the blue sea on the other, — what words can suggest its charm? On a jutting promontory on the ruins of the Palazzo di Donna Ana are seen the palace whose convenient location made it possible for the royal hosts to throw their guests into the sea whenever they became tiresome, an accommodation that the modern hostess might, at times, appreciate. On this road, winding up the Posilipo, is the villa where Garibaldi passed the last winter of his life and which is marked by a tablet. And everywhere and at every turn are the beautiful views, commanding Bagnoli, Camaldoli, Ischia, Baia and Procida, Capri, Nisida and the Neapolitan waters. The hill slopes are overgrown with myrtles and orange trees and roses. Here and there a defile is filled with a vineyard under careful culture.

In the presence of all this marvel of nature's loveliness the visitor hardly remembers the historic interest; yet it was on the little island of Nisida that Brutus and Cassius concocted the conspiracy against Cæsar. The vast Phlegræan Plain before the eye is invested with Hellenic traditions and is the region of many scenes in the poems of Virgil and Homer. In the years of the first and second centuries this plain was dotted with the rich villas of the Roman aristocracy. Here, too, lay the celebrated Lacus Avernus, a volcanic lake which the ancients regarded as the entrance to Avernus itself. Truly it required little imagination to see here the approach to the infernal regions. The air was so poisonous that no bird could fly over the lake and live. Virgil's scene of the descent of Æneas, guided by the sibyl, into the infernal depths is laid here; and near this lake are

ANCIENT TEMPLE, BAIÆ

Page 241

resorts of the latter-day tourist, known as the "Sibyl's Grotto," the "Grotto della Pace," the "Bagni di Sibyl," and the "Inferno."

Baia, on the coast, was the Newport of Rome in the days of Augustus, Hadrian, Cicero, and Nero. It was then the most magnificent summer watering-place known to the world. The glory of the Roman Empire was reflected in the glory of Baia. In one of the Epistles of Horace a Roman noble is made to say: "Nothing in the world can be compared with the lovely bay of Baia." Some five hundred years ago this region became so malarial that no one could dwell in it. Fragments and ruins still remain of the imposing baths and villas of the Roman occupancy. An old crater called the Capo Miseno is described by Virgil as the burial place of Misenus: —

"*At pius Æneas ingenti mole sepulcrum*
Inponit, suaque arma viro remumque tubamque
Monte sub aereo, qui nunc Misenus ab illo
Dicitur aeternumque tenet per saecula nomen."

Cumæ was the most ancient Greek colony of Italy on the coast, and the last survivors of the Tarquinii died here. This is the most classic of all these legendary coast towns near Naples, as it was here that the Cumæan Sibyl dwelt with the mysterious sibylline leaves, — the books that were carried to Rome. A colossal Acropolis was once here, fragments of whose walls are now standing; and the rocky foundation is honeycombed with secret passages and openings. It is here that Virgil's "Grotto of the Sibyl" is supposed to have stood, — the grotto "whence resound as many voices, the oracles of the prophetess."

The journey from Naples to Herculaneum is easily made by electric train cars within an hour, and while there is not much to see it is still an excursion well worth making. Dr. de Petra, of the chair of Archæology in the University of Naples, and formerly the Director of the National Museum, is warmly in favor of the proposed excavation of this buried city, as is Professor Spinazzola of the San Martino museum, who believes that Italy may well become one vast museum of antiquities. "As the theatre of Herculaneum is actually at present a subterranean excavation," he observed, "why not excavate in a similar way the entire city underneath modern Resina? In this way a

perfectly unique underground museum would
be formed, which would have the merit of
leaving magnificent Roman art treasures exactly
in their proper places in the villas. Such a
work ought to be perfectly practicable, with
the resources of modern engineering, and would
certainly be unique in the world.

"There would be no need to build a special
museum for the objects discovered. Not only
would this money be saved, but I feel convinced
that so many visitors would be attracted as to
more than pay for the maintenance. A sub-
terraneous Herculaneum — surely a perfectly
unique place of pilgrimage, just as it was nearly
two thousand years ago — might be lighted by
electric arc lights. I feel certain it would attract
sight-seers from the ends of the world. At the
same time work might go on in the open parts
of the city.

"Pompeii was more of an industrial town,
while Herculaneum was a favorite resort of the
Roman patricians, who did not bring their treasures with them from their northern homes, but
had them executed by Greek artists in the south."

Under the mighty floods of *lava d'acqua* that
buried Herculaneum doubtless lie temples, a

splendid forum, magnificent villas, and most valuable art and literary treasures. In the eighteenth century excavations brought to light rare bronzes, mosaics, and papyri. The famous equestrian statue of Bulbi, in the Naples Museum, was excavated from Herculaneum. Professor Lanciani and Commendatore Boni of Rome — the latter the present director of the Forum, succeding Lanciani — believe that some of the richest art of ancient times may be found in Herculaneum; as does Professor Dall' Osso, inspector of excavations at Pompeii.

Herculaneum is held to have been founded by Hercules when he landed at Campania, returning from Iberia, some three hundred years B.C., and it was in 63 A.D. that it was destroyed. Of this cataclysm Pliny, the Younger, wrote: —

"The sea seemed to roll back on itself by the convulsions of the earth. On the other side hung a black and dreadful cloud, bursting with fiery and serpentine vapors. Naught was heard in the darkness but the shrieks of women, the screams of children, and the frenzied cries of men calling for children, for wives, for parents,

ITALY, THE MAGIC LAND

— all lifting hands to the gods, praying and wishing for death."

Dr. Charles Waldstein of Cambridge University, the eminent archæologist, whose efforts toward initiating the excavation of Herculaneum were a notable event of 1906, thus writes of this buried city: —

"It is important to bear in mind that naturally all the best works in the Museum of Naples, especially the bronzes, came from Herculaneum and not from Pompeii.

"What is most striking is the marvellous preservation of these works. This fact of itself ought to counteract the strange but widespread misapprehension that, while Pompeii was covered with cinders and ashes, Herculaneum was covered with lava, and that the hardness of that material made excavation difficult, if not impossible. All geologists and archæologists are agreed that no lava issued from the eruption of 79 A.D. Herculaneum was covered by a torrent of mud consisting of ashes and cinders mixed with water. The mass which covers it, so far from being less favorable to the preservation of objects, is much more favorable than that which covers Pompeii. Pompeii was partially covered with hot ashes and pumice stones, which burnt or damaged the works of art. As it was not wholly covered, moreover, the inhabitants returned and dug up some of their greatest treasures. Herculaneum, on the other hand, had its actual life, arrested at the highest point, securely preserved from depredation, to a depth of eighty feet, by a material which preserved intact the most delicate specimens which have come down to us in a state so perfect as to be really remarkable.

"The most important of these delicate objects are manuscripts, of which that one villa produced 1750. The state of preservation is illustrated by one specimen, giving two pages from the works of the philosopher Philademus. Unfortunately, the possessor of the villa was a specialist, a student of Epicurean philosophy. While his taste in art was fortunately so catholic, his taste in literature was narrowed down by his special bent. Piso was the friend and protector of the philosopher Philo. Already sixty-five copies of that author's works have been found among the papyri.

ITALY, THE MAGIC LAND

"Yet the city of Herculaneum contained many such villas, and herein it differed from Pompeii. Pompeii was a commonplace provincial town devoted exclusively to commerce; it was not the resort of wealthy and cultured Romans. It was essentially illiterate. No manuscript can be proved to have been found there. It is true a wax tablet with writing has been found; yet this contains — receipts of auctions. Herculaneum, on the other hand, was the favorite resort of wealthy Romans, who built beautiful villas there as in our times people from modern Rome settle for the summer at Sorrento and Castellammare."

The present descent into the theatre of Herculaneum is made by a flight of more than a hundred steps, slippery and cold, in total darkness save for the candle that is carried by the guide, and the visitor sees only the stone seats of the amphitheatre and the stage with the two vacant niches, the statues that filled each being now placed in the Museum in Naples.

The journey of thirteen miles from Naples to Pompeii is through a succession of densely populated villages that seem to be an integral part of Naples itself, for there is no line of demarcation. Portici, Torre del Greco, Torre dell' Annunziata, and others all blend with each other and with Naples. However familiar one has become with the literature of Pompeii, with both archæological descriptions and imaginative interpretations in romance, and however familiar with its aspects he may have become from replicas in art museums, and from pictures, one can yet hardly approach this silent, phantom city without being thrilled by its deep significance. At a distance of a few miles over the gently undulating plain rises Vesuvius; one gazes on the paths where the rivers of molten fire must have rolled down. George S. Hillard, visiting Pompeii in 1853, thus described a house which the visitors of to-day study and admire: —

"The finest house we saw within the walls is one which had been discovered and laid bare about four months previous to the date of our visit, called the house of the Suonatrice, from a painting of a female playing on a pipe, at the entrance. This house was deemed of such peculiar interest that it was under the charge of a special custode, and was only to be seen on payment of an extra fee. It was not of large size, but had evidently been occupied by a person of ample fortune and exquisite taste. The paintings on the walls were numerous, and in the most perfect preservation. In the rear was a minute garden not more than twenty or thirty feet square, with a fairy fountain in the centre; around which were several small statues of children and animals, of white marble, wrought with considerable skill. The whole thing had a very curious effect, like the tasteful baby-house of a grown-up child. Everything in this house was in the most wonderful preservation. The metal pipes which distributed the water, and the cocks by which it was let off, looked perfectly suited for use. Nothing at Pompeii seemed so real as this house, and nowhere else were the embellishments so numerous and so costly.

"Pompeii, though a Roman city in its political relations, was everywhere strongly marked with the impress of the Greek mind. It stood on the northern edge of that part of Italy which, from the number of Grecian colonies it contained, was called Magna Græcia, — a region of enchanting beauty, in which the genius of

Greece attained its most luxurious development. It has been conjectured that Pompeii had an unusually large proportion of men of property, who had been drawn there by the charms of its situation and climate, and that it thus extended a liberal patronage to Greek architects, painters, and sculptors. At any rate, the spirit of Greece still lives and breathes in its ashes. Its temples, as restored by modern architects, are Greek. Its works in marble and bronze claim a place in that cyclus of art of which the metopes of the Parthenon are the highest point of excellence. The pictures that embellish the walls, the unzoned nymphs, the bounding Bacchantes, the grotesque Fauns, the playful arabesques, all are informed with the airy and creative spirit of Greek art.

"The ruins of Pompeii are not merely an open-air museum of curiosities, but they have great value in the illustration they offer to Roman history and Roman literature. The antiquarian of our times studies the great realm of the past with incomparable advantage, by the help of the torch here lighted."

From Pompeii to Castellammare, the beauti-

ful seaside summer resort of the Neapolitans,
"a lover of nature could hardly find a spot of
more varied attractions. Before him spreads
the unrivalled bay, — dotted with sails and un-
folding a broad canvas, on which the most
glowing colors and the most vivid lights are
dashed, — a mirror in which the crimson and
gold of morning, the blue of noon, and the
orange and yellow-green of sunset behold a
livelier image of themselves, — a gentle and
tideless sea, whose waves break upon the
shore like caresses, and never like angry blows.
Should he ever become weary of waves and
languish for woods, he has only to turn his
back upon the sea and climb the hills for an
hour or two, and he will find himself in the
depth of sylvan and mountain solitudes, — in
a region of vines, running streams, deep-shad-
owed valleys, and broad-armed oaks, — where
he will hear the ringdove coo, and see the sensitive hare dart across the forest aisles. A
great city is within an hour's reach; and the
shadow of Vesuvius hangs over the landscape,
keeping the imagination awake by touches of
mystery and terror."

The road to Sorrento, on a cliff a hundred

feet or more above the sea, with mountains on the other side, towering up hundreds of feet high; a road cut in many places out of the solid rock, supported by galleries and viaducts from below, — a road that crosses deep gorges and chasms, always with the iridescent colors of the sea below, — and from Sorrento to Amalfi again, only, if possible, even more wonderful, — is there in the world any drive that can rival this picturesque and sublime route? Of it George Eliot wrote: —

"It is an unspeakably grand drive round the mighty rocks with the sea below; and Amalfi itself surpasses all imagination of a romantic site for a city that once made itself famous in the world."

Sorrento, with its memories and associations of Tasso, seems a place in which one cares only to sit on the balcony of the hotel overhanging the sea and watch the magic spectacle of a panorama unrivalled in all the beauty of the world. Flowers grow in riotous profusion; the fairy sail of a flitting boat is caught in the deepening dusk; the dark outline of Vesuvius is seen against the horizon; and orange orchards gleam against gray walls. Here Tasso was born, in 1544, fit haunt for a poet, with tangles of gay blossoms and the aerial line of mountain peaks. A low parapet borders the precipice, and over it one leans in the air heavy with perfume of locust blossoms. Has the lovely town anything beside sunsets and stars and poets' dreams? Who could ask for more?

To La Cava, — to Amalfi, — still all a dream world!

> "O summer day, beside the joyous sea!
> O summer day so wonderful and white,
> So full of gladness and so full of pain!"

How Amalfi sets itself to song and music! Who can enter it without hearing in the air Longfellow's beautiful lines? —

> "Sweet the memory is to me
> Of a land beyond the sea,
> Where the waves and mountains meet,
> Where, amid her mulberry-trees,
> Sits Amalfi in the heat,
> Bathing ever her white feet
> In the tideless summer seas.
>
> .   .   .   .
>
> 'T is a stairway, not a street,
> That ascends the deep ravine,

ITALY, THE MAGIC LAND

Where the torrent leaps between
Rocky walls that almost meet.

.   .   .   .

This is an enchanted land!
Round the headlands, far away,
Sweeps the blue Salernian bay
With its sickle of white sand;
Further still and furthermost
On the dim discovered coast,
Pæstum with its ruins lies,
And its roses all in bloom."

If ever a region was dropped out of paradise designed, solely, for a poet's day-dreams, it is Amalfi, and the even more beautiful Ravello just above. One fancies that it must have been in the mystic loveliness of this eyrie that the poet lost himself in a day-dream while Jupiter was dividing all the goods of the world. When he reproached the god for not saving a portion for him, Jupiter replied that all the goods were gone, it was true, but that his heaven was always open to the poet.

The ancient Amalfi, the city of activities and merchandise, is gone.

"Where are now the freighted barks
From the marts of east and west?
Where the knights in iron sarks

ITALY, THE MAGIC LAND

Journeying to the Holy Land,
Glove of steel upon the hand,
Cross of crimson on the breast?
Where the pomp of camp and court?
Where the pilgrims with their prayers?
Where the merchants with their wares?

.   .   .   .   .

Vanished like a fleet of cloud,
Like a passing trumpet-blast,
Are those splendors of the past,
And the commerce and the crowd!
Fathoms deep beneath the seas
Lie the ancient warves and quays,
Swallowed by the engulfing waves."

It is impossible to realize that Amalfi was once a flourishing city of Oriental trade. One looks in vain for any trace of ruin or shrine that still suggests the ancient splendors of activity. The strata of the past, so visible in other mediæval cities, are not apparent here. The great cathedral is a most interesting study in the art of architecture, — its exquisite arcades, its delicate, lofty campanile glittering in the sun. The green-roofed cupola is a distinctive feature, and up the many flights of stairs the old Capuccini convent lies, — the unique, romantic hotel where the cells of the monks are now the rooms of the perpetual procession of guests. Does the wraith of Cardinal Capuano, who founded this convent, still wander in midnight hours through the dim cloisters? Does he still keep watch by the body of St. Andrew, the apostle, which he is said to have found and brought to the cathedral where the saint lies, as a saint should lie, gloriously entombed. St. Andrew was the patron saint of Amalfi, but at his death his body was carried from Patras to the Bosphorus, where it was placed in a church in Constantinople. The legend runs that Cardinal Capuano, being in Constantinople, entered the Church of the Holy Apostles to pray, and knowing that the body of the saint was in that city, he besought the heavenly powers to guide him to it. Rising from his devotions he was approached by an aged priest, who announced to the Cardinal that the object of his search was in that very church in which he was praying for guidance; and, aided by unseen powers, he was able to recover it and convey it to Amalfi. All Italian towns that respect themselves offer the allurement of an entombed saint and if, occasionally, the same identical saint does duty for more than one city, who is to decide the local genuineness of the claim? Nothing in

all Italy is so curious as is this town of staircases instead of streets; of houses perched on
the angles of impossible eyries suggesting that,
as the Venetians go about in gondolas, so the
Amalfians must have airships, or the wings of
Icarus, with which to circle in air from their
dwellings to the beach.

The precipitous gorges and dark ravines have
on their crests low parapets of stone walls over
which the visitor lingers and leans watching the
bluest of seas lying fair under the bluest of skies.
The main road, — there is only one, — descending from the hill to the water's edge, makes its
progress through a tunnel.

The old Amalfi, with its palaces, its arches
and colonnades, lies under the sea. Just as the
Pensione Caterina with its rose walks and terraces slipped into the sea in December of 1899,
when two guests and several fishermen lost
their lives, so the ancient Amalfi fell, its cliffs
swallowed up in the waters below.

> "Hidden from all mortal eyes,
>   Deep the sunken city lies;
>   Silent streets and vacant halls,
>   Ruined roofs and towers and walls;
>   Even cities have their graves!"

ITALY, THE MAGIC LAND

When, on a May evening, the white moonlight falls in cascades of silver sheen over terraces and sea, with Amalfi all alabaster and pearl like a dream city in the ethereal air; when the stars hang low in the skies and the fairy lights of the fishermen's boats twinkle far out at sea; when the summer silence is suddenly thrilled by the melody of Neapolitan songs on the air, as if it were a veritable *chant d'amour* of sirens, — then does one believe in the buried city. These rich baritone voices are surely those of some singers of the buried ages. They are floating across the centuries since Amalfi had its pride and place among the great centres of activity. Atrani, Amalfi's twin city, lies in the adjoining defile of the mountains which arch above them. The strange old houses are all dazzlingly white, transfigured under the moon to an unearthly loveliness.

The tragedy of the ruin of Amalfi is related by Petrarca, who was then living in Naples. It was in 1343 that a terrible cataclysm — an earthquake accompanied by a tempest — caused the destruction and the submergence of the city in the sea.

The believers in astrology will find their faith re-enforced by the fact that a bishop, who

was also an astrologist, had read in the stars
that in December of 1343 a terrible disaster
would occur on the Naples coast. It arrived
on schedule time. Petrarca, writing of it to
Giovanni Colonna, states that in consequence
of the prediction of the bishop, the people were
in a condition of wild terror, endeavoring to.
repent of their sins and aspiring to a purer
moral life. In this tide of religious emotion,
ordinary occupations were neglected. On the
very day of the calamity people were crowding
the churches and kneeling in prayer. At night,
after the people were in bed, the shock came.
The sunset had been fair, the evening quiet,
and the people were reassured. But they were
awakened from sleep by the violence of falling
walls and the terror of the tempest. Petrarcha
was lodging in a convent, and he heard the
monks calling to one another as they rushed
from cell to cell. They hastily gathered crosses
and sacred relics in their hands, and, preceded
by the prior, sought the chapel, where they passed
the night in prayer while the tempest raged
outside. The sea broke against the rocks with
a fury that seemed to tear the very foundations
of the earth. The thunder pealed, and mingled

with it were the shrieks of the frightened populace. The rain fell in torrents, deluging the city
as if the sea itself were pouring on it. When
the morning came the darkness still continued.
In the harbor broken ships crashed helplessly together. The sands were strewn with mutilated
dead bodies. Between Capri and the shore the
sea ran mountains high. Amalfi was completely
destroyed, and has never regained her prestige.

The cathedral at Revello has traces of the
rich art it once enshrined, and the rose gardens
of the Palazzo Rufelo might enchant Hafiz himself. The terrace on the very crest of the mountain commands one of the wonderful views of the
world. The cloistered colonnades of this old
Saracenic palace reveal views even to the plains
of Pæstum. There are rare mosaics and fragments of bronzes and marbles yet remaining.

The noble Greek ruins at Pæstum — the three
temples — stand in all the majesty of utter desolation. They are overgrown with flowers, however, and they stand "dewy in the light of the
rising dawn-star."

> "The shrine is ruined now, and far away
> To east and west stretch olive groves, whose shade,
> Even at the height of summer noon, is gray.

ITALY, THE MAGIC LAND

"Yet this was once a hero's temple, crowned
  With myrtle boughs by lovers, and with palm
By wrestlers, resonant with sweetest sound
Of flute and fife in summer evening's calm,
And odorous with incense all the year,
With nard and spice and galbanum and balm."

The detour to Pæstum is full of significance.
The massive columns of the temples stand like
giants of the ages. "It is difficult," writes John
Addington Symonds, "not to return again and
again to the beauty of coloring at Pæstum.
Lying basking in the sun on a flat slab of stone,
and gazing eastward, we overlook a foreground
of dappled light and shadow; then come two
stationary columns built, it seems, of solid gold,
where the sunbeams strike along their russet
surface. Between them lies the landscape, a
medley first of brakefern and asphodel and
feathering acanthus and blue spikes; while beyond and above is a glimpse of mountains,
purple almost to indigo with cloud shadows,
and flecked with snow."

The sail from Amalfi to Pæstum is one incomparable in loveliness. The sunshine is all
lurid gold. The faint, transparent blue haze
fills all the defiles of the mountains; the cliffs

disclose yawning caverns where vast clusters of stalactites hang; and as the boat floats toward Capri from the Sorrento promontory its rocky headlands rise and flame into purple and rose against the glowing sky. Across the Bay of Naples rises the great city. It stands in some subtle way reminding one of the scene where one

> " . . . rowing hard against the stream,
> Saw distant gates of Eden gleam."

Capri is the idyllic island of prismatic light and shade, of gay and joyous life. Here Tiberius had his summer palace, and it was from these shores that he sent the historic letter which revolutionized the life of Sejanus. The letter — *verbosa et grandis epistola* — is still vivid in the historic associations of Rome. Capri is one of the favorite resorts both for winter and summer. Its former modest prices are now greatly increased, like all the latter-day expenses of Italy; but its beauty is perennial, and the artist and poet can still command there a seclusion almost impossible to secure elsewhere in Italy. The distinguished artist, Elihu Vedder of Rome, has a country house on Capri, and another well-known artist, Charles

Caryl Coleman, makes this island his home.
There are days — sometimes several days in
succession — that the sea is high and the boats
cannot run between Naples, Sorrento, and Capri;
and the enforced seclusion is still the seclusion
of the poet's dream. For he shares it with
Mithras, the "unconquered god of the sun,"
whose cult influenced all the monarchs of
Europe and who holds his court in the Grotto
de Matrimonia. Into this grotto one descends
by a flight of nearly two hundred feet; he strolls
among the ruins of the villa of Tiberius, where
the very air is still vital and vocal with those
strange and tragic chapters of Roman life.
The Emperor Augustus first founded here palaces and aqueducts. Tiberius, who retired
to Capri in the year 27 A.D., had his architects
build twelve villas, in honor of the gods, the
largest of these being for Jupiter and known as
the Villa Jovis. In 31 A.D. occurred that
dramatic episode in Roman history, the fall of
Sejanus, and six years later Tiberius died. The
vast white marble baths he had built for him
are now submerged on the coast, and boats glide
over the spot where they stood. The Villa
Jovis stood on a cliff seven hundred feet above

the sea, and the traditions of the barbarities and atrocities that took place there still haunt the island. The natives apparently regard them as a certain title to fame, but the wise tourists persistently ignore horrors; life is made for joy, sweetness, and charm; it is far wiser to think on these things.

And there is charm and joy to spare on lovely Capri. "Sea-mists are frequent in the early summer mornings, swathing the cliffs of Capri and brooding on the smooth water till the day wind rises," says John Addington Symonds. "Then they disappear like magic, rolling in smoke-wreaths from the surface of the sea, condensing into clouds and climbing the hills like Oceanides in quest of Prometheus, or taking their station on the watchtowers of the world as in the chorus of the Nephelai. Such a morning may be chosen for the *giro* of the island. The Blue Grotto loses nothing of its beauty, but rather gains by contrast, when passing from dense fog you find yourself transported to a world of wavering subaqueous sheen. It is only through the very topmost arch that a boat can glide into this cavern; the arch itself spreads downward through the

water so that all the light is transmitted from
beneath and colored by the sea. Outside the
magic world of pantomime there is nothing to
equal these effects of blue and silver. . . .
Numberless are the caves at Capri. The so-
called Green Grotto has the beauty of moss
agate in its liquid floor; the Red Grotto shows
a warmer chord of color; and where there is
no other charm to notice, endless beauty may
be found in the play of sunlight upon roofs
of limestone, tinted with yellow, orange, and
pale pink, mossed over, hung with fern, and
catching tones of blue or green from the still
deeps beneath. . . . After a day upon the
water it is pleasant to rest at sunset in the
loggia above the sea. The Bay of Naples
stretches far and wide in front, beautiful by
reason of the long fine line descending from
Vesuvius, dipping almost to a level, and then
gliding up to join the highlands of the north.
Now sun and moon begin to mingle: waning
and waxing splendors. The cliffs above our
heads are still blushing like the heart of some
tea-rose; when lo, the touch of the huntress
is laid upon those eastern pinnacles, and the
horizon glimmers with her rising. Was it on

such a night that Ferdinand of Aragon fled from his capital before the French, with eyes turned ever to the land he loved, chanting, as he leaned from his galley's stern, that melancholy psalm, 'Except the Lord keep the city, the watchman waketh but in vain,' and seeing Naples dwindle to a white blot on the purple shore?'"

The roses of Capri would form a chapter alone. What walks there are where the air is all fragrance of acacia and rose and orange blossoms! Cascades of roses in riotous luxuriance festoon the old gray stone walls; the pale pink of the early dawn or of a shell by the seashore, the amber of the Banskeia rose, the great golden masses of the Maréchal Niel, their faint yellow gleaming against the deep green leaves of myrtle and frond. The intense glowing scarlet of the gladiolus flames from rocks and roadside, and rosemary and the purple stars of hyacinths garland the ways, until one feels like journeying only in his singing robes. The deep, solemn green of stone pines forms canopies under the sapphire skies, and through their trunks one gazes on the sapphire sea. Is Capri the isle of Epipsychidion?

ITALY, THE MAGIC LAND

"Is there now any one that knows
What a world of mystery lies deep down in the heart of a rose ?"

One walks among these rose-lined lanes, hearing in the very air that exquisite lyric by Louise Chandler Moulton: —

"Roses that briefly live,
    Joy is your dower;
Blest be the Fates that give
    One perfect hour.
And, though too soon you die,
    In your dust glows
Something the passer-by
    Knows was a Rose."

Monte Cassino is one of the most interesting inland points in Southern Italy, — the monastery lying on the crest of a hill nearly two thousand feet above the sea. Dante alludes to this in his Paradiso (XXII, XXXVII), and in the prose translation made by that eminent Dantean scholar, Professor Charles Eliot Norton, this assurance of Beatrice to Dante is thus rendered: —

"That mountain on whose slope Cassino is, was of old frequented on its summit by the deluded and ill-disposed people, and I am he

who first carried up thither the name of Him
who brought to earth the truth which so high
exalts us; and such grace shone upon me that
I drew away the surrounding villages from the
impious worship which seduced the world.
Those other fires were all contemplative men,
kindled by that heat which brings to birth holy
flowers and fruits. Here is Macarius, here is
Romuald, here are my brothers, who within the
cloisters fixed their feet, and held a steadfast
heart. And I to him, 'The affection which
thou displayest in speaking with me, and the
good semblance which I see and note in all
your ardors, have so expanded my confidence
as the sun does the rose, when she becomes
open so much as she has power to be. Therefore I pray thee, and do thou, father, assure me
if I have power to receive so much grace,
that I may see thee with uncovered shape.'
Whereon he, 'Brother, thy high desire shall be
fulfilled in the last sphere, where are fulfilled
all others and my own. There perfect, mature,
and whole is every desire; in that alone is every
part there where it always was: for it is not in
space, and hath not poles; and our stairway
reaches up to it, wherefore thus from thy sight

it conceals itself. Far up as there the patri-
arch Jacob saw it stretch its topmost part when
it appeared to him so laden with Angels. But
now no one lifts his feet from earth to ascend it;
and my rule is remaining as waste of paper.
The walls, which used to be an abbey, have
become caves; and the cowls are sacks full of
bad meal. But heavy usury is not gathered in
so greatly against the pleasure of God, as that
fruit which makes the heart of monks so foolish.
For whatsoever the Church guards is all for the
folk that ask it in God's name, not for one's
kindred, or for another more vile. The flesh
of mortals is so soft that a good beginning
suffices not below from the springing of the oak
to the forming of the acorn. Peter began without gold and without silver, and I with prayers
and with fasting, and Francis in humility his
convent; and if thou lookest at the source of
each, and then lookest again whither it has run,
thou wilt see dark made of the white. Truly,
Jordan turned back, and the sea fleeing when
God willed, were more marvellous to behold
than succor here.'"

Dante adds that the company "like a whirlwind gathered itself upward," and that "the sweet lady urged me behind them, with only a sign, up over that stairway; so did her virtue overcome my nature. But never here below, where one mounts and descends naturally, was there motion so rapid that it could be compared unto my wing."

The time was when Dante and Beatrice met, and he "was standing as one who within himself represses the point of his desire, and attempts not to ask, he so fears the too-much." And then he heard: "If thou couldst see, as I do, the charity which burns among us thy thoughts would be expressed. But that thou through waiting mayst not delay thy high end, I will make answer to thee, even to the thought concerning which thou art so regardful."

The vast monastery of Monte Cassino, lying on the crest of a hill nearly two thousand feet above the sea, has one of the most magnificent locations in all Italy. This monastery was founded (in 529 A.D.) by St. Benedict, on the site of an ancient temple to Apollo. Dante alludes to this also in the Paradiso (Canto XX, 11). As seen from below this monastery has the appearance of a vast castle, or fortress. Its

location is one of the most magnificent in all
Italy. The old entrance was a curious passage
cut through solid rock and it is still used for
princes and cardinals — no lesser dignitaries being allowed to pass through it — and within
the past thirty years a new entrance has been
constructed. In the passageway of the mediæval entrance St. Benedict is said to have had his
cell, and of recent years the German Benedictines, believing they had located the original cell,
had it located, restored, and decorated with
Egyptian frescoes. Several of the courts of this
convent are connected by beautiful arcades with
lofty arches, and adorned with statues, among
which are those of St. Benedict and his sister,
St. Scholastica. Still farther up the hill, upon
the monastery, stands the church which is built
on the site of the ancient one that was erected
by St. Benedict himself — this present edifice
dating back to 1637. Above the portals there
is a long inscription in Latin relating the history
of the monastery and the church. These portals are solid bronze, beautifully carved, with
inlaid tablets of silver on which are inscribed a
list of all the treasures of the abbey in the year
1006. The church is very rich in interior deco-

ration of mosaics, rare marbles, and wonderful monumental memorials. Either side of the high altar are monuments to the Prince of Mignano (Ginodone Trieramosca) and also to Piero de Medico. Both St. Benedict and his sister, St. Scholastica, are entombed under the high altar, which is one of the most elaborately sculptured in all the churches of Italy.

Among the pictorial decorations of this church are a series of fresco paintings by Luca Gindano, painted in the seventeenth century, representing the miracles wrought by St. Benedict. In the refectory is the "Miracle of the Loaves," by Bassano; and in the chapel below are paintings by Mazzarappi and Marco da Siena. Nothing can exceed the richness and beauty of the carvings of the choir stalls. These were executed in the seventeenth century by Coliccio.

The library of this monastery is renowned all over Europe — indeed, it is famous all over the world — for its preservation of ancient manuscripts done by the monks. These are carefully treasured in the archives. Among them is the record of a vision that came to the monk Alferic, in the twelfth century, on which it is believed that Dante founded his immortal

"Divina Commedia;" there is also a fourteenth-
century edition of Dante with margined notes;
and the Commentary of Origen (on the Epistle
to the Romans), dating back to the sixteenth
century; there is the complete series of Papal
bulls that were sent to the monastery of Monte
Cassino from the eleventh century to the
present time, many of them being richly illuminated and decorated with curiously elaborate
seals. There is an autograph letter of the Sultan Mohammed II to Pope Nicholas IV, with
the Pope's reply, — the theme of the correspondence being the Pope's threat of war. The
imperial Mohammed seems to have been in
terror of this, and in his epistle he expresses
his willingness, and, indeed, his intention, to
be converted as soon as he shall visit Rome!
Apparently the Holy Father of that day laid
little stress on the sincerity of this offer on the
part of the Sultan. Here, too, is a wonderful
correspondence between Don Erasmo Gattola,
the historian of the abbey, and a great number
of the celebrated men of his time; and there
are hundreds of other letters, manuscripts, and
documents relating to kings, nobles, emperors,
and many of the nobility of the age.

ITALY, THE MAGIC LAND

In this monastery there is a most interesting collection of relics, in bronze, silver, gold, and *rosso antico*. The library proper contains some eleven thousand volumes, dating back to the very dawn of the discovery of the art of printing.

Mr. Longfellow, whose poet's pen has pictured so many of the Italian landscapes and ancient monuments, thus set Monte Cassino to music, picturing the entire landscape of the Terre di Lavorno region: —

> "The Land of Labor and the Land of Rest,
>   Where mediæval towns are white on all
> The hillsides, and where every mountain's crest
>   Is an Etrurian or a Roman wall.

> . . . . .

> "There is Aquinum, the old Volscian town,
>   Where Juvenal was born, whose lurid light
> Still hovers o'er his birthplace like the crown
>   Of splendor seen o'er cities in the night.

> "Doubled the splendor is, that in its streets
>   The Angelic Doctor as a school-boy played,
> And dreamed perhaps the dreams that he repeats
>   In ponderous folios for scholastics made.

> "And there, uplifted, like a passing cloud
>   That pauses on a mountain summit high,
> Monte Cassino's convent rears its proud
>   And venerable walls against the sky.

ITALY, THE MAGIC LAND

"Well I remember how on foot I climbed
  The stony pathway leading to its gate;
Above, the convent bells for vespers chimed,
  Below, the darkening town grew desolate.

. . . . .

"The silence of the place was like a sleep,
  So full of rest it seemed; each passing tread
Was a reverberation from the deep
  Recesses of the ages that are dead.

"For, more than thirteen centuries ago,
  Benedict fleeing from the gates of Rome,
A youth disgusted with its vice and woe,
  Sought in these mountain solitudes a home.

"He founded here his Convent and his Rule
  Of prayer and work, and counted work as prayer;
The pen became a clarion, and his school
  Flamed like a beacon in the midnight air.

. . . . .

"From the high window, I beheld the scene
  On which Saint Benedict so oft had gazed, —
The mountains and the valley in the sheen
  Of the bright sun, — and stood as one amazed.

. . . . .

"The conflict of the Present and the Past,
  The ideal and the actual in our life,
As on a field of battle held me fast,
  Where this world and the next world were at strife."

ITALY, THE MAGIC LAND

The monastery of Monte Cassino entertains, as its guests, for dinner or for a night, all gentlemen who visit it; but there is an alms box on the ancient gate into which the guest is supposed to place whatever contribution he pleases for the poor of the place. The Italian government, in 1866, declared this monastery to be a "Monumento Nazionali," and it is now a famous ecclesiastical school with some two hundred students and a resplendent faculty of fifty learned monks under the direction of the Abbot. Some of the most celebrated prelates in Europe have been educated at Monte Cassino.

Quite near Monte Cassino, as Longfellow depicts in his lines, is Monte Aquino, a picturesque hillside where the "Doctor Angelicus," Thomas Aquinas, was born (in 1224), the son of Count Landulf, in the Castel Roccasecca. He was educated in the monastery, and one finds' himself recalling here these lines of Thomas William Parsons, entitled "Turning from Darwin to Thomas Aquinas:" —

"Unless in thought with thee I often live,
Angelic doctor! life seems poor to me.
What are these bounties, if they only be
Such boon as farmers to their servants give?

ITALY, THE MAGIC LAND

That I am fed, and that mine oxen thrive,
That my lambs fatten, that mine hours are free —
These ask my nightly thanks on bended knee;
And I do thank Him who hath blest my hive,
And made content my herd, my flock, my bee.
But, Father! nobler things I ask from Thee.
Fishes have sunshine, worms have everything!
Are we but apes? Oh! give me, God, to know
I am death's master; not a scaffolding,
But a true temple where Christ's word could grow."

It was at Aquinum, too, at the foot of Monte
Aquino, Juvenal was born. Near the peaks of
Monte Cassino and Monte Aquino is that of
Monte Cairo, five thousand five hundred feet
high, from whose summit one of the finest
views of all southern Europe is attained. The
Gulf of Gaeta, the valley of San Germano, the
wild and romantic mountain region of the
Abruzzi and a view, too, of the blue sea are in
the panorama, bathed in the opalescent, gleaming lights that often invest the Italian landscape with jewelled splendor.

"I ask myself, Is this a dream?
    Will it all vanish into air?
Is there a land of such supreme
    And perfect beauty, anywhere?"

ITALY, THE MAGIC LAND

It might have been in this pictured dream-region that Hercules came to rest.

"When Heracles, the twelve great labors done,
   To Calpe came, and there his journey stayed,
He raised two pillars toward the evening sun,
   And carved them by a goddess' subtle aid.
Upon their shafts were sacred legends traced,
And round the twain a serpent cincture placed:
'T was at this bound the primal world stood still,
And of Atlantis dreamed, with baffled will."

But still in unmeasured space, still beyond and afar and unattained, still lost in the unpenetrated realms of the poet's fancy, —

"Atlantis lies beyond the pillars yet!"

> *" Here Ischia smiles*
> *O'er liquid miles."*

High o'er the sea-surge and the sands,
  Like a great galleon wrecked and cast
Ashore by storms, thy Castle stands
  A mouldering landmark of the Past.

Upon its terrace-walk, I see
  A phantom gliding to and fro;
It is Colonna, — it is she
  Who lived and loved so long ago.

LONGFELLOW.

We are the only two that, face to face,
Do know each other, as God doth know us both.
— O fearless friendship, that held nothing back!
O absolute trust, that yielded every key,
And flung each curtain up, and drew me on
To enter the white temple of thy soul,
So vast, so cold, so waste! — and give thee sense
Of living warmth, of throbbing tenderness,
Of soft dependencies! O faith that made
Thee free to seek the spot where my dead hopes
Have sepulture, and read above the crypt
Deep graven, the tearful legend of my life!
There, gloomed with the memorials of my past,
Thou once for all didst learn what man accepts
Lothly — (how should he else?) — that never woman,
Fashioned a woman, — heart, brain, body, soul, —
Ever twice loved.

"*Vittoria Colonna to Michael Angelo.*"

MARGARET J. PRESTON.

IV

A PAGE DE CONTI FROM ISCHIA

"Unto my buried lord I give myself."

———

Michael Angelo!
A man that all men honor, and the model
That all should follow; one who works and prays,
For work is prayer, and consecrates his life
To the sublime ideal of his art
Till art and life are one.
> LONGFELLOW, from *"Michael Angelo ; A Fragment."*

IN that poetic sail along the Italian coast
between Naples and Genoa the voyager feels
that it is

"On no earthly sea with transient roar"

that his bark is floating; that

"Unto no earthly airs he trims his sail,"

as he flits along this coast when violet waves
dash against a brilliant background of sky.
Ischia reveals herself through the blue, trans-

parent air, gleaming with opalescent lights, quivering, fading and flaming again as the afterglow in the east rivals in its coloring the sunset splendors of the west. Is there in the air a faint, lingering echo of the *chant d'amour* of sirens on the rocky shores? Is Parthenope still to be descried? Gazing upon Ischia there is a rush of romantic impressions as if one were transported into ideal regions of song, before this impression begins to resolve itself into definite remembrance of fact and incident. Surely some exquisite associations in the past had enchanted this island in memory and invested it with the magic light that never was on sea or land. Traditions of beauty; of the lives of scholar and savant and princes of the church; of a court of nobility enriched and adorned by prelate and by poet; traditions, too, of a woman's consecration to an immortal love and the solace of grief by poetic genius and exalted friendships, — all these seem to cling about Ischia in a vague, atmospheric way till memory, still groping backward in the twilight of the richly historic past, suddenly crystallized into recognition that it was Ischia which was the home of Vittoria Colonna, the greatest woman poet of the Italian

ISCHIA, FROM THE SEA

Page 282

Renaissance. Lines, long since read, arose like an incantation; and like bars of music, each note of which vibrated in the air, came this fragment of one of her songs: —

"If in these rude and artless songs of mine
I never take the file in hand, nor try
With curious care and nice, fastidious eye
To deck and polish each uncultured line,
'T is that it makes small merit of my name
To merit praise. . . .

. . . . . .

But it must be that heaven's own gracious gift
Which, with its breath, divine, inspires my soul,
Strikes forth these sparks unbidden by my will."

Vittoria Colonna was called the most beautiful and gifted woman of her time in all Italy. Her life of nearly sixty years (1490–1547) lay entirely in that period when the apathy of ten centuries was broken, when the darkness fled before the dawning of a glorious day. New methods of thought, revised taste in poetry, new discoveries of science, a nobler progress in criticism, great discoveries, and a lofty and unprecedented freedom of conviction marked the century between 1450 and 1550, stamping it as the marvellous time which we know as the Renaissance, "that solemn fifteenth century which can hardly be studied too much, not merely for its positive results in the things of the intellect and the imagination, its concrete works of art, its special and prominent personalities, with their profound æsthetic charm, but for its general spirit and character, for the ethical qualities of which it is a consummate type."

It was peculiarly fitting that Italy should take the initiative in inaugurating this *vita nuova*. Italy had a language and literature and art. Dante had delivered his solemn message and Petrarca his impassioned song. Boccaccio had taught the gospel of gladness. Who shall analyze the secret springs of their inspiration and reveal to what degree Ovid and Horace and Virgil influenced the later literature? A new solar system was established by Copernicus. America was discovered. Science entered on her definite and ceaseless progress, and religion and art became significant forces in human life. Printing had been invented and the compass discovered.

Into this time of new forces, when everything was throbbing and pulsating with life, was

ITALY, THE MAGIC LAND

Vittoria Colonna born into social prestige and splendor. Her father, Fabrizio Colonna, and her mother, Agnesina di Montefeltro, a daughter of the Duke of Urbino, were then domiciled in the castle of Marino, on the Lago d' Albano, a magnificent palace some twelve miles from Rome, in which the Duke d' Amalfi (the father of Fabrizio Colonna) lived, and which is still standing, filled with memorials and relics of historic interest. Urbino, the seat of the Montefeltro, is renowned as having been the birthplace of Raphael, who

> "Only drank the precious wine of youth,"

but who

> ". . . lives immortal in the hearts of men,
>   . . . and the world is fairer
>   That he lived in it."

The Colonna date back to the eleventh century, and they gave many princes and cardinals to the country. At the close of the thirteenth century they were arrayed against Boniface VIII, the Pope, who accused them of crime, while they disputed the validity of his election to the holy office. In retaliation, the Pope excommunicated the entire family, anathematized them as heretics and declared their estates forfeited to the church. The Colonna, far from being intimidated, commanded three hundred armed horsemen, attacked the papal palace, which they plundered, and made him a prisoner, — an incident referred to by Dante in the "Inferno." The Colonna and the Orsino were also at warfare, and when a member of the former family was elevated to the papacy under the name of Martin V, they despoiled property of the Orsini.

Gay excursionists to-day, who fly over the Campagna in their twentieth-century touring cars to the lovely towns of the Alban hills, may look down from Castel Gondolfo on the gloomy, mediæval little town of Marino, part way up a steep hillside, whose summit is crowned by the castle once belonging to the Colonna and in which Vittoria passed her early childhood. "Nothing," in his "Roba di Roma," says Story, "can be more rich and varied than this magnificent amphitheatre of the Campagna of Rome, . . . sometimes drear, mysterious, and melancholy in desolate stretches; sometimes rolling like an inland sea whose waves have suddenly become green with grass, golden with grain, and gracious with myriads of wild flowers, where scarlet poppies blaze and pink daisies cover vast meadows and vines shroud the picturesque ruins of antique villas, aqueducts, and tombs, or drop from mediæval towers and fortresses."

Flying in the swift motor-car of the time toward the Alban hills, Marino may be easily reached in less than an hour from the Porta San Giovanni, and in the near distance Monte Albani, rising into the cone of Monte Cavi, is a picture before the eye, while on the lower slopes gleam the white villages of Albani, Marino, Castel Gondolfo, and Frascati, with the campanile of a cathedral, a fortress-like ruin, or gardens and olive orchards clambering up the heights. The Papal town of Rocca di Papa crowns one summit where once Tarquin's temple to Jupiter stood and on whose ruins now gleam afar in the Italian sunshine the white walls of the Passionist convent of Monte Cavi, built by Cardinal York. From this height Juno gazed upon the great conflict of contending armies, if Virgil's topography be· entitled to authority. And here, through a defile in the hills, one may look toward Naples, "and then rising abruptly with sheer limestone cliffs and crevasses, where transparent purple shadows sleep all day long, towers the grand range of the Sabine mountains, whose lofty peaks surround the Campagna to the east and north like a curved amphitheatre. . . . Again, skirting the Pontine Marshes on the east, are the Volscian mountains, closing up the Campagna at Terracina, where they overhang the road and affront the sea with their great barrier. Following along the Sabine hills, you will see at intervals the towns of Palestrina and Tivoli, where the Anio tumbles in foam, and other little mountain towns nestled here and there among the soft airy hollows, or perched on the cliffs."

In this landscape there are three ruined villages — Colonna, Gallicano, and Zagarda — perched on their respective hills. The castle of the Colonna family is now restored and modernized to a degree that leaves little trace of that former stately grandeur which is transmuted into modern convenience and comfort.

In this scene of romantic beauty, with the vista of· beauty almost incomparable in any inland view in Italy, Vittoria passed her infancy, until, at the age of four, her childhood was

transplanted to fairy Ischia. In all this chain
of Alban towns, including Marino, Viterbo, Ariccia, and Rocca di Papa, the great family of the
Colonna owned extensive estates, each crowning some height, while the defiles between were
filled, then as now, with the foam and blossom
of riotous greenery. Then, as now, across the
mystic Campagna, the dome of St. Peter's silhouetted itself against a golden background of
western sky.

One needs not to have had privileged access
to the sibylline leaves of the Cumæan sooth-
sayer to recognize that Vittoria Colonna was
born under the star of destiny. Her horoscope
seemed to be inextricably entwined with that of
Italy; and the events which created and determined the conditions of her life and its pano-
ramic series of circumstances were the events
of Italy and of Europe as well — in political
aspects and in the influence on general progress,
brought to bear by strong and prominent individualities whose gifts, genius, or force domi-
nated the movements of the day.

To her father's change of political allegiance,
from the French to the Spanish side, in the
war raging between those countries in 1494,

Vittoria owed all her life in Ischia; and her marriage, and all that resulted from her becoming a member of the d'Avalos family, was due to this espousal of a new political faith on the part of Fabrizio Colonna. To the fact that in 1425 the war with France again broke out was due the loss of her husband and the conditions that consecrated her life to poetry, to learning, and that made possible the beautiful and sympathetic friendship between herself and Michael Angelo. Her life presents the most forcible illustration of the overruling power on human life and destiny.

It was the political change of faith on the part of Fabrizio Colonna that initiated an unforeseen and undreamed-of drama of life for his infant daughter, the first act of which included the command of the King of Naples that the little Vittoria should be betrothed to Francesco d'Avalos, the son of Alphonso, Marchese di Pescara, of Ischia, one of the nobles who stood nearest to the king in those troubled days. Francesco was born in the castle on Ischia in 1489, and was one year older than Vittoria. Fabrizio exchanged his castle at Marino for one in Naples, which city made him the Grand

Constable. The d'Avalos castle in Ischia had
at this time for its chatelaine the Duchessa di
Francavilla, who is said by some authorities
to have been the elder sister and by others to
have been the aunt of Francesco. Donna Con-
stanza d'Avalos, later the Duchessa di Francavilla, had been made the Castellana of the
island for her courage in refusing to capitulate
to the French troops when, after the death of
her father, she was left in sole charge of the
d'Avalos estates, and Emperor Charles V elevated her rank to that of Principessa. The
Duchessa was one of the most remarkable
women of the day. She was a classical scholar,
and herself a writer, the author of a book entitled "*Degli Infortuni e Travagli del Mondo.*"
To the care of this learned and brilliant woman,
a great lady in the social life of the time, the
care of the little Vittoria was committed, and
she studied and played and grew up with
Francesco, her future husband. The d'Avalos
family ranked among the highest nobility of
the Court of Naples, and the Principessa reigned
as a queen of letters and society in her island
kingdom. It was under her care that the two
children, Francesco and Vittoria, pursued their

studies together and acquired every grace of scholarship and accomplishment of society. The circles which the Duchessa drew around her included many gentlewomen from Sicily and from Naples; and "the life at Castel d' Ischia was synonymous with everything glorious and elegant," recorded Visconti, "and its fame has been immortalized." Although Francesco (the future Marchese di Pescara) was born in Italian dominions, yet the d' Avalos family were of Spanish ancestry and traditions. The musical Castilian was the language of the household. The race ideals of Spain — the poetic, the impassioned, the joy in color and movement — pervaded the very atmosphere of Castel d' Ischia. Vittoria's earliest girlhood revealed her exceptional beauty and charm, and gave evidence that the gods loved her and had dowered her with their immortal gifts and genius, which flowered, under the sympathetic guidance and stimulus of such a woman as the Principessa (the Duchessa di Francavilla) and the society she drew around her, as the orange and the myrtle flower under the southern sunshine.

The literature of biography presents no chapter that can rival this in the idyllic beauty of

the lives of those two children on the lovely
island in the violet sea. The perpetual conflicts that were waged in both Rome and Naples awakened no echoes in this romantic and
isolated spot, whose atmosphere was that of
the peace of scholarly pursuits and lofty thought
that is found where the arts and the muses
hold their sway.

But in 1496 came the tragedy of the death
of the young king and queen of Naples; four
years later Rome celebrated a jubilee in which
Naples took part, sending a splendid procession
as escort to the famous Madonna that was
carried from Naples to Rome and back, working miracles, it is said, on both journeys, as a
Madonna should. A year later Frederick of
Naples and the queen, and two of the king's
sisters, — ladies of high nobility, — came as
guests to the castle in Ischia, — royal exiles
seeking shelter. Five years later the new king
and queen were welcomed with gorgeous parade
and acclamation. A pier was thrown out over
one hundred feet into the sea; on this a tent of
gold was erected, and all the nobility of Naples,
in the richest costumes of velvet and jewels,
thronged to meet the royal guests. Over the

sunlit Bay of Naples resounded the thunder of the guns in military salute and the cheers of the people. Among the distinguished nobility present, Costanza, Duchessa and Principessa di Francavilla, was a marked figure with her young charge, Vittoria Colonna, at her side. She made a deep reverence and kissed the hand of the king as he passed, as did many of the ladies of highest rank, and at the fête of that evening Vittoria's beauty charmed all eyes. Although it was well understood that she had been betrothed since childhood to Francesco d'Avalos, yet many princes and nobles sued for her hand and were refused by her father, who was at this time established magnificently in Naples. Pope Julius II refused the pleadings of two dukes, both of whom wished to seek Vittoria in marriage, as he considered the love of the young girl for her betrothed a matter to be held sacred. Three years later, when Vittoria was nineteen and Francesco twenty, their marriage was celebrated in Castel d'Ischia with the richest state and beauty of ceremonial observance. A few months previous to this time she had returned to her father's country home in the family castle at Marino, whither

LA ROCCA, ISCHIA
Page 294

both Fabrizio and Agnese Colonna accompanied their daughter. When the time appointed for her bridal came, Vittoria was escorted to Ischia by princes, and dukes, and ladies of honor, and the marriage gifts to the bride included a chain of rubies, diamonds, and emeralds, linked with gold; a writing desk of solid gold; wonderful bracelets; costumes of velvets, and brocades and rich embroideries, and a portion of fourteen thousand ducats.

"The noted pair had not their equals in Italy at this time," writes a contemporary historian. "Their life in Naples was all magnificence and festivity, and when they desired to exchange it for the country they left Naples for Pietzalba on Monte Emo, where they assembled pleasant parties of ladies and gentlemen. Much time was passed in their beloved Ischia, where the Duchessa, as Castellana, was obliged to receive much company. And here were found the flower of chivalry and the men most noted in letters. . . . They listened to the poets Sanazzaro, il Rota, and Bernardo Tasso; or they heard the admirable discourses on letters of Musefico, il Givoio, and il Minturo. It was an agreeable school for the youthful minds of Vittoria and Pescara. Thus passed in great happiness the first three years of their married life."

It is not strange that to the young Marchesa di Pescara, Ischia had become an enchanted island. The scene of her happy childhood, of her studies, of her first efforts in lyric art, of her stately and resplendent bridal; the home, too, of her early married life, — it is little wonder that in after years she translated into song its scenic loveliness and the thoughts and visions it had inspired.

Again, the ever-recurring war came on, and in the spring of 1512 the King of Naples conferred the doubtful privilege on the Marchesa di Pescara of serving as the royal representative. It is said that Vittoria personally superintended her young husband's outfit, — in horses, attendants, armor, and other details belonging to a gentleman of rank. Her father and her uncle, Prospero Colonna, were also among the military who led Italian troops. In the terrible battle of Ravenna (which was fought on the Easter Sunday, April 11, of 1512), Pescara was wounded, taken prisoner, and carried to the fortress of Porta Gobbia. A messenger was sent to Ischia, where Vittoria lived between her books and the orange groves; and the twentieth-century cynic of 1907 will smile at the form in which she expressed her sorrow, — that of a poem of some forty stanzas, which began: —

> *"Eccelso Mio Signor! Questa ti scrivo*
> *Per te narrar tre quante dubbie voglie,*
> *Fra quanti aspri martir, degliosa io vivo!"*

A translation of this lyric epistle, made in prose, gives it more fully as follows: —

"Eccelso Mio Signor: I write this to thee to tell thee amid what bitter anxieties I live. . . . I believed that so many prayers and tears, and love without measure, would not have been displeasing to God. . . . Thy great valor has shone as in a Hector or an Achilles."

In this letter Vittoria tells him that when the messenger reached her, she was lying on a point of the island ("*I*, in the *body*, my *mind* always with *thee*," she says), and that the whole atmosphere had been to her that day "like a cavern of black fog," and that "the marine gods seemed to say to Ischia, 'To-day, Vittoria, thou shalt hear of disgrace from the confines:

thou now in health and honor, thou shalt be turned to grief; but thy father and husband are saved, though taken prisoners.'"

This presentiment she related to her husband's aunt, the Duchessa Francavilla, the Castellana of Ischia, who begged her not to think of it and said, "It would be strange for such a force to be conquered."

Just after this conversation between the youthful Marchesa and the Duchessa, the messenger arrived. The psychic science of to-day would see in this occurrence a striking instance of telepathy. In her poetic epistle to her husband, Vittoria also says: —

"A wife ought to follow her husband at home and abroad; if he suffers trouble, she suffers; if he is happy, she is; if he dies, she dies. What happens to one happens to both; equals in life, they are equals in death. His fate is her fate."

These letters — in keeping with the times — were, on both sides, expressed in literary rather than in personal form. Pescara, from his captivity, wrote to her a "Dialogue on Love," —

a manuscript for which Visconti notes that he has searched in vain.

The Marchesa di Pescara went from Ischia to Naples, after learning of the misfortunes that had overtaken her husband, in order that she might be able constantly to receive direct communication regarding his fate. A few months later the Marchese returned, making the day "brilliant with joy" to Vittoria, but after a year of happiness he was again called to service, and the Marchesa returned to her beloved Ischia. She gave herself to the study of the ancient classics; she wrote poems, and "considered no time of value but so spent," says Rota. The age was one of a general revival of learning. Royalty, the Pope, the princes and nobility were all giving themselves with ardor to this higher culture. Under Dante the Italian language assumed new perfection. This period was to Vittoria one of intense stimulus, and it must have had a formative influence on her gifts and her mental power. Having no children, she adopted a young cousin of her husband, the Marchese del Vasto, to educate and to be the heir of their estates. In 1515, Pescara again returned and the entire island of Ischia was "aflame with bonfires, and the borders of the beautiful shore bright and warm with lights," in honor of the event. Of this event, Vittoria wrote: —

". . . My beloved returns to us . . . his countenance radiant with piety to God, with deeds born of inward faith."

At a magnificent wedding festival in the d'Avalos family about this time, it is recorded that the Marchesa di Pescara "wore a robe of brocaded crimson velvet, with large branches of beaten gold wrought on it, with a headdress of wrought gold and a girdle of beaten gold around her waist."

When the coronation of Charles V was to be celebrated at Aix-la-Chapelle the Marchese di Pescara was appointed ambassador to represent the House of Aragon on this brilliant occasion, when the new emperor was to be invested with the crown and the sceptre of Charlemagne. Charles had decided to journey by sea and to visit Henry VIII on the way, an arrangement of which Cardinal Wolsey was aware, although he had kept Henry in ignorance of it, according to those curious mental processes of his mind where his young monarch was concerned. Shakespeare, in the play of "King Henry VIII," describes the meeting of the two kings, which occurred at Canterbury, "at a grand jubilee in honor of the shrine of Thomas à Becket." One historian thus describes this scene: —

"The two handsome young sovereigns rode into Canterbury under the same canopy, the great Cardinal riding directly in front of them, and on the right and left were the proud nobles of Spain and England, among whom was Pescara. The kings alighted from their horses at the west door of the cathedral and together paid their devotions before that rich shrine blazing with jewels. They humbly knelt on the steps worn by the knees of tens of thousands of pilgrims."

On the return to Naples of the Marchese di Pescara he told the story of his regal journey to an assemblage of nobles in the Church of Santa Maria di Monte Oliveto, and he then joined the Marchesa in Rome, where she had gone to visit her family and to pay her devotions to Leo X, who had just created Pompeo Colonna a cardinal.

Pope Leo aspired to draw around him a court distinguished for its culture and brilliancy in both art and literature. In this court the Marchesa di Pescara shone resplendent. "She was at the height of her beauty, and her charms were sung by the poets of the day," says a contemporary.

A year later Leo X died, succeeded by Adrian (who had been tutor to Charles V), to the intense and bitter disappointment of Cardinal Wolsey, who had made the widest — and wiliest — efforts to gratify his own ambition of reigning in the Papal chair. Again the war between France and Italy, that which seemed to be a perpetually smouldering feud, and the Marchese di Pescara, again summoned to battle, was wounded at Pavia. For some time he lay between life and death at Milan, and a messenger was sent to beg Vittoria to come to him. She set out on this journey, leaving Naples in great haste; but on reaching Viterbo another messenger met her with the tidings of the death of the Marchese, which had occurred on Nov. 25, 1525. Overcome with grief, Vittoria was carried back to Rome and for the solace of entire seclusion she sought the cloistered silence of the convent of San Silvestre, which lay at the foot of the Monte Cavallo in Rome, almost adjoining the gardens of the Colonna palace. To the Marchese di Pescara, who had the military rank of general, was given a funeral of great pomp and splendor in Milan, and his body was brought to the famous Naples church of Santa Domenica Maggiore, where it was entombed with the princes and nobles of his house.

Before the death of the Marchese there had been a political plot to join the Papal, Venetian, and Milanese forces and rescue Italy from the Emperor's rule, and the Pope himself had sent a messenger to Pescara asking him to unite with the league. The Marchese, Spanish by ancestry and by sympathies, used this knowledge to frustrate the Italian designs and to warn Spain. The Italian historians have execrated him for this act, which they regard as that of a traitor. Vittoria, however, did not take this view apparently, as in a letter to her husband she wrote: —

"Titles and kingdoms do not add to true

honor. . . . I do not desire to be the wife of a king, but I glory in being the wife of that great general who shows his bravery in war and, still more, by magnanimity in peace, surpasses the greatest kings."

The inducement of the throne of Naples had been held out to Marchese di Pescara. He evidently regarded this in the nature of a dishonorable bribe, and it is this view which the Marchesa plainly shared.

After his death her first impulse was to take the vows of a cloistered nun. The Pope himself intervened to dissuade her, and she consented to enter, only temporarily, the convent of San Silvestre on the Monte Cavallo.

In the will of the Marchese di Pescara there was a clause directing that anything in his estate unlawfully acquired should be restored to the owner; and under this, Vittoria gave back to the monastery of Monte Cassino the Monte San Mano that had formerly been its property.

From the cloistered shades of the convent Vittoria removed to the family castle of the Colonna at Marino, where, on the shore of this beautiful lake (which was the scenery of Virgil's Æneid), she passed some months, engaged in writing sonnets. Of one of these a translation runs in part: —

"I write solely to assuage my inward grief, which destroys in my heart the light of this world's sun; and not to add light to *mio vel solo*, to his glorified spirit. It is fit that other tongues should preserve his great name from oblivion."

In another, perhaps her most perfect sonnet, she beseeches the winds to convey to her beloved the message she sends: —

"*Ch'io di lui sempre pensi; o pianga, o parli,*" — That I always think of him, or weep for him, or speak of him.

Again, a year later, Vittoria returned to lovely Ischia, which, as one writer has described, "rises out of the blue billows of the Mediterranean like giant towers. The immense blocks of stone are heaped one upon another, in such a supernatural manner as to give a coloring to the legend, that beneath them, in those vast volcanic caverns, dwells the giant Tifeo." The castle where the Duchessa Francavilla and the Marchesa Pescara lived is built on a towering mass of rock joined to the island by a causeway. The castle includes the palace, a church, and other buildings for the family and their guests and dependants.

For some three years the Marchesa did not again leave Ischia. In the mean time volumes of her poems were published. She received the acclamation of all the writers of her time. The crown of immortelles, often laid but on a tomb, was continually pressed upon her brow. She was the most famous woman of her time. Her beauty, her genius, her noble majesty of character impressed the contemporary world. Her days were filled with correspondence with the most distinguished men of the day. Ariosto, Castiglione, Ludovico Dolce, Cardinal Bembo, Cardinal Contarini, and Paolo Giovio were among her nearer circle of friends.

Stormy times fell upon Italy, in all of which the Colonna family bore prominent part, and all of which affected the life of Vittoria Colonna in many ways. Her biography, if written with fulness and accuracy, would be largely a his-

CASTELLO DI ALFONSO, ISCHIA

Page 306

tory of the Italy of that time, for her life seemed
always inseparably united with great events.

In the year 1530 (Clement VII being the
Pope) a full Papal pardon had been extended
to all the Colonna, and their castles and estates
had also been restored to them. For years past
Rome had been in a state of conflict. Benvenuto Cellini, who had watched the terrible
scenes from Castel San Angelo where he was
immured, has described the terrors. The Eternal City, whose population under Leo X had
been 90,000, was now — in 1530 — reduced to
half that number. Palaces and temples had
been the scenes of riot and destruction, yet to
this very lawlessness of the time the Roman
galleries of the present owe their ancient statues,
which were uncovered by these assaults. The
Coliseum was left in the ruined state in which
it is now seen, and by the sale of the stones
taken from it the Palazzo Barberini was
erected.

Vittoria, coming again to Rome and revisit-
ing its classic greatness, exclaimed that happy
were they who lived in times so full of grandeur;
to which the poet Molza gallantly replied that
they were less happy, as they had not known

her! Everywhere was she received with the highest honors. She made a tour, visiting Bagni di Lucca, Bologna, and Ferrara, where she was the guest of the Duca and Duchessa Ercole in the ducal palace. The Duchessa was the Princesse Renée, the daughter of Louis XII of France, and an ardent friend of Calvin, who visited her in Ferrara. It was to this visit that Longfellow refers in his poem entitled "Michael Angelo," when he pictures Vittoria as sitting for her portrait to the artist and conversing with her friend Giulia, the Duchess of Trajetto, Michael Angelo begs them to resume the conversation interrupted by his entrance, and Vittoria says: —

> "Well, first, then, of Duke Ercole, a man
> Cold in his manners, and reserved and silent,
> And yet magnificent in all his ways."

To which the Duchessa replies: —

> "How could the daughter of a king of France
> Wed such a duke?"

> MICHAEL ANGELO.
> "The men that women marry,
> And why they marry them, will always be
> A marvel and a mystery to the world."

ITALY, THE MAGIC LAND

"And then the Duchess, — how shall I describe her,
Or tell the merits of that happy nature
Which pleases most when least it thinks of pleasing?
Not beautiful, perhaps, in form and feature,
Yet with an inward beauty, that shines through
Each look and attitude and word and gesture;
A kindly grace of manner and behavior,
A something in her presence and her ways
That makes her beautiful beyond the reach
Of mere external beauty; and in heart
So noble and devoted to the truth,
And so in sympathy with all who strive
After the higher life."

　　　　　"She draws me to her
As much as her Duke Ercole repels me."

"Then the devout and honorable women
That grace her court, and make it good to be there;
Francesca Bucyronia, the true-hearted,
Lavinia della Rovere and the Orsini,
The Magdalena and the Cherubina,
And Anne de Parthenai, who sings so sweetly;
All lovely women, full of noble thoughts
And aspirations after noble things.

　　·　　　·　　　·　　　·

　　　　　With these ladies
Was a young girl, Olympia Morata,
Daughter of Fulvio, the learned scholar,
Famous in all the universities:

309

ITALY, THE MAGIC LAND

A marvellous child, who at the spinning-wheel,
And in the daily round of household cares,
Hath learned both Greek and Latin; and is now
A favorite of the Duchess and companion
Of Princess Anne. This beautiful young Sappho
Sometimes recited to us Grecian odes
That she had written, with a voice whose sadness
Thrilled and o'ermastered me, and made me look
Into the future time, and ask myself
What destiny will be hers."

JULIA.

                    "And what poets
Were there to sing you madrigals, and praise
Olympia's eyes?" . . .

VITTORIA.
"None; for great Ariosto is no more."

.   .   .   .   .

JULIA.

"He spake of you."

VITTORIA.

          "And of yourself, no less,
And of our master, Michael Angelo."

MICHAEL ANGELO.
"Of me?"

VITTORIA.

          "Have you forgotten that he calls you
Michael, less man than angel, and divine?
You are ungrateful."

MICHAEL ANGELO.

                    "A mere play on words."

310

DETAIL FROM "PARNASSUS," RAPHAEL STANZE, PALAZZO VATICANO, ROME
Raphael Sanzio
Page 311

ITALY, THE MAGIC LAND

The Duca and Duchessa of Ferrara invited
the most distinguished persons in Venice and
Bologna and Lombardy to meet their honored
guest. Bishop Ghiberto of Verona besought
her to visit that city. Vittoria accepted and
was for some time the Bishop's guest in his
palace, and she took great interest in the historic
city. With the Bishop she visited the ancient
Duomo, which in 1160 had been restored by Pope
Urban II, and reconsecrated. It was a strong
desire of the Marchesa at this time to make a
pilgrimage to Jerusalem; but the journey was
then so perilous and so long — none too easy,
indeed, at the present time — that she was dis-
suaded from the attempt.

Verona, to do her honor, had a medal struck
bearing her portrait. The group of great artists
— Titian, Tintoretto, and Giorgione in Venice;
Fra Angelico, Bartolommeo, and others of that
day — were creating their wonderful works which
Vittoria must have seen and enjoyed during
this tour. Raphael, whose death had occurred
in 1520, Vittoria had, doubtless, known; but
whether it was she who was the original of the
Muse in his great picture of "Parnassus," as
is alleged, is not fully established.

ITALY, THE MAGIC LAND

"Unto my buried lord I give myself,"

wrote Vittoria Colonna in one of the sonnets
to her husband's memory, and this line is the
keynote to her entire life, both as woman and
poet. It was no translation of her life into
another key, no reckoning by stars that flashed
from different skies, when there fell upon her
the baptism and crown of that immortal friendship with Michael Angelo.

The Marchesa di Pescara returned to Rome,
from this notable tour in Northern Italy, in
1538. She was received with the honors that
her fame inspired. Michael Angelo was then
deeply absorbed in painting his "Last Judgment," in the Capella Sistina.

"Every one in Rome took an interest in the
progress of this magnificent fresco, from the
Pope (who continually visited the artist) down
to the humblest of the people. We may imagine Vittoria standing by the great painter to
view his sublime work; but Michael Angelo
did not require the patronage, even of a Colonna,
and it is possible that Vittoria herself first
sought out his friendship."

In the Casa Buonarroti, in Florence, hangs

that exquisite picture painted of Italy's greatest woman poet, in her early youth; and in its rare and precious collection of manuscripts are the letters of Vittoria to the poet and sculptor. Her influence is said to have produced a great change in his religious views, influencing his mind to a more lofty and more spiritual comprehension of the divine laws that govern the universe.

Condivi, in referring to this chapter in their lives, has said: —

"In particular he was most deeply attached to the Marchesa di Pescara, of whose divine spirit he was enamoured, and he was beloved by her in return with much affection."

It was about 1535 when Michael Angelo left Florence for Rome, appointed by the Pope, Paul III, as the chief architect, sculptor, and painter of the Vatican. He was enrolled in the Pontifical household, and he at once began his work in the Sistine Chapel. Mr. Symonds believes that he must have been engaged upon the "Last Judgment" through 1536, 1537. The great artist was not without a keen wit of his own as well; for on receipt of a letter from Pietro

Aretino, from Venice, in September of 1537, with praises of his work that Michael Angelo deemed extravagant, he replied that while he rejoiced in Aretino's commendation, he also grieved; "as having finished a large part of the fresco," he said, "I cannot realize your conception which is so complete that if the Day of Judgment had come and you had been present and seen it with your eyes, your words could not have described it better."

Vittoria Colonna now passed some years between Rome and Orvieto, that picturesque town with its magnificent cathedral rich in mediæval art, where she lived in the convent of St. Paolo d' Orvieto. She varied this residence by remaining at times in the convent of San Caterina di Viterbo, in that city. In Rome she had lived both at the convent of Santa Anna and also at the Palazzo Cesarini, which was the home of members of the Colonna family. A sonnet of Michael Angelo's written to Vittoria reflects the feeling that she inspired in him: —

"Da che concetto ha l' arte intera e diva
    La forma e gli atti d' alcun, poi di quello
    D' umil materia un semplice modello
È 'l primo parto che da quel deriva.

ITALY, THE MAGIC LAND

Ma nel secondo poi di pietra viva
    S' adempion le promesse del martello;
    E sì rinasce tal concetto e bello,
Che ma' non è chi suo eterno prescriva.
Simil, di me model, nacqu' io da prima;
    Di me model, per cosa più perfetta
    Da voi rinascer poi, donna alta e degna.
Se 'l poco accresce, 'l mio superchio lima
    Vostra pietà; qual penitenzia aspetta
    Mio fiero ardor, se mi gastiga e insegna?"

Of this sonnet the following beautiful translation is made by John Addington Symonds: —

"When divine Art conceives a form and face,
    She bids the craftsman for his first essay
    To shape a simple model in mere clay:
This is the earliest birth of Art's embrace.
From the live marble in the second place
    His mallet brings into the light of day
    A thing so beautiful that who can say
When time shall conquer that immortal grace?
Thus my own model I was born to be —
    The model of that nobler self, whereto
    Schooled by your pity, lady, I shall grow.
Each overplus and each deficiency
    You will make good. What penance then is due
    For my fierce heat, chastened and taught by you?"

The correspondence between Vittoria and Michael Angelo was undated, and all that now remains is fragmentary.

ITALY, THE MAGIC LAND

The great artist, writing to his nephew, Sionardo, in 1554, says: —

"Messer Giovan Francisco Fattucci asked me about a month ago if I possessed any writings of the marchioness. I have a little book bound in parchment which she gave me some ten years ago. It has one hundred and three sonnets, not counting another forty she afterward sent on paper from Viterbo. I had these bound into the same book, and at that time I used to lend them about to many persons so that they are all of them now in print. In addition to these poems I have many letters which she wrote from Orvieto and Viterbo. These, then, are the writings I possess of the marchioness."

In Rome, 1545, Michael Angelo thus writes to Vittoria: —

"I desired, lady, before I accepted the things which your ladyship has often expressed the will to give me — I desired to produce something for you with my own hand in order to be as little as possible unworthy of this kindness. I have now come to recognize that the grace of God is not to be bought, and that to keep it waiting is a grievous sin. Therefore I acknowledge my error and willingly accept your favors. When I possess them — not, indeed, because I shall have them in my house, but for that I myself shall dwell in them — the place will seem to encircle me with paradise. For which felicity I shall remain ever more obliged to your ladyship than I am already, if that is possible.

"The bearer of this letter will be Urbino, who lives in my service. Your ladyship may inform him when you would like me to come and see the head you promised to show me."

With this letter Michael Angelo sent to Vittoria a sonnet which, in the translation made by John Addington Symonds, is as follows: —

> "Seeking at least to be not all unfit
>   For thy sublime and boundless courtesy,
>   My lowly thoughts at first were fain to try
>   What they could yield for grace so infinite.
>   But now I know my unassisted wit
>   Is all too weak to make me soar so high,
>   For pardon, lady, for this fault I cry,
>   And wiser still I grow remembering it.

ITALY, THE MAGIC LAND

Yea, will I see what folly 't were to think
That largess dropped from thee like dews from heaven,
Could e'er be paid by work so frail as mine!
To nothingness my art and talent sink;
He fails who from his mental stores hath given
A thousandfold to match one gift divine."

As a gift to Vittoria Colonna, Michael Angelo designed an episode from the Passion of our Lord, which Condivi describes as "a naked Christ at the moment when, taken from the cross, our Lord would have fallen at the feet of His most holy mother if two angels did not support Him in their arms. She sits below the cross with a face full of tears and sorrow, lifting both her widespread arms to heaven while on the stem of the tree above is written this legend: '*Non vi si pensa quanto sangue costa.*' The cross is of the same kind as that which was carried by the White Friars at the time of the plague of 1348, and afterward deposited in the Church of Santa Croce at Florence."

In presenting this cross to her he wrote: —

"Lady Marchioness, being myself in Rome, I thought it hardly fitting to give the Crucified Christ to Messer Tommaso, and to make him an intermediary between your ladyship and me, especially because it has been my earnest wish to perform more for you than for any one I ever knew upon the world. But absorbing occupations, which still engage me, have prevented my informing your ladyship of this. Moreover, knowing that you know love needs no task-master, and that he who loves doth not sleep, I thought the less of using go-betweens. And though I seemed to have forgotten, I was doing what I did not talk about, in order to effect a thing that was not looked for, my purpose has been spoiled. He sins who faith like this so soon forgets."

In reply Vittoria Colonna wrote: —

"Unique Master Angelo and my most singular friend: I have received your letter and examined the crucifix which truly hath crucified in my memory every other picture I ever saw. Nowhere could one find another figure of our Lord so well executed, so living, and so exquisitely finished. I cannot express in words how subtly and marvellously it is designed. Wherefore I am resolved to take the work as coming from no other hand but yours. . . . I have examined it minutely in full light and by the lens and mirror, and never saw anything more perfect."

She added: —

". . . Your works forcibly stimulate the judgment of all who would look at them. My study of them made me speak of adding goodness to things perfect in themselves, and I have seen now that 'all is possible to him who believes.' I had the greatest faith in God that He would bestow upon you supernatural grace for the making of this Christ. When I came to examine it I found it so marvellous that it surpasses all my expectations. Wherefore, emboldened by your miracles I conceived a great desire for that which I now see marvellously accomplished: I mean that the design is in all parts perfect and consummate. I tell you that I am pleased that the angel on the right hand is by far the fairer, since Michael will place you, with all angels, upon the right hand of the Lord some day. Meanwhile I do not know how else to serve you, than by making orisons to this

VITTORIA COLONNA, GALLERIA BUONARROTI, FLORENCE
Page 312

sweet Christ, whom you have drawn so well
and exquisitely, and praying you to hold me
yours to command as yours in all and for all."

Again Vittoria wrote to him: —

"I beg you to let me have the crucifix a short
while in my keeping, even though it be unfinished. I want to show it to some gentlemen who have come from the most reverend,
the Cardinal of Mantua. If you are not working will you not come at your leisure to-day
and talk with me?"

It is an interesting fact to the visitor in the
Rome of to-day that the convent of San Silvestre
where Vittoria Colonna lived was attached to
the church of San Silvestre in Capite, now used
as the English-speaking Catholic church in the
Eternal City. The wing which was formerly
the convent (founded in 1318) is now converted
into the central post office.

It was in the sacristy of San Silvestre, decorated with frescoes by Domenichino, that a
memorable meeting and conversation took place,
one Sunday afternoon in those far-away days of

nearly five hundred years ago, between Michael
Angelo and Francesco d' Ollanda, a Spanish
miniature artist, — the meeting brought about
by Vittoria Colonna. The Spanish artist was
a worshipper of Michael Angelo, who "awakened such a feeling of love," that if d' Ollanda
met him in the street "the stars would come out
in the sky," he says, "before I would let him go
again." This fervent worship was hardly enjoyed by its object, who avoided the Spanish
enthusiast. One Sunday, however, d' Ollanda
had gone to San Silvestre finding there Tolomei,
to whom he was also devoted, and Vittoria
Colonna, both of whom had gone to hear the
celebrated Fra Ambrosia of Siena expound the
Epistles of St. Paul. The Marchesa di Pescara
observed that she felt sure their Spanish friend
would far rather hear Michael Angelo discuss
painting than to hear Fra Ambrosia on the
wisdom of St. Paul. Summoning an attendant
she directed him to find Michael Angelo and tell
him how cool and delightful was the church
that morning and to beg him to join Messer
Tolomei and herself; but to make no mention
of the presence of d' Ollanda. Her woman's
tact and her faultless courtesy were successful

in procuring this inestimable privilege for the Spanish painter. Michael Angelo came, and began the conversation — which was a monologue, rather, as all three of the friends wished only to listen to the master — by defending artists from the charge of eccentric and difficult methods. With somewhat startling candor Michael Angelo proceeded: —

"I dare affirm that any artist who tries to satisfy the better vulgar rather than men of his own craft will never become a superior talent. For my part, I am bound to confess that even his Holiness wearies and annoys me by begging for too much of my company. I am most anxious to serve him, . . . but I think I can do so better by studying at home than by dancing attendance on my legs in his reception room."

Another meeting of this little group was appointed for the next Sunday in the Colonna gardens behind the convent, under the shadow of the laurel trees in the air fragrant with roses and orange blossoms, where they sat with Rome spread out like a picture at their feet. That beautiful terrace of the Colonna gardens, to which the visitor in Rome to-day always makes his pilgrimage, with the ruined statues and the broken marble flights of steps, is the scene of this meeting of Vittoria Colonna, Michael Angelo, and Francesco d' Ollanda. On this second occasion the sculptor asserted his belief that while all things are worthy the artist's attention, the real test of his art is in the representation of the human form. He extolled the art of design. He emphasized the essential nature of nobleness in the artist, and added: —

"In order to represent in some degree the adored image of our Lord, it is not enough that a master should be great and able. I maintain that he must also be a man of good conduct and morals, if possible a saint, in order that the Holy Ghost may rain down inspiration on his understanding."

Of the relative degree of swiftness in work Michael Angelo said: —

"We must regard it as a special gift from God to be able to do that in a few hours which other men can only perform in many days of labor. But should this rapidity cause a man to fail in his best realization it would be better to proceed slowly. No artist should allow his eagerness to hinder him from the supreme end of art — perfection."

Mr. Longfellow, in his unfinished dramatic poem, "Michael Angelo" (to which reference has already been made), has one scene laid in the convent chapel of San Silvestre, in which these passages occur: —

VITTORIA.

"Here let us rest awhile, until the crowd
Has left the church. I have already sent
For Michael Angelo to join us here."

MESSER CLAUDIO.

"After Fra Bernardino's wise discourse
On the Pauline Epistles, certainly
Some words of Michael Angelo on Art
Were not amiss, to bring us back to earth."

.   .   .   .   .   .

MICHAEL ANGELO, *at the door.*

"How like a Saint or Goddess she appears!
Diana or Madonna, which I know not,
In attitude and aspect formed to be
At once the artist's worship and despair!"

ITALY, THE MAGIC LAND

VITTORIA.

"Welcome, Maestro. We were waiting for you."

MICHAEL ANGELO.

"I met your messenger upon the way,
And hastened hither."

VITTORIA.

                    "It is kind of you
To come to us, who linger here like gossips
Wasting the afternoon in idle talk.
These are all friends of mine and friends of yours."

MICHAEL ANGELO.

" If friends of yours, then are they friends of mine.
Pardon me, gentlemen. But when I entered
I saw but the Marchesa."

Vittoria tells the master that the Pope has
granted her permission to build a convent, and
Michael Angelo replies: —

                    "Ah, to build, to build!
That is the noblest art of all the arts.
Painting and sculpture are but images,
Are merely shadows cast by outward things
On stone or canvas, having in themselves
No separate existence. Architecture,
Existing in itself, and not in seeming
A something it is not, surpasses them
As substance shadow. . . .

ITALY, THE MAGIC LAND

> . . . Yet he beholds
> Far nobler works who looks upon the ruins
> Of temples in the Forum here in Rome.
> If God should give me power in my old age
> To build for Him a temple half as grand
> As those were in their glory, I should count
> My age more excellent than youth itself,
> And all that I have hitherto accomplished
> As only vanity."

To which Vittoria responds: —

> "I understand you.
> Art is the gift of God, and must be used
> Unto His glory. That in art is highest
> Which aims at this."

The poet, with his characteristically delicate divination, has entered into the inner spirit of these two immortal friends.

Walter Pater, writing of Michael Angelo, truly says: —

"Michael Angelo is always pressing forward from the outward beauty — *il bel del fuor che agli occhi piace* — to apprehend the unseen beauty; *trascenda nella forma universale* — that abstract form of beauty about which the Platonists reason. And this gives the impression in him of something flitting and unfixed, of the

houseless and complaining spirit, almost clair-
voyant through the frail and yielding flesh."

Again we find Pater saying: —

"Though it is quite possible that Michael
Angelo had seen Vittoria, that somewhat shadowy figure, as early as 1537, yet their closer
intimacy did not begin till about the year 1542,
when Michael Angelo was nearly seventy years
old. Vittoria herself, an ardent Neo-Catholic,
vowed to perpetual widowhood since the news
had reached her, seventeen years before, that
her husband, the youthful and princely Mar-
quess of Pescara, lay dead of the wounds he
had received in the battle of Pavia, was then
no longer an object of great passion. In a
dialogue written by the painter, Francesco
d' Ollanda, we catch a glimpse of them together
in an empty church at Rome, one Sunday afternoon, discussing indeed the characteristics of
various schools of art, but still more the writings
of St. Paul, already following the ways and
tasting the sunless pleasures of weary people,
whose hold on outward things is slackening.
In a letter still extant he regrets that when he

visited her after death he had kissed her hands
only. He made, or set to work to make, a
crucifix for her use, and two drawings, perhaps
in preparation for it, are now in Oxford. . . .
In many ways no sentiment could have been
less like Dante's love for Beatrice than Michael
Angelo's for Vittoria Colonna. Dante's comes
in early youth; Beatrice is a child, with the
wistful, ambiguous vision of a child, with a
character still unaccentuated by the influence
of outward circumstances, almost expression-
less. Vittoria is a woman already weary, in
advanced age, of grave intellectual qualities.
Dante's story is a piece of figured work inlaid
with lovely incidents. In Michael Angelo's
poems frost and fire are almost the only images
— the refining fire of the goldsmith; once or twice
the phœnix; ice melting at the fire; fire struck
from the rock which it afterwards consumes."

Visconti notes that among Italian poets,
Vittoria Colonna was the first to make religion
a subject of poetic treatment, and the first to
introduce nature's ministry to man into poetry.
Rota, her Italian biographer, states that she
died in February of 1547, in the Palazzo Cesa-

rini. This palace is in Genzano, on Lago di Nemi, and has been one of the Colonna estates; but from Visconti and other authorities it is evident that she died in Rome, either in the convent of Santa Anna or in the palace of Cesarini, the husband of her kinswoman, Giulio Colonna, which must have been near the convent in Trastevere, the old portion of Rome across the Tiber. Visconti records that on the last evening of her life when Michael Angelo was beside her, she said: "I die. Help me to repeat my last prayer. I do not now remember the words." He clasped her hand and repeated it to her, while her own lips moved, she gazed intently on him, smiled and passed away. This translation has been made of Vittoria Colonna's last prayer: —

"Grant, I beseech Thee, O Lord, that I may ever worship Thee with such humility of mind as becometh my lowliness and such elevation of mind as Thy loftiness demandeth. . . . I entreat, O Most Holy Father, that Thy most living flame may so urge me forward that, not being hindered by any mortal imperfections, I may happily and safely again return to Thee."

ITALY, THE MAGIC LAND

It is recorded by an authority that her body, "enclosed in a casket of cypress wood, lined with embroidered velvet," was placed in the chapel of Santa Anna which has since been destroyed. Visconti says: "She desired, with Christian humility, to be buried in the manner in which the sisters were buried when they died. And, as I suppose, her body was placed in the common sepulchre of the nuns of Santa Anna." Grimm declares that he cannot discover the place of her burial, and Visconti declares that her tomb remains unknown.

But it is apparently a fact that the body of Vittoria Colonna is entombed in the sacristy of Santa Domenica Maggiore in Naples, the sarcophagus containing it resting by the side of the one containing the body of her husband, Francesco d'Avalos, Marchese of Pescara. This church is one of the finest in Naples, with twenty-seven chapels and twelve altars, and it is here that nearly all the great nobles of the kingdom of Naples are entombed. Here is the tomb of the learned Thomas Aquinas and here is shown, in relief, the miracle of the crucifix by Tommaso de Stefani, which — as the legend runs — thus addressed the learned doctor: —

"*Bene scripsisti de me, Thoma; quam ergo mercedem recipris?*"

To which he replied: "*Non aliam nisi te.*"

It is in the sacristy in which lie all the Princes of the House of Aragon that the sarcophagi of the Marchese and the Marchesa di Pescara are placed side by side in the high gallery near the ceiling. The altar has a fine Annunciation ascribed to Andrea da Salerno. The ceiling (whose coloring is as fresh and vivid as if painted yesterday) is by Solimena. Around the walls near the ceiling are two balconies or galleries, filled with very large wooden sarcophagi, whose scarlet velvet covers have faded into yellow browns with pink shades, many of which are tattered and are falling to pieces. The casket containing the body of Fernando Francesco d'Avalos, Marchese of Pescara (the husband of Vittoria Colonna), has on it an inscription by Ariosto; and his portrait (showing in profile a young face with blonde hair and a full reddish brown beard) and a banner, also, is suspended above the casket. That containing the body of the Marchesa, his wife (Vittoria Colonna), has an aperture at the top where the wood is worn away and the embalmed form, partly crumbled, may be seen. This seems strange to the verge of fantasy, but it is, apparently, true. The writer of this volume visited the Church of Santa Domenica Maggiore in Naples in December of 1906, and was assured by the sacristan that this sarcophagus contains the body of the Marchesa. Inquiries were then made of other prelates and of the Archbishop, who gave the same assurance. Later, learned archæologists in Rome were appealed to, regarding this assertion made in Naples, and the consensus of opinion obtained declares their assertion true. Professor Lanciani has himself publicly expressed this conviction. Still, it remains a curious question as to when this sarcophagus was placed in the sacristy, for the date goes back into long-buried centuries.

Adjoining Santa Domenica Maggiore is the monastery in which Thomas Aquinas lived and lectured (in 1272), and the cell of the great doctor of philosophy is now made into a chapel. His lectures called together men of the highest rank and learning and were attended by the king and the members of the royal family.

The entire locality of this church is replete with historic association. The most distinguished of the nobility of Naples have, for centuries, held their chapels in this church, and in these are many notable examples of Renaissance sculpture.

The Accadémia des Arcades of Rome, founded in the seventeenth century to do honor to lyric art, celebrated the placing of a bust of Vittoria Colonna in a gallery of the Capitoline, in May of 1865, by a resplendent poetic festa. According to the gentle, leisurely customs of the land, where it is always afternoon and time has no value, thirty-two poets read their songs, written in Latin or in Italian, for this occasion, which were published in a sumptuous volume to be preserved in the archives of the Arcadians, who take themselves more seriously than the world outside quite realizes. This bust of Vittoria Colonna was the gift of the Duca and Duchessa of Torlonia of that period. It was crowned with laurel, as that of Petrarca had been, and the government took official recognition of the event.

Goethe was made a member of this Accadémia that regarded itself as reflecting the glories of the Golden Age of Greece, and which was a century old at the time of his visit to Italy. "No stranger of any consequence was readily permitted to leave Rome without being invited to join this body," he recorded, and he wrote a humorous description of the formalities of his initiation.

Mrs. Horatio Greenough was honored by being made a member of this Accadémia in recognition of her musical accomplishments, and the record of it is placed on the memorial marble over her grave in the Protestant cemetery in Rome. Every year, on Tasso's birthday (April 25), the Accadémia holds a festa in a little amphitheatre near "Tasso's oak," on the Janiculum, at which his bust is crowned with laurel. The gardens in which the seventeenth-century Arcadians disported themselves are now known among the Romans as *il Bosco Parrasio degli Arcadi.*

Throughout Italy the fame of Vittoria Colonna only deepens with every succeeding century. Her nobility of character, her lofty spirituality of life, fitly crowned and perfected her intellectual force and brilliant gifts. Although from the customs of the time the Marchesa lived much in convents, she never, in any sense, save that of her fervent piety, lived the conventual life. Her noble gifts linked her always to the larger activities, and her gifts and rank invested her with certain demands and responsibilities that she could not evade. She was one of the messengers of life, and her place as a brilliant and distinguished figure in the contemporary world was one that the line of destiny, which pervades all circumstances and which, in her case, was so marked, absolutely constrained her to fill. She had that supreme gift of the lofty nature, the power of personal influence. Her exquisite courtesy and graciousness of manner, her simple dignity and unaffected sincerity, her delicacy of divination and her power of tender sympathy and liberal comprehension all combined to make her the ideal companion, counsellor, and friend, as well as the celebrity of letters and lyric art.

No poet has more exquisitely touched the friendship between Vittoria Colonna and Michael Angelo than has Margaret J. Preston, in a poem supposed to be addressed to the sculptor by Vittoria, in which occur the lines: —

ITALY, THE MAGIC LAND

"We twain — one lingering on the violet verge,
And one with eyes raised to the twilight peaks —
Shall meet in the morn again.

.   .   .   .   .   .

            . . . Supremest truth I gave;
Quick comprehension of thine unsaid thought,
Reverence, whose crystal sheen was never blurred
By faintest film of over-breathing doubt;
.   .   .   . helpfulness
Such as thou hadst not known of womanly hands;
And sympathies so urgent, they made bold
To press their way where never mortal yet
Entrance had gained, — even to thy soul."

This is the *Page de Conti* that one reads in
the air as he sails past Ischia on the violet sea;
and the *chant d'amour* of the sirens catches
the echo of lines far down the centuries: —

"I understood not, when the angel stooped,
Whispering, 'Live on! for yet one joyless soul,
Void of true faith in human happiness,
Waits to be won by thee, from unbelief.'

"Now, all is clear. For *thy* sake I am glad
I waited. Not that some far age may say, —
'*God's benison on her, since she was the friend
Of Michael Angelo!*'"

So sometimes comes to soul and sense
The feeling which is evidence
That very near about us lies
The realm of spiritual mysteries.
The sphere of the supernal powers
Impinges on this world of ours.
The low and dark horizon lifts,
To light the scenic terror shifts;
The breath of a diviner air
Blows down the answer of a prayer: —
That all our sorrow, pain, and doubt
A great compassion clasps about,
And law and goodness, love and force,
Are wedded fast beyond divorce.
Then duty leaves to love its task,
The beggar Self forgets to ask;
With smile of trust and folded hands,
The passive soul in waiting stands
To feel, as flowers the sun and dew,
The One true Life its own renew.

WHITTIER.

"*For Thou only art holy. Thou only art the Lord. Thou only, O Christ, with the Holy Ghost, art most high in the Glory of God the Father.*"

Sometimes in heaven-sent dreams I do behold
    A city with its turrets high in air,
    Its gates that gleam with jewels strange and rare,
And streets that glow with burning of red gold;
And happy souls, through blessedness grown bold,
    Thrill with their praises all the radiant air,
    And God himself is light, and shineth there
On glories tongue of man hath never told.

And in my dreams I thither march, nor stay
    To heed earth's voices, howsoe'er they call,
Or proffers of the joys of this brief day,
    On which so soon the sunset shadows fall;
I see the Gleaming Gates, and toward them press —
What though my path lead through the Wilderness ?

                              LOUISE CHANDLER MOULTON.

V

VOICES OF ST. FRANCIS OF ASSISI

Oh, Italy! thy strength, thy power, thy crown
Lie in the life that in Assisi stirs .
The heart, with impulse of self-sacrifice;
Where still St. Francis gathers weary souls
In his great love, which reaches out to all.
            .   .   .   His blessing falls
In clear sweet tones: "*Benedicat tibi*
Convertat vultum suum ad te et
Det Pacem! " Hushed and holy silence breathes
About the wanderer who lifts his heart
To catch the echo of that voice of love.

CELIA RICHMOND.

THE mystic pilgrimage to Assisi, the "Seraphic
City," prefigures itself almost as a journey to
the Mount of Vision. "Any line of truth that
leads us above materialism," says Dr. Wilberforce, Venerable Archdeacon of Westminster
Abbey, "that forces us to think, that encourages the imagination to pierce the world's
cobwebs, that forces us to remember that
we are enwrapped by the supernatural, is
helpful and stimulating. A human life lived

only in the seen and felt, with no sense of the
invisible, is a fatally impoverished life, a poor,
blind, wingless life, but to believe that ever
around us is a whole world full of spiritual
beings; that this life, with its burdens, is but
the shadow which precedes the reality; that
here we are but God's children at school, is
an invigorating conviction, full of hope, pro-
ductive of patience and fruitful in self-control."

To an age imprisoned in the fear of God
the "sweet saint," Francis, brought the message
of the love of God. To an age crushed under
the abuses of religion as an organization of
feudal bishops and ecclesiastics, St. Francis
brought the message of hope and of joy. He
revealed to his age the absolute reality of the
spiritual world that surrounds us. He was
born into a time when there existed on the
one hand, poverty and misery; on the other,
selfish and debasing self-indulgence of wealth
and its corresponding oppression of the poor.
The Church itself was a power for conquest
and greed. Its kingdom was of this world.
St. Bernard and others had nobly aimed to
effect a reform and had illustrated by their own
lives the beautiful example of simplicity and

unselfishness, but their work failed in effectiveness and permanent impress.

> "Oh, beauty of holiness!
> Of self-forgetfulness, of lowliness."

Not only in beauty, but in power does it
stand. St. Francis brought to the sad and
problematic conditions of his time that resist-
less energy of infinite patience, of a self-control
based on insight into the divine relationships
of life, and of unfailing fidelity to his high purpose. Through good report or through evil
report he kept the faith, and pressed onward
to the high calling of God. The twelfth and the
thirteenth centuries had been a period of religious unrest and chaos. As Archdeacon Wilberforce has so impressively said in the words
quoted from him, a life lived with no sense of
the invisible is blind and impoverished. The
movement initiated by St. Francis proclaimed
anew the divine grace and love.

> "Tokens are dead if the things live not. The light everlasting
> Unto the blind is not, but is born of the eye that has vision."

Something not unlike this trend of thought
must drift through the mind of every one

who journeys through the lovely Umbrian country to Assisi, one of those picturesquely beautiful hill towns of Italy whose romantic situation impresses the visitor. Seen from a little distance, one could hardly imagine how it could be reached unless he were the fortunate possessor of an airship. The entire region is most picturesque in character. Journeying from Rome to Assisi there is a constant ascent from the Campagna to the Apennines, and the road passes through wild defile and valley with amethyst peaks shining fair against the sky, with precipitous rocks, and the dense growth of oak and pine trees. In some places the valley is so narrow that the hills, on either side, rise almost within touch of the hand from the car window. The hill towns are frequent, and the apex of these towns is invariably crowned with a castle, a cathedral, or a ruin, and around it, circling in terraces, is built the town. The charm largely vanishes when fairly in these circling roads, for on either side are high walls, so that one's view is completely bounded by them; but from the summit and from the upper floors of the houses the most beautiful views are obtained. The Umbrian region, in which are located Perugia, Assisi, Spello, Foligno, Spoleto, Terni, Narni, and others, is simply the gem region of all Italy. The Umbrians are the most ancient of the Italian people, and Assisi claims to have been founded eight hundred and sixty-five years before the founding of Rome. It was the scene of constant warfare, and the streets are all underlaid by subterranean passages, in which the inhabitants could disappear from their enemies.

To this ancient Umbrian city, from which went out the life and light that carried wonderful currents of vitality and illumination to all Italy and into almost all parts of the world, one comes as to a special and a sacred pilgrimage. For this mediæval town, perched on the top of a rocky hill, is the birthplace of St. Francis, the founder of the Franciscan order; in it were the scenes of his early life, and here, in 1226, at the age of forty-four years, he died. The convent-church of San Francesco, built to his memory in 1230; the lower church, completed at that date, while the upper was finished in 1253; the magnificent Cathedral of Santa Maria Degli Angeli, completed in 1640; the Church of Santa Chiara and the Duomo, are the points of interest.

ITALY, THE MAGIC LAND

The purple Apennines, on one spur of which Assisi is built, are a picturesque feature of lovely Umbria. The old houses of Assisi rise white in the sunshine. The ancient walls still surround the city, and its towers stand as they stood before the eyes of St. Francis, almost seven centuries ago. The peak of Mt. Subasio, a neighboring peak of the Apennines, looms above the colossal rock that crowns the hill around whose top Assisi clusters in winding terraces. The massive pile of the Francescan church and monastery — the two churches, one above the other — forms an architectural group whose imposing aspect arrests the eye of every traveller for miles around. The pointed arches of the cloisters and the square campanile contrast rather than blend in an effective and harmonious manner and resemble military fortifications rather than an edifice of the church. The old walls still surround Assisi, and the houses all rise white under the blue Italian sky. The narrow streets, hardly wide enough for one carriage to pass another, are so intricate in their curves as they climb the steep hill, that it requires a faith hardly less than the traditional degree said to move mountains to lead the

SAN FRANCESCAN CONVENT-CHURCH, ASSISI

Page 346

visitor to suppose that he will ever emerge from
one that he has entered. Many of the houses
along these curious thoroughfares have no windows, the only light and air coming through the
open door. The bells from the campanile
of the Francescan convent-church, from the
Duomo and from the Church of Santa Chiara
ring every quarter of an hour; and this constant
clash of bells is almost the only sound that
breaks the silence of the mediæval town, which
lends itself to visions and to dreams. On the
very air is stamped the impress of St. Francis.
His personality, his teachings, his faith pervaded the atmosphere in a way that no one
could believe until he had himself entered into
the experience. In narration it cannot but
seem like a pleasing and half-poetic fancy;
but the lingerer in this shrine of religion
and art will realize that the actual personality
of the man who trod these streets nearly
seven hundred years ago is strangely before
him. Canon Knox Little, in a series of lectures on St. Francis of Assisi delivered in
the Ladye Chapel of Worcester Cathedral a
few years since, says of the panorama of the
town: —

ITALY, THE MAGIC LAND

"The scene which from Assisi presented itself daily to his youthful eyes must have had, did have, as we know, a lasting effect upon his mind. From thence the eye surveys a noble coronet of stately mountains. You look from Radicofani, above Trena, to Monte Catria, famous as the scene of some of Dante's saddest times of solitude, and ever is the eye satisfied with the grace and grandeur of the curves of mountain outline, and the changing hues of an incomparable sky. There are rivers and cities and lakes, — from Thrasymene, just hidden by a line of crests, to the Paglia and Tiber beneath, where Orvieto crowns its severe and lonely rock. With the changing lights and shadows always beautiful in the vivid spring or burning summer, tender-tinted autumn or clear and sparkling winter, with the bright and pure and buoyant atmosphere always giving life and vigor, what spot on earth more fitted as the birthplace of the saint who was, above all things, bright and tender and strong?"

Assisi was an important town in the twelfth century when Francis, the son of Pietro Bernardone di Mercanti, wandered over its hills, and after severe fasting and prayer communed with

ITALY, THE MAGIC LAND

God. Born in the midst of the constant warfare between Assisi and Perugia, he was first a
soldier. He was captured and thrown into
prison, and it was a remarkable dream, or vision,
that came to him before he was set free, that
determined his life of consecration. Tradition
invested his birth with legends, one of which is,
that in his infancy an aged man came to the
door and begged to be permitted to take the
child in his arms, prophesying that he was
destined to accomplish a great work. Pietro
Bernardone was a wealthy merchant of Assisi.
Pica, the mother of Francis, is said to have been
of noble origin and of a deeply religious nature.
The early youth of Francis was given to games,
festivals, and pleasures that degenerated into
dissipation, but the mother continually affirmed
her assurance that, if it pleased God, her
son would become a Christian. In this atmosphere was nurtured "the sweet-souled saint
of mediæval Italy," who is described as a figure of magical power, whose ardent temperament and mystic loveliness attracted to him
all men.

There is also a legend that Pica went to pray
at the Portiuncula and that, for seven years,

she prayed for a son. Her prayer was answered in the coming of the infant who was to be the great saint of all the ages. Francis, in his childhood, also knelt and prayed at this shrine. In the year 1211, when Francis was twenty-nine years of age and had entered on his ministry, this chapel was given to him, "and no sooner had they come to live here," it is said, "than the Lord multiplied their number from day to day." At one time he had gone to his devotions in great depression of spirits, "when, suddenly, an unspeakable ecstasy filled his breast. 'Be comforted, my dearest,' he said, 'and rejoice in the Lord, and let us not be sad that we are few; for it has been shown to me by God that you shall increase to a great multitude and shall go on increasing to the end of the world. I see a multitude of men coming to me from every quarter — French, Spaniards, Germans, English — each in their different tongues encouraging the others.'"

At a distance of perhaps a mile and a half from Assisi, down in the valley near the railroad station, four holy pilgrims founded a shrine in the fourth century. Later, on this site, St. Benedict erected a tiny chapel, called "St.

Maria della Portiuncula" (St. Mary of the
Little Patron), and once, when praying in the
chapel, Benedict had a vision of a vast crowd of
people kneeling in ecstasy, chanting hymns of
praise, while outside greater multitudes waited
to kneel before the shrine, and he took this to
mean that a great saint would one day be honored there.

So the legends, still conversationally told in
Assisi, run on and are locally current. Undoubtedly the dwellers in this curious old town,
whose streets have hardly one level spot but
climb up and down the steep hillside, realize
that their saint is their title to fame and their
revenue as well; yet through all the tales there
breathes a certain sincerity and simplicity of
worship. The little dark primitive shops teem
with relics, which make, it is true, a great
draft on imagination, and by what miracle
modern photography has contrived to present
the saint of Assisi in various impressive attitudes
and groups it would be as well not to inquire
too closely. It is a part of the philosophy of
travel to take the goods the gods provide, and
the blending of amused tolerance and unsus-
pected depths of reverential devotion by which

the visitor will find himself moved, while in Assisi, can hardly be described. For, surely, here

> ". . . there trod
> The whitest of the saints of God,"

and Catholic or Protestant, one equally enters into the beauty of his memory. The double and triple arches of the convent church enclose cloistered walls continually filled with visitors. No shrine in Italy holds such mysterious power. Simplicity and joy were the two keynotes of the life taught by St. Francis. "Poverty," he asserted, "is the happy state of life in which men are set free from the trammels of conventionalism, and can breathe the pure air of God's love. The richest inward life is enjoyed when life is poorest outwardly. Be poor," he continued, "try a new principle; be careless of having and getting; try *being*, for a change. Our life in the world ought to be such that any one on meeting us should be constrained to praise the heavenly Father. Be not an occasion of wrath to any one," he often said, "but by your gentleness may all be led to press onward to good works."

ITALY, THE MAGIC LAND

The supreme aim of Francis was that of service to humanity. He gave himself with impassioned fervor to this one work. For him there were no ideals of cloistered seclusion or of devotion to learning and art, but the ideal alone to uplift humanity. It was literally and simply, indeed, the Christ ideal. Of the "Rule" made, one of his biographers says: —

"Amid all these encouragements the Rule was made. It consists, like other monastic rules, of the three great vows of poverty, chastity, and obedience, differing only in so far that the poverty ordained by Francis was absolute. In other rules, though the individual was allowed to possess nothing, the community had often rich possessions, and there was no reason why the monks should not fare sumptuously and secure to themselves many earthly enjoyments, notwithstanding their individual destitution and their vow. But among the Brothers Minor there was not to be so much as a provision secured for the merest daily necessities. Day by day they were to live by God's providence, eating what was given to them, taking no thought how they were to be fed, or wherewithal clothed;

'neither gold nor silver in your purses;' not even the scrip to collect fragments in — as if God could not provide for every returning necessity. There had been monasteries in Italy for centuries, and the Benedictines were already a great and flourishing community; but this absolute renunciation of all things struck a certain chill to the hearts of all who heard of it, except the devoted band who had no will but that of Francis. His friend, the Bishop of Assisi, was one of those who stumbled at this novel and wonderful self-devotion. 'Your life, without a possession in the world, seems to me most hard and terrible,' said the compassionate prelate. 'My lord,' said Francis, 'if we had possessions, arms and protection would be necessary to us.' There was a force in this response which perhaps we can scarcely realize, but the Assisan bishop, who knew something of the temper of the lords of Umbria, and knew how lonely were the brethren dwelling on the church lands — the little plot (Portiuncula) a whole half league from the city gates — understood and perceived the justice of the reply.

"Another grand distinction of the Rule drawn up by Francis was the occupation it prescribed to its members. They were not to shut themselves up, or to care first for their own salvation. They were to preach — this was their special work; they were to proclaim repentance and the remission of sins; they were to be heralds of God to the world, and proclaim the coming of His kingdom. It is not possible to suppose that when he thus began to organize the mind of Francis did not make a survey of the establishments already in existence — the convents bound by the same three great vows, where life at this moment was going on so placidly, with flocks and herds and vineyards to supply the communities, and studious monks in their retirement, safe from all secular anxieties, fostering all the arts in their beginning, and carrying on the traditions of learning; while all around them the great unquiet, violent world heaved and struggled, yet within the convent walls there was leisure and peace. Blessed peace and leisure it was often, let us allow, preserving for us the germs of many good things we now enjoy, and raising little centres of safety and charity and brotherly kindness through the country in which they were placed. But such quiet was not in the nature of Francis. So far

as we can make out, he had thought little of
himself — even of his own soul to be saved —
all his life. The trouble on his mind had been
what to do, how sufficiently to work for God
and to help men. His fellow creatures were
dear to him; he gave them his cloak from his
shoulders many a day, and the morsel from
his own lips, and would have given them the
heart from his bosom had that been possible."

These are the "voices" that still echo in the air
of Assisi. In the suburbs is still shown the spot
where the chapel of St. Damian stood up a rocky
path on the hillside in an olive grove. It was
here that the scene of the miracle of the crucifix
is laid. Before the altar Francis knelt, praying:
"Great and Glorious Father, and thou, Lord
Jesus, I pray ye, shed abroad your light in the
darkness of my mind. May I in all things act
in accordance with thy holy will."

It is recorded that while he thus knelt in deep
prayer, he was unable to turn his eyes from the
cross, conscious that something marvellous was
taking place. The image of the Saviour assumed life; the eyes turned attentively on him;
a voice spoke accepting his service and he felt

at once endowed with the most marvellous tide of vitality, of joy, and of exhilaration. At this moment he entered on that life whose impress is left on the ages. Of the character and the peculiar quality of its influence Mrs. Oliphant well says: —

"It is not always possible to follow with our sympathy that literal, childlike rendering of every incident in the life of the Master, which sometimes looks fantastical and often unmeaning. He was a man of his time, and could live only under the conditions which that time allowed. He made visible to a literal, practical, unquestioning age the undeniable and astounding fact that the highest of all beings chose a life of poverty, hardship, and humbleness; that He chose submission instead of resistance, love instead of oppression, peace and forgiveness instead of revenge and war. Christ had died in their hearts, as said the legend of that Christmas at Greccia; and, as in one of the bold and artless pictures just then beginning to yield to a more refined and subtle art, Francis set forth before the world the image of his Master. The Son of man was lifted up, as on another cross, before the eyes of Umbria, before all Italy, warlike and wily, priest and baron, peasant and Pope. In this world Francis knew nothing, acknowledged nothing, cared for nothing save Christ and Him crucified — except, indeed, Christ's world, the universe redeemed, the souls to be saved, the poor to be comforted, the friends to be cherished, the singing birds and bubbling fountains, the fair earth and the sweet sky. Courteous, tender, and gentle as any paladin, sweet-tongued and harmonious as any poet, liberal as any prince, was the barefooted beggar and herald of God. We ask no visionary reverence for the Stigmata, no wondering belief in any miracle. As he stood, he was as great a miracle as any then existing under God's abundant, miraculous heavens; more wonderful than are the day and night, the sun and the dew; only less wonderful than that great Love which saves the world, and which it was his aim and destiny to reflect and show forth."

That mystic union to which all the ages attest, the union that may, at any moment, be formed between the soul and God, that mystery which the church calls conversion and which

finds its perfect interpretation in the words of
St. Paul, when he said, that if any man be in
Christ he is a new creation, had been accomplished in the life of Francis. He realized the
fulness of the knowledge of God's will; he longed
only for wisdom and for spiritual understanding.
Nor is this experience one to be relegated to the
realm of miracle. It is simply entering into
the supreme completeness of life. It is not
alone St. Paul, but every man, who may truly
say, "I can do all things through Christ, who
strengtheneth me." Nor does this experience,
when translated aright into daily life and action,
require any abnormal form of expression. It
does not, in its truest significance, mean a life
apart from the ordinary duties, but rather
it means that these duties shall be fulfilled in
the larger and nobler way. The exceptional
man may be called to be the standard bearer;
to renounce all domestic ties and give his service to the world; but such a life as this differs
only in degree from that which in the ordinary
home and social relations finds ample means
for its best expression. The persistent aim
after perfection should be the keynote of every
life. No one should be satisfied to hold as his

supreme ideal any lesser standard of ultimate achievement than is involved in the divine command, "Be ye therefore perfect, even as your Father in heaven is perfect." This is the soul's ideal, whatever ages and eternities it may require for it to recognize this trackless path.

St. Francis recognized joy as a factor of the nobler life. "It was his constant effort," writes one biographer, "that there should be bright looks and cheerful tones about him. To one of his brethren, who had the habit of walking about sadly with his head drooping, he said, — it is evident, with a spark of the impatience natural to his own vivacious spirit, — 'You may surely repent of your sins, my brother, without showing your grief so openly. Let your sorrow be between God and you: pray to Him to pardon you by His mercy, and to restore to your soul the joy of His salvation. But before me and the others be always cheerful, for it does not become a servant of God to have an air of melancholy and a face full of trouble.'"

An incident in the early life of St. Francis, which had determining significance, was his meeting with Dominic. The story is told "that Dominic, praying in a church in Rome, saw, in

a vision, our Lord rise from the right hand of
the Father in wrath, wearied at last with the
contradiction of sinners, with a terrible aspect
and three lances in his hand, each one of which
was to destroy from the face of the earth a distinct class of offenders. But while the dreamer
gazed at this awful spectacle, the Virgin Mother
arose and pleaded for the world, declaring that
she had two faithful servants whom she was
about to send into it to bring sinners to the
feet of the Saviour; one of these was Dominic
himself, the other was a poor man, meanly
clad, whom he had never seen before. This
vision came to the devout Spaniard, according
to the legend, during the night, which he spent,
as he was wont, in a church, in prayer. Next
morning, while he mused on the dream which
had been sent to him, his eye fell all at once
upon a stranger in a brown tunic, of aspect as
humble and modest as his garb, coming into
the same church to pray. Dominic at once ran
to him, fell on his neck, and, saluting him with
a kiss, cried, 'Thou art my companion: thy work
and mine is the same. If we stand by each
other, nothing can prevail against us.'"

No magic mirror, however, revealed to Francis the wonderful panorama of his future. No sibyl turned the leaves of the records yet to unfold. "He was preparing himself for a life of penitence rather than a life of activity," in the opinion of Paul Sabatier, and he had dreamed no dream of becoming a religious founder. He was so entirely without any personal ambition, save that of being obedient to the Heavenly Vision, that this absolute consecration of purpose enabled the divine power to work through him without obstruction. He became a very perfect instrument, so to speak, in the divine hand. After repairing the little chapel called the Portiuncula, on the level ground at the foot of the hill, some two miles from Assisi, his plan was to there pass his time in meditation and prayer. But the legend runs that on the feast of St. Mathias (February 24), in the winter of 1209, a Benedictine monk was celebrating mass and on his turning to read, "Wherever ye go preach, saying, The kingdom of heaven is at hand," Francis was profoundly and peculiarly impressed, and he exclaimed: "This is what I desire, O Father; from this day forth I set myself to put this command in practice." He felt that Jesus himself had spoken to him through the priest. Love and sacrifice became to him the supreme ideals, and in this moment, in that poor and bare little chapel, was inaugurated one of the greatest and most far-reaching religious movements of the entire world.

> "Not always as the whirlwind's rush
>   On Horeb's mount of fear,
> Not always as the burning bush
>   To Midian's shepherd seer,
> Not as the awful voice which came
>   To Israel's prophet bards,
> Nor as the tongues of cloven flame,
>   Nor gift of fearful words, —
>
> "Not always thus with outward sign
>   Of fire or voice from Heaven
> The message of a truth divine,
>   The call of God is given!"

That great ministry of St. Francis, whose influence pervades all time, — that lies between the opening years of the thirteenth and the opening years of the twentieth centuries, — was initiated the next morning in Assisi, when Francis preached for the first time. He spoke simply, emphasizing the truths he had learned to realize through his own experience: the absolute duty of following after perfection; the importance of realizing the shortness of life and the need of repentance. The first disciple of Francis was a wealthy resident of Assisi, named Bernardo. He was impressed with the conviction that he should distribute his possessions and unite with Francis in all his aims and work. Without definite organization, others joined them. They passed that spring and summer going up and down the country, sometimes assisting the harvesters and haymakers, and everywhere entering into the common life of the people. The Bishop of Assisi, however, remonstrated with Francis, saying that to him it seemed very harsh and unwise to try to live without owning anything. To which Francis replied that he did not desire temporal possessions, as these required arms for their defence and were an obstacle to the love of God and one's neighbor. It has remained for later years to discern the still truer significance of the teachings of Jesus, that neither possessions nor the lack of possessions form the real test, but the use which is made of them. As spiritual insight is developed it is more and more clearly realized that the quality of the life lived is the sole matter of importance, and not the conditions that surround it.

The brotherhood increased. The abbot of the Benedictines on Monte Subasio ceded to Francis and his order the little chapel called the Portiuncula, now enclosed within the vast and magnificent church of Santa Maria degli Angeli. M. Paul Sabatier, in his admirable biography of St. Francis, points out clearly that the founder of the Franciscans contemplated a laboring and not a mendicant order. During the decade 1211 to 1221, which Francis and his followers passed at the Portiuncula, a portion of the time was constantly passed in industrial pursuits. "With all his gentleness, Francis knew how to show an inflexible severity toward the idle," says Sabatier, "and he even went so far as to dismiss a friar who refused to work." Although Francis espoused poverty, declaring that she was his bride, he was unfalteringly loyal to the ideals of honest industry and integrity.

The mystic legends of the life of their saint that abound in Assisi are touched with poetic romance in that a companion figure is always seen by his side, that of Santa Chiara. Not more inseparable in popular thought are Dante and

Beatrice, or Petrarca and Laura, than are Francis and Clara. Their statues stand side by side in the Duomo; they are represented together by both painter and sculptor in the churches of Santa Chiara and Santa Maria degli Angeli in the old hill town. Chiara was the daughter of a noble family, and as a girl of sixteen, coming under the influence of Francis from hearing one of his sermons, she, too, became one of his followers and left her father's palace in Assisi to take the vows of perpetual and voluntary poverty at the altar of the Portiuncula. Followed by two women, she passed swiftly through the town in the dead of the night, and through dark woods, her hurrying figure seeming like some spirit driven by winds towards an unknown future. One thing alone was clear before her — that she was nearing the abode of Francis Bernardone whose preaching at San Giorgio only a month before had thrilled her, inspiring her in this strange way to seek the life he had described in fiery words. Just as she came in sight of the Portiuncula the chanting of the brethren, which had reached her in the wood, suddenly ceased, and they came out with lighted torches in expectation of her coming.

ST. FRANCIS D'ASSISI, THE DUOMO, ASSISI
Giovanni Dupré
Page 366

Swiftly and without a word she passed in to attend the midnight mass which Francis was to serve, and the scene is thus described: —

"The ceremony was simple, wherein lies the charm of all things Franciscan. The service over and the last blessing given, St. Francis led Clare toward the altar, and with his own hands cut off her long, fair hair and unclasped the jewels from her neck. But a few minutes more and a daughter of the proud house of Scifi stood clothed in the brown habit of the order, the black veil of religion falling about her shoulders, lovelier far in this nun-like severity than she had been when decked out in all her former luxury of silken gowns and precious gems.

"It was arranged that Clare was to go afterward to the Benedictine nuns of San Paolo, near Bastia, about an hour's walk farther on in the plain. So when the final vows had been taken, St. Francis took her by the hand and they passed out of the chapel together just as dawn was breaking, while the brethren returned to their cells gazing half sadly, as they passed, at the coils of golden hair and the little heap of jewels which still lay upon the altar cloth."

Clara founded a convent and lived as its abbess, and the great church of Santa Chiara is built on the site of this convent. She was born in Assisi in 1194, and died in 1253, surviving Francis by twenty-seven years. Her father was the Count Favorini Scifi, and he had destined his daughter — who had great beauty — to a rich and brilliant marriage. He violently opposed her choice of the religious life, but no earthly power, she declared, should sever her from it.

The beauty of the lifelong friendship between Francis and Clara is thus touched upon by Mrs. Oliphant: —

"It was one of those tender and touching friendships which are to the student of history like green spots in the desert; and which gave to the man and the woman thus voluntarily separated from all the joys of life a certain human consolation in the midst of their hardships. They can have seen each other but seldom, for it was one of the express stipulations

of the Franciscan Rule that the friars should
refrain from all society with women, and have
only the most sparing and reserved intercourse
even with their sisters in religion. And Francis
was no priest, nor had he the privilege of hearing
confession and directing the spiritual life of
his daughter in the faith. But he sent to her to
ask enlightenment from her prayers, when any
difficulty was in his way. He went to see her
when he was in trouble; especially once on his
way to Rieti to have an operation performed
on his eyes. Once the two friends ate together
at a sacramental meal, the pledge and almost
the conclusion on earth of that tenderest, most
disinterested, and unworldly love which existed
between them. That he was sure of her sympathy in all things, of her prayers and spiritual
aid, whatsoever he might be doing, whereso-
ever he might be, no doubt was sweet to Francis
in all his labors and trials. As he walked many
a weary day past that church of St. Damian,
every stone of which was familiar to him, and
many laid with his own hands, must not his
heart have warmed at thought of the sister
within, safe from all conflict with the world,
upon whose fellow-feeling he could rely abso-

lutely as man can rely only on woman? The world has jeered at the possibility of such friendships from its earliest age; and yet they have always existed, — one of the most exquisite and delicate of earthly ties. Gazing back into that far distance over the graves, not only of those two friends, but of a hundred succeeding generations, a tear of grateful sympathy comes into the student's eye. He is glad to believe that, all those years, Francis could see in his comings and goings the cloister of Clara; and that this sacred gleam of human fellowship, — love purified of all self-seeking, — tender, visionary, celestial affection, sweetened their solitary lives."

Legends innumerable, attesting supernormal manifestations regarding Francis, sprang up and have been perpetuated through the ages. One is as follows: —

"Hardly more than three years from the moment when the pale penitent was hooted through Assisi amid the derisive shouts of the people, and driven with blows and curses into confinement in his own father's house, we find that it has already become his custom on Sunday to preach in the cathedral; and that, from his little convent at the Portiuncula, Francis has risen into influence in the whole country, which no doubt by this time was full of stories of his visit to Rome and intercourse with the Pope, and all the miraculous dreams and parables with which that intercourse was attended. Already the mind of the people, so slow to adopt, but so ready to become habituated to, anything novel, had used itself to the sight of the brethren in their brown gowns, and, leaping from one extreme to the other, instead of madmen, learned to consider them saints. The air about the little cloister began to breathe of miracles, — miracles which must have been a matter of common report among the contemporaries of the saint, for Celano wrote within three years of Francis's death. Once, when their leader was absent, a sudden wonder startled the brethren. It was midnight between Saturday and Sunday, and Francis, who had gone to preach at Assisi, was at the moment praying in the canon's garden. A chariot of fire, all radiant and shining, suddenly entered the house, awaking those who lay asleep, and moving to wonder and awe those who watched, or labored, or prayed. It was the heart and thoughts of their leader returning to them in the midst of his prayer, which were figured by this appearance."

When Francis died a pathetic scene is thus described: —

"All the clergy of Assisi, chanting solemn hymns, came out to meet the bier, and thus they climbed the hill to the birthplace of the saint, the city of his toils and tears and blessing. When they came to St. Damian an affecting pause was made. Clara within, with all her maidens, waited the last visit of their father and friend. Slowly the triumphant crowd defiled into the church of the nuns, hushing, let us hope, their songs of joy, their transports of gratulations, out of respect to the grief which dwelt there, and could scarcely, by all the arguments of family pride, or the excitement of this universal triumph, be brought to rejoice. The bier was set down within the chancel, the coffin opened, and opened also was the little window through which the nuns received the sacrament on ordinary occasions. To this little opening

the pale group of nuns, ten of them, with Clara
at their head, came marching silently, with
tears and suppressed cries.   Clara herself, even
in face of that multitude, could not restrain her
grief. 'Father, father, what will become of us?'
she cried out; 'who will care for us now, or
console us in our troubles?' 'Virgin modesty,'
says Celano, stopped her lamentations, and with
a miserable attempt at thanksgiving, reminding
herself that the angels were rejoicing at his
coming, and all was gladness on his arrival in
the city of God, the woman who had been his
closest friend in this world, whose sympathy
he had sought so often, kissed the pale hands —
'splendid hands,' says Celano, in his enthusiasm, 'adorned with precious gems and shining
pearls' — and disappeared from the little window with her tears into the dim convent behind,
where nobody could reprove her sorrow.''

The personality of Chiara comes down to us
through the ages invested with untold charm.
It is said that when she was dying there came
"a long procession of white-robed virgins, led
by the Queen of Heaven, whose head was
crowned with a diadem of shining gold, each of

the celestial visitors stooped to kiss Chiara as her soul passed to its home."

During all the life of Francis, whenever any new movement or work was to be undertaken, he invariably sent to ask the counsel and the prayers of Chiara.

The miraculous preservation of the body of Santa Chiara is one of the articles of faith in Assisi. In 1850 — six hundred years after her death — a tomb believed to be hers was found and opened in the presence of a distinguished group of ecclesiastics, among whom was Cardinal Pecci, later Pope Leo XIII. In this tomb a form is said to have been found, and it has been placed in a reliquary of alabaster and Carrara marble especially constructed for it. This sanctuary is placed in the church of Santa Chiara, in the crypt, behind a glass screen, where candles are kept perpetually burning. Lina Gordon Duff, writing the history of Assisi, says of this curious spectacle: —

"As pilgrims stand before a grating in the dimly lighted crypt, the gentle rustle of a nun's dress is heard; slowly invisible hands draw the curtain aside, and the body of Santa Chiara is

SANTA CHIARA, THE DUOMO, ASSISI
Amalia Dupré
Page 375

seen lying in a glass case upon a satin bed, her face clearly outlined against her black and white veils, whilst her brown habit is drawn in straight folds about her body. She clasps the book of her Rule in one hand, and in the other holds a lily with small diamonds shining on the streamers."

In all these churches — the great convent church, upper and lower, of the Franciscans elaborately adorned with frescoes by Cimabue and by Giotto; in the ancient Duomo; in Santa Chiara and in Santa Maria degli Angeli — statues of the two saints, Francis and Chiara, are placed side by side. She shares all the exaltation of his memory and the fulness of his fame.

The strange problem of the stigmata has, perhaps, never been absolutely solved. Canon Knox Little says that as to the miracles of St. Francis generally speaking, there is no intrinsic improbability; that "his holy life, his constant communion with God, the abundant blessings with which it pleased God to mark his ministry, all point in the same direction." Latter-day revelations of psychic science disclose contemporary facts of the power of mental influence on the physical form that are, in many instances, hardly less wonderful than this alleged miracle of St. Francis. Whether the story is accepted literally or only in a figurative sense does not affect the transcendent power of his influence. His entire life and work illustrate the beauty of holiness. "Art in its widest sense gained a marvellous impulse from his work and effort," says Canon Knox Little. The French and Provençal literature and the schools of Byzantine art preceded the life of Francis; but his influence imparted a powerful wave of sympathetic and vital insight and awakened a world of new sensibilities of feeling. Indeed, it is a proverb of Italy, "Without Francis, no Dante." Certainly the life of Francis was the inspiration of the early Italian art. Cimabue and Giotto drew from the inspiration of that unique and lovely life the pictorial conceptions that have made Assisi the cradle of Italian painting. The great works of Giotto are in the lower church of the Franciscan monastery. One of these frescoes represents chastity as a maiden kneeling in a shrine, while angels bring to her branches of palm.

ITALY, THE MAGIC LAND

Obedience is depicted as placing a yoke upon
the bowed figure of a priest, while St. Francis,
attended by two angels, looks on; Poverty,
whom Francis declared to be his bride, is pictured as accompanied by Hope and Charity,
who give her in marriage to St. Francis, the
union being blessed by Christ, while the
heavenly Father and throngs of angels gaze
through the clouds on this nuptial scene. The
fresco called Gloriosus Franciscus is perhaps
the crowning work of Giotto. Francis is seen
in a beatitude of glory, with a richly decorated
banner bearing the cross and seven stars floating above his head and bands of angels in the
air surrounding him. Canon Knox Little, al-
luding to these interesting works of Giotto, says
that "even in their faded glories they give an
immense interest to the lower church of Assisi.
No one can look at them now unmoved, or
wander on the hillside to the west of the little
city, with the rugged rocks above one's head, and
beneath one's feet the rich carpets of cyclamen,
and before one's eyes long dreamy stretches of
the landscape of Umbria, without being touched
by the feeling of that beautiful and loving life
devoted to God and man and nature, in utter

truth, which therefore left such an impress on Christian art."

The Madonna and saints painted by Cimabue are faded almost to the point of obliteration, yet there still lingers about them a certain grace and charm. The visitor to this Franciscan monastery church realizes that he is beholding the art which was the very pledge and prophecy of the Renaissance, and he realizes, too, that the Renaissance itself was the outgrowth of the new vitality communicated to the world by the life and character of St. Francis. He gave to the world the realization of the living Christ; he taught that religion was in action, not in theology. He liberated the spirit; and when this colossal church was being built (1228–53) the artists who had felt the new thrill of life opened by his teaching hastened to Assisi to express their appreciation by their pictorial work on its walls. The qualities of spiritual life — faith, sacrifice, sympathy, and love — began, for the first time, to be interpreted into artistic expression.

The tomb of St. Francis is in the crypt of the church. The stone sarcophagus containing his body was discovered in 1818, and then placed here in a little chamber especially prepared, surrounded by an iron latticework with candles perpetually burning.

From the sacristy of the lower church, stairs ascend to the upper, with its beautiful nave and transept with a high altar, and the choir stalls. While the lower church with its great arches is always dark, the upper is flooded with light from vast windows. There is a series of frescoed panels on either side, accredited to pupils of Giotto, full of forcible action and a glow of color. But the upper church, while it is magnificent, lacks somewhat of that mystic atmosphere one is so swiftly conscious of in the gloom and mystery of the lower church.

Stretching behind the churches, along the crest of the high hill, is the colossal monastery itself, with that double row of arches and colonnades that makes it so conspicuous a feature of all the Umbrian valley. Formerly hundreds of monks dwelt here; but the Italian government suppressed this monastery in 1866, and since that time it has been used as a school for boys.

The ancient Duomo, whose façade is of the twelfth century, has three exquisite rose windows, and on either side, as one approaches

the high altar, stand the statues of St. Francis
and of Santa Chiara. In the little piazza in
front of the church is a bronze copy of Dupré's
famous statue of St. Francis.

The colossal church of Santa Maria degli
Angeli, with its magnificent dome, is a contrast,
indeed, to the primitive little Portiuncula where
Francis knelt in prayer, and which is now preserved in the centre of this vast cathedral, —
the rude structure encased in marble, and
decorated, above the entrance, with a picture
by Overbeck, whose motive is St. Francis as he
stands, hushed and reverent, listening to the
voice that tells him to embrace poverty. There
is a fine Perugino in the church, representing
the Saviour. The cell in which St. Francis
died, enclosed in the little chapel which St.
Bonaventuri built over it, is preserved in this
great cathedral.

"And who was he that opened that door
in heaven?" questions Canon Knox Little in
reference to St. Francis. "Who was he that
gave that fresh life and thought? Who but the
man who had brought down in his own person
the living Christ into his century, who had
taught men again the love of God, and then the

love of man and the love of nature; who had lifted the people out of their misery and degradation, and awakened the church out of its stiffness and worldliness; it was he, too, who inspired, who may at most be said to have created, Italian art, — the great St. Francis! Such are the deep, such are the penetrating, such are the far-reaching effects of sanctity. If a soul is, by divine grace, given wholly to God, it is impossible for us to say to what heights it may attain, or what good, in every region of human effort, it may do."

Perugia, the neighboring city only fifteen miles from Assisi, is the metropolis of all this Umbrian region. Like Assisi, it is a "hill town," built on an acropolis of rock, its foundations laid by the Etruscans more than three thousand years before the Christian era, and its atmosphere is freighted with the records of artists and scholars. The Perugians were the forerunners. They held the secret of artifice in metals and gems; they were architects and sculptors. The only traces of their painting that have come down to us are their works on sarcophagi, on vases or funeral urns, — traces that indicate their gifts for line and form. It was about 310 B.C. that all Umbria became a Roman province. The colossal porta of Augustus — a gateway apparently designed for the Cyclops — still retains its inscription, "Augustus Perusia." The imperishable impress of the great Roman conqueror is still seen in many places. Perugia was a firm citadel, as is attested by the fact that Totila and his army of Goths spent seven years in besieging it. The centuries from the thirteenth to the fifteenth inclusive, when it was under the sway of the Guelphs and the Ghibellines, were years of tragic violence. Even the cathedral became the scene of riot, and its interior was entirely washed with wine, and it was reconsecrated before it could be again used for holy offices. The little piazza in front of the cathedral, now dreaming in the sun, has been the scene of strange and contrasting crises of life. Strife and warfare have desolated it; the footsteps of Bernardino of Siena have consecrated it, as he passed within the great portals to preach the gospel of peace. He was one of the most potent of the Francescan disciples, and Bernardino (born of the noble family of the Albizzeschi, in 1380, in Siena, the year after St. Catherine's death) for forty years

BAIÆ AND ISCHIA, FROM CAMALDOLI

Page 382

wandered over Italy, preaching peace and repentance. Vespasiano da Bisticci, a contemporary historian, records that Bernardino "converted and changed the minds and spirits of men marvellously and had a wondrous power in persuading men to lay aside their mortal hatreds." Bernardino died at the age of sixty-four in Aquila, and the towns in which he had faithfully carried on his apostolic work placed the sacred sign of the divine name (I.H.S.) upon their gates and palaces, in his memory. In the Sienese gallery is a portrait of San Bernardino by Sano, painted in 1460, representing the saint as the champion of the Holy Name, with the inscription, "I have manifested Thy name to men." In one of his impressive and wonderful sermons San Bernardino said: —

"There still remain many places for us to make. Ah! for the love of God, love one another. Alas! see you not that, if you love the destruction one of the other you are ruining your very selves? Ah! put this thing right for the love of God. Love one another! What I have done to make peace among you and to make you like brothers, I have done with that

zeal I should wish my own soul to receive. I
have done it all to the glory of God. And let
no one think that I have set myself to do anything at any person's request. I am only moved
by the bidding of God for His honor and glory."

Opposite the Duomo of Perugia, on the other
side of the piazza, is the Palazzo Municipio,
with a Gothic façade, a beautiful example of
thirteenth-century architecture. Here also is
the colossal fountain with three basins, decorated with pictorial designs from the Bible by
Niccolo Pisano and Arnolfo of Florence, and
in the shadow of this fountain St. Dominic, St.
Francis, and St. Bernardino often met and held
converse.

Perugia easily reads her title clear to artistic
immortality in having been the home of Perugino, the master of Raphael. Here he lived
for several years working with Pinturicchio in
the frescoes that adorn the Collegio del Cambio,
now held as a priceless treasure hall of art.
They still glow with rich coloring, — the Christ
seen on the Mount of Transfiguration; the
Mother and Child with the adoring magi; and
the chariot of the dawn driven by Apollo a

century before Guido painted his "Aurora" in the Palazzo Rospigliosa in Rome.

From the parapets of Perugia are views of supreme poetic beauty. The play of light and color on the picturesque hills and mountains of the Umbrian country; the gray-green gleam of olive orchards and the silver threads of winding streams; the towers and ruins and castles of a dozen towns and villages that crown the slopes, and the violet shadows of deepening twilight, with Assisi bathed in a splendor of rose and gold, — all combine to make this an ever-changing panorama for the poet and painter.

No journey in Italy is quite like that to the lovely Umbrian valley and its Jerusalem, Assisi, the shrine which, with the single exception of Rome, is the special place of pilgrimage for the entire religious world. Perugia offers the charm of art, and attracts the visitor, also, by an exceptional degree of modern comfort and convenience; but Assisi is the shrine before which he kneels, where the footsteps of saints who have knelt in prayer make holy ground, and where he realizes anew the consecration of faith and sacrifice. The very air is filled with divine messages, and in lowly listening he will hear, again, those wonderful and thrilling words of St. Francis: —

"By the holy love which is in God I pray all to put aside every obstacle, every care, every anxiety, that they may be able to consecrate themselves entirely to serve, love, and honor the Lord God, with a pure heart and a sincere purpose, which is what He asks above all things."

White phantom city, whose untrodden streets
    Are rivers, and whose pavements are the shifting
        Shadows of palaces and strips of sky;
I wait to see thee vanish like the fleets
    Seen in mirage, or towers of clouds uplifting
        In air their unsubstantial masonry.

                                        LONGFELLOW.

Fair as the palace builded for Aladdin,
Yonder St. Mark uplifts its sculptured splendor —
Intricate fretwork, Byzantine mosaic,
Color on color, column upon column,
Barbaric, wonderful, a thing to kneel to!
Over the portal stand the four gilt horses,
Gilt hoof in air, and wide distended nostril,
Fiery, untamed, as in the days of Nero.
Skyward, a cloud of domes and spires and crosses;
Earthward, black shadows flung from jutting stonework.
High over all the slender Campanile
Quivers, and seems a falling shaft of silver.

                        THOMAS BAILEY ALDRICH.

As one who parts from Life's familiar shore,
  Looks his last look in long-beloved eyes,
  And sees in their dear depths new meanings rise
And strange light shine he never knew before;
As then he fain would snatch from Death his hand
  And linger still, if haply he may see
  A little more of this Soul's mystery
Which year by year he seemed to understand;
So, Venice, when thy wondrous beauty grew
  Dim in the clouds which clôthed the wintry sea
I saw thou wert more beauteous than I knew,
  And long to turn and be again with thee.
But what I could not then I trust to see
In that next life which we call memory.

PHILLIPS BROOKS.[1]

---

[1] From "Life of Phillips Brooks," by kind permission of Messrs. E. P. Dutton & Co.

VI

THE GLORY OF A VENETIAN JUNE

I have been between Heaven and Earth since our arrival at Venice. The Heaven of it is ineffable — never had I touched the skirts of so celestial a place. The beauty of the architecture, the silver trails of water up between all that gorgeous color and carving, the enchanting silence, the music, the gondolas, — I mix it all up together, and maintain that nothing is like it, nothing equal to it, no second Venice in the world.

MRS. BROWNING, in the June of 1850.

THE first glimpse of enchanted Venice, as her towers and marble palaces rise wraith-like from the sea, is an experience that can never fade from memory. Like a mirage, like a vision invoked by some incantation or magician's spell, the scene prefigures itself, bringing a thrill of some vague and undefined memory, as if a breath floated by, —

"An odor from Dreamland sent,
That makes the ghost seem nigh me,
  Of a splendor that came and went;
Of a life lived somewhere, — I know not
  In what diviner sphere, —
Of memories that stay not and go not,"

389

which eludes all translation into words. Nor does the spell dissolve and vanish when put to the test of one's actual sojourn in the Dream City. It is an experience outside the boundaries of the ordinary day and daylight world, as if one were caught up into the ethereal realm to find a city

> ". . . of gliding and wide-wayed silence
> With room in the streets for the soul."

The sense of remoteness from common life could hardly be greater if one were suddenly swept away to some far star, blazing in the firmament; or if Charon had rowed him over the mystic river and he had entered the abodes of life on the plane beyond. Even the hotel becomes an enchanted palace whose salons, luxuriously decorated, open by long windows on marble balconies overhanging the Grand Canal. Dainty little tables piled with current reading matter, in French, English, and Italian, stand around; the writing-desks are sumptuous, filled with every convenience of stationery; and the matutinal coffee and rolls are served the guest in any idyllic niche wherein he chooses to ensconce himself, regardless of

the regulation *salle-à-manger*.   One looks across
the Grand Canal to the beautiful Church of
Santa Maria della Salute.   The water plashes
against the marble steps as gondolas glide past;
the blue sky of Italy reflects itself in the waters
below, until one feels as if he were floating in
the air between sea and sky.   In the heart of
the city, with throngs of people moving to and
fro, all is yet silence, save the cry of the gon-
dolier, the confused echo of voices from the
people who pass, and here and there the faint
call of a bird.   No whir and rush of electric
cars and motors; no click of the horses' feet on
the asphalt pavement — no pavement, indeed,
and no horses, no twentieth-century rush of life.
It is Venice, it is June, and the two combine
to make an illuminated chapter.   To live in
Venice is like being domesticated in the heart
of an opal.   How wonderful it is to drift — a
sky above and a sky below — on still waters at
sunset, with the Dream City mirrored in the
depths, every shade of gold and rose and amber
mirrored back, — the very atmosphere a sea of
color, recalling to one Ruskin's words that "none
of us appreciate the nobleness and the sacredness of color.   Of all God's gifts to man," he

continues, "color is the holiest, the most divine, the most solemn. Color is the sacred and saving element." If the enthusiasm in these words savor of exaggeration, Venice is the place that will lure one to forgetfulness of it. One is simply conscious of being steeped in color and revelling in a strange loveliness. One no longer marvels at the glory of Tintoretto and Paolo Veronese. They but interpreted on canvas the shining reality. A charming writer on Venice has well said: —

"The aspects of Venice are as various, as manifold, as the hues held in solution upon her waters beneath a sirocco sky. There is a perpetual miracle of change; one day is not like another, one hour varies from the next; there is no stable outline such as one finds among the mountains, no permanent vista, as in a view across a plain. The two great constituents of the Venetian landscape, the sea and the sky, are precisely the two features in nature which undergo most incessant change. The cloud-wreaths of this evening's sunset will never be repeated again; the bold and buttressed piles of those cloud-mountains will never be built again just so for us; the grain of orange and crimson that stains the water before our prow, we cannot be sure that we shall look upon its like again. . . . One day is less like another in Venice than anywhere else. The revolution of the seasons will repeat certain effects; spring will chill the waters to a cold, hard green; summer will spread its breadth of golden light on palace front and water way; autumn will come with its pearly-gray sirocco days, and sunsets flaming a sombre death; the stars of a cloudless winter night, the whole vast dome of heaven, will be reflected in the mirror of the still lagoon. But in spite of this general order of the seasons, one day is less like another in Venice than anywhere else; the lagoon wears a different aspect each morning when you rise, the sky offers a varied composition of cloud each evening as the sun sets. Words cannot describe Venice, nor brush portray her ever-fleeting, ever-varying charm. Venice is to be felt, not reproduced; to live there is to live a poem, to be daily surfeited with a wealth of beauty enough to madden an artist to despair."

It was in the autumn of 1882 that the Rev.

ITALY, THE MAGIC LAND

Dr. Phillips Brooks, later Bishop of Massachusetts, visited Venice and wrote of San Marco: —

"Strange how there is nothing like St. Mark's in Venice, nothing of the same kind as the great church. It would have seemed as if, standing here for so many centuries, and always profoundly loved and honored, it would almost of necessity have influenced the minds of the generations of architects, and shown its power in their works. But there seems to be no sign of any such influence. It stands alone."

Dr. Brooks noted that Venice had "two aspects, one sensuous and self-indulgent, the other lofty, spiritual, and even severe. Both aspects," he continues, "are in its history and both are also in its art. Titian often represents the former. The loftier, nobler Tintoretto gives us the second. There is something in his greatest pictures, as, for instance, in the Crucifixion, at St. Rocco, which no other artist approaches. The lordly composition gives us an impression of intellectual grasp and vigor. The foreground group of prostrate women is full of a tenderness. The rich pearly light, which floods the centre, glows with a solemn picturesqueness, and the great Christ, who hangs like a benediction over the whole, is vocal with a piety which no other picture in the world displays. And the Presentation of the Virgin, in Santa Maria dell' Orto, is the consummate presentation of that beautiful subject, its beauty not lost in its majesty."

Of other pictures Dr. Brooks said: —

"In the Academia there is the sunshine of three hundred years ago. Paris Bordone's glowing picture of the Fisherman who brings the Ring of St. Mark to the Doge, burned like a ray of sunlight on the wall. Carpaccio's delightful story of St. Ursula brought the old false standards of other days back to one's mind, but brought them back lustrous with the splendor of summers that seemed forever passed, but are perpetually here. Tintoretto's Adam and Eve was, as it always is, the most delightful picture in the gallery, and Pordenone's great St. Augustine seemed a very presence in the vast illuminated room."

Tennysón loved best, of all the pictures in Venice, a Bellini, — a beautiful work, in the

Church of Il Redentore; and he was deeply
impressed by the "Presentation of the Virgin,"
from Tintoretto, in the Church of the Madonna
dell' Orto. "He was fascinated by St. Mark's,"
writes the poet's son, "by the Doge's Palace
and the Piazza, and by the blaze of color in
water and sky. He climbed the Campanile,
and walked to the library where he could
scarcely tear himself away from the Grimani
Breviary."

Venice, though not containing any single
gallery comparable with the Pitti and the
Uffizi, is still singularly rich in treasures of art,
and rich in legend and story. The school of
encrusted architecture is nowhere so wonderfully represented as here, and it is only in this
architecture that a perfect scheme of color decoration is possible. In all the world there is no
such example of encrusted architecture as that
revealed in St. Mark's. It is a gleaming mass
of gold, opal, ruby, and pearl; with alabaster
pillars carved in designs of palm and pome-
granate and lily; with legions of sculptured
angels looking down; with altars of gold ablaze
with scarlet flowers and snowy lilies, while
clouds of mystic incense fill the air. One most

impressive place is the baptistery, where is the tomb of St. Mark and also that of the Doge Andrea Dandolo, who died at the age of forty-six, having been chosen Doge ten years before. His tomb is under a window in the baptistery, and the design is that of his statue in bronze, lying on a couch, while two angels at the head and the feet hold back the curtains.

The sarcophagus that is said to contain the body of St. Mark is of the richest description, encrusted with gold and jewels on polished ebony and marble. There is a legend that after St. Mark had seen the people of Aguilia well grounded in religion he was called to Rome by St. Peter; but before setting off he took with him in a boat the holy Bishop Hennagoras and sailed to the marshes of Venice. The boat was driven by wind to a small island called Rialto, on which were some houses, and St. Mark was suddenly snatched into ecstasy and heard the voice of an angel saying, "Peace be to thee, Mark; here shall thy body rest."

There is also a legend that in the great conflagration which destroyed Venice in 976 A.D., the body of St. Mark was lost and no one knew where to find it. Then the pious Doge and the people gave themselves to fasting and prayer, and assembled in the church, asking that the place be revealed them. It was on the 25th of June that the assemblage took place. Suddenly one of the pillars of the church trembled, and opened to disclose the sarcophagus, — a chest of bronze. The legend goes on to say that St. Mark stretched his hand out through the side and that a noble, Dolfini by name, drew a gold ring off the finger.

The place where this miracle is said to have been wrought is now marked by the Altar of the Cross.

Ruskin declares that "a complete understanding of the sanctity of color is the key to European art." Nowhere is this sanctity of color so felt as at San Marco. The church is like the temple of the New Jerusalem.

The origin of Venice is steeped in sacred history. It is pre-eminently the city founded in religious enthusiasm. The chronicles of De Monici, written in 421, give this passage: "God, who punishes the sins of men by war, sorrow, and whose ways are past finding out, willing both to save the innocent blood, and that a great power, beneficial to the whole world, should arise in a place strange beyond belief, moved the chief men of the cities of the Venetian province both in memory of the past, and in dread of future distress, to establish states upon the nearer islands of the Adriatic, to which, in the last extremity, they might retreat for refuge. . . . They laid the foundation of the new city under good auspices on the island of the Rialto, the highest and nearest to the mouth of the Brenta, on March 25, 471."

The first Doge of Venice was Paolo Lucio Anopeste, elected by the tribunal of commonalty, tribunals, and clergy, at Heraclea, in 697. The period of the subjection of the ecclesiastical to the ducal and patrician powers followed. The "Council of Ten" was established in 1335, and the last Doge elected was Lodovico Manin in 1789, who exclaimed, "*Tolè questo: no la doperò più*," as the French Revolution destroyed the Republic of Venice.

The finest example of Renaissance architecture in Venice is that of the *Libreria Vecchia*, the work of Jacobo Sansovino, completed in the sixteenth century. Never were the creations of poet and philosopher more fittingly enshrined. The rich Doric frieze, the Ionic columns, the stately balustrade, with statues and obelisks, the resplendent richness of ornamentation, offer a majesty and beauty seldom found even in the best classical architecture of Europe. On the ceiling of one sala is a picture by Titian representing "Wisdom" as a woman, reclining on a cloud, her right hand outstretched to take a book that Genius is offering her. There are two beautiful caryatides by Vittoria and rich mural work by Battesta Franco and De Moro.

Petrarca, returning from his wanderings in 1362, pleaded with the Senate of Venezia to give him a house, in return for which he offered the inheritance of his library. This was the nucleus of the fine collection which since 1812 has been included in the Palace of the Doges. In it are some magnificent works by Paolo Veronese, one portrait by Tintoretto, and others by Salviati and Telotti.

The Doge's Palace is a treasure house of history. One enters the Porta delta Carta, which dates back to 1638, erected by Bartolomeo Buon. The portal is very rich in sculpture, and among the reliefs is a heroic one of Francesco Foscari, kneeling before the lion at St. Mark's. One recalls his tragic fate and passes

on. Perhaps, *en passant*, one may say that his
pilgrimage through Venice and Florence is so
constantly in the scenes of tragedy that he is
prone to sink almost into utter sadness, even,
rather than seriousness. The air is full of
ghosts. One feels the oppression of all the life
that has there been lived, all the tragedies that
have been enacted in these scenes.

In Renaissance nothing more wonderful in
Europe can be found than the court of the
Palace of the Doges. Antonio Rizzo began the
east façade of the building in 1480, and it was
continued by Lombardo, and completed by
Scarpagnino. "Words cannot be found to
praise the beauty of these sculptures," says Salvatico, "as well as of the single ornaments of
the walls and of the ogres which have been
carved so delicately and richly that they cannot
be excelled by the Roman antique friezes."

By the golden staircase one goes to the council
chambers, — the hall of the Senate, the Council
of Ten, and the Council of Three. In the great
council chamber is that most celebrated mural
painting in the world, "The Glory of Venice,"
by Paolo Veronese, which covers the ceiling. In
a frieze are the portraits of seventy-six of the

Doges, but in one space is a black tablet only, with the inscription: "This in place of M. F., who was executed for his crimes."

The "Sala del Maggior Consiglio" (hall of the grand council) is very rich in paintings. Above the throne is Tintoretto's "The Glory of Paradise," and the walls are covered with battle pieces and symbolic and allegorical paintings. There is "Venice Crowned by Fame," by Paolo Veronese, "Doge Niccolò da Ponte Presenting the Senate and Envoys of . Conquered Cities to Venice," by Tintoretto; "Venice Crowned by the Goddess of Victory," by Palma Giovane, and many another of the richest and most wonderful beauty.

Descending into the prisons and dungeons brings one into a vivid realization of the grim history of which these were the scenes. The Bridge of Sighs has two covered passages, one for the political and one for the criminal prisoners. Here is shown a narrow ledge on which the condemned man stood, with a slanting stone passageway before him, which, when the guillotine had done its swift and deadly work, conveyed the crimson flood into the dark waters of the canal below, while the body was thrown in the water on the other side. There are the "Chambers of Lead," where prisoners were confined, intensely hot in the summer, and as intensely cold in the winter. Many of these dark, close, narrow cells — in which the one article of furniture allowed was the wooden slanting rack, that served as a bed — still remain. In many of these are inscriptions that were written by the prisoners. One reads (in translation): "May God protect me against him whom I trust; I will protect myself against him whom I do not trust."

The murderer, Giovanni M. Borni, wrote in his cell: "G. M. B. was confined very unjustly in this prison; if God does not help it will be the last desolation of a poor, numerous, and honest family."

All visitors to these gloomy dungeons recall the lines of Byron: —

> "I stood in Venice on the Bridge of Sighs,
> A palace and a prison on each hand."

The piazza of St. Mark's is a distinctive feature, even in all Europe. It is not large; it is surrounded on three sides with shops, which are merely glittering bazaars of jewels and bric-a-brac; the sidewalk is blockaded with cafés *al fresco*, the ground is half covered with the dense flocks of white doves, but here all lingers and loiters. The façade of St. Mark's fills one end — a mass of gleaming color. At one corner is the tall clock tower (Torre dell' Orologio) in the Renaissance style of 1400, crowned with the gilded lion of St. Mark. On the festa days three figures, the Three Wise Men, preceded by an angel, come forth on the tower and bow before the Madonna, in a niche above, — a very ingenious piece of mechanism. With its rich architecture and sculptures and masses of color, the piazza of San Marco is really an open-air hall, where all the town congregates from morning till midnight.

To study the art of the Venetian school is a work of months, and one that would richly repay the student. The churches and galleries of Venice give a truly unique opportunity. In the Church of San Sebastiano lies Paolo Veronese, the church in which he painted his celebrated frescoes, now transformed into a temple for himself. Here one finds his "Coronation of the Virgin," "The Virgin in the Gloria," "Adoration of the Magi," "Martyrdom of San

Sebastian," and many others. In the Scuola
di San Rocco are the great works of Tintoretto,
"St. Magdalene in the Wilderness," the "Visitation," and the "Murder of the Innocents."

In the San Maria dei Frari is the tomb of
Titian, — an exquisite grouping of sculpture in
Carrara marble, erected in 1878–80 by the command of the Emperor of Austria, the work of
Zandomenighi. In this church is Titian's most
famous painting, the "Madonna of the Pessaro,"
the work of which is probably, too, the greatest
in all Venetian art. The Hall of Heaven is
shown, supported by colossal columns. St.
Peter, Maucis, and Antoninus are commending
the Pessaro family to the Virgin, who is enthroned on high. The beauty of line, the splendor of color, and the marvellous composition
render this immortal masterpiece something
whose sight marks an epoch in life. Canova's
tomb in San Maria dei Frari is a wonderful
thing. It is a pyramid of purest marble, with
a door opening for the sarcophagus, above which
is a portrait of Canova in relief, and on either
side the door angels and symbolic figures are
sculptured.

The Church of Santa Maria della Salute, to

which one is always returning, is a wonderful
example of artistic architecture, as its snowy.
towers and dome seem to rise out of the water
and float in the air.

The fall of the Campanile in 1904 was regarded as a calamity by all the civilized world.
For a thousand years it had stood at the side of
St. Mark's; but the disaster aroused the attention of experts to the condition of the great
cathedral itself, and it was found that the vast
area of over fifty thousand square feet of matchless mosaic needed restoration in order that
they should be preserved.

The Palazzo Rezzonico, which dates to Clement XIII, usually known as the "Browning
Palace," has been for many years one of the
special interests to the visitor in Venice. In
the early months of 1907 it passed out of the
hands of Robert Barrett Browning, who had
purchased it in 1888, and had held it sacredly,
with its poetic and personal associations, since
the death of his father, the poet, in 1889. To
Mr. Barrett Browning is due the grateful appreciation of a multitude of tourists for his generous and never-failing courtesy in permitting
them the privilege of visiting this palace in

which his father had passed many months of enjoyment. It was from this residence that the poet Browning wrote, in October of 1880, to a friend: —

"Every morning at six I see the sun rise; far more wonderfully, to my mind, than his famous setting which everybody glorifies. My bed-room window commands a perfect view; the still, gray lagune, the few sea-gulls flying, the islet of San Giorgio in deep shadow and the clouds in a long purple rock behind which a sort of spirit of rose burns up till presently all the rims are on fire with gold, and last of all the orb sends before it a long column of its own essence apparently; so my day begins."

Later, of his son's palace, Mr. Browning wrote: —

"Have I told you that there is a chapel which he has restored in honor of his mother — putting up there the inscription by Tommaseo,[1] now above Casa Guidi in Florence?"

[1] This inscription and a description in detail of all the memorials of Elizabeth Barrett Browning are given in full in a volume entitled "A Study of Elizabeth Barrett Browning." Boston: Little, Brown, & Co.

ITALY, THE MAGIC LAND

In this palace Mr. Browning wrote some of
his later poems, and it may well be that it was
when he was clad in his singing robes that he
perhaps most deeply felt the ineffable charm of
Venice:—

> "For the stars help me, and the sea bears part;
>   The very night is clinging
>   Closer to Venice' streets to leave one space
>   Above me. . . ."

It was from these lofty salons in the Browning Palace that the poet passed to the "life
more abundant" on that December day of
1889, on the very day that his last volume,
"Asolando," was published and also the last
volume of Tennyson's. Regarding these Mr.
Gladstone said, in a letter to Lord Tennyson:
"The death of Browning on the day of the
appearance of your volume, and we hear of
one of his own, is a touching event."

From the time of Mrs. Browning's death in
Florence (in June of 1861) Mr. Browning never
felt that he could see Italy again, until the
autumn of 1878, when he, with his sister, Miss
Sarianna Browning, came to Venice by way
of the Italian lakes and Verona. At this time

they only remained for a fortnight, domiciled in the old Palazzo Brandolin-Rota, which was transformed into the Albergo dell' Universo. This palace was on the Grand Canal below the Accadémia, and here he returned through two or three subsequent years. Mr. Browning became very fond of Venice, and he explored its winding ways and gardens and knew it, not merely from the gondola view, but from the point of view of the curious little dark and narrow byways, the bridges, and the piazzas.

It was in 1880 that Mr. Browning first met, through the kind offices of Mr. Story, a most charming and notable American lady, Mrs. Arthur Bronson (Katherine DeKay), who had domiciled herself in Casa Alvisi, an old palace on the Grand Canal opposite the Church of Santa Maria della Salute. She was a woman of very interesting personality, and had drawn about her a circle including many of the most distinguished people of her time, authors, artists, poets, and notable figures in the social world. She was eminently *simpatica* and her lovely impulses of generous kindness were rendered possible to translate into the world of the actual by the freedom which a large fortune confers on its possessor. Between Mrs. Bronson and Mr. Browning there sprang up one of those rare and beautiful friendships that lasted during his lifetime, and to her appreciation and many courtesies he owed much of the happiness of his later years. In the autumn of 1880 Mrs. Bronson made Mr. Browning and his sister her guests, placing at their disposal a suite of rooms in the Palazzo Giustiniani Recanati — a palace adjoining her own — and each night they dined and passed the evening with her, with music and conversation to enchant the hours. After Mr. Browning's death, Mrs. Bronson was the friend whom all pilgrims to his shrine in Venice felt it a special privilege to meet and to hear speak of him. In her palace was a large easy-chair, with a ribbon tied across the arms, in which Browning was accustomed to sit, and which was held sacred to him. Mrs. Bronson was an accomplished linguist, and the *habitués* of her salon represented many nationalities. Among these was the Princess Montenegro, the mother of the present Queen of Italy.

It is little wonder that the Browning Palace was for so many years a focus for all who revered and loved the wedded poets, Robert and Elizabeth Barrett Browning.

In the marble court, roofed only by the blue Venetian sky, stood Mr. Barrett Browning's statue of "Dryope" in bronze, on its marble pedestal, — a beautiful conception of the Dryope of Keats, — the dweller in forest solitudes whom the Hamadryads transformed into a poplar. Here a fountain makes music all day long, and the court is also adorned in summer by great Venetian jars of pink hydrangeas in full bloom. The grand staircase, with its carved balustrade and the wide landing where a rose window decorates the wall, leads to the lofty salons which were yet as homelike as they were artistic during the residence of the Brownings. Mr. Story's bust of Mrs. Browning, other portrait busts of both the poets, sculptured by their artist son, and by others, and other memorials abound. In the library were gathered many interesting volumes, autographed from their authors, and many rare and choice editions, among which was one of the "Sonnets from the Portuguese" in a sumptuous volume whose artistic beauty found a fitting setting to Mrs. Browning's immortal sonnets. Among other volumes were a collection of signed "Etchings" by Sir Laurence Alma-Tadema; presentation copies from Tennyson, Matthew Arnold, Aubrey De Vere, Walter Savage Landor, and many another known to fame; and a copy, also, of a study of Mrs. Browning's poetry[1] by an American writer.

There is one memento over which the visitor always smiled — a souvenir of a London evening in 1855 when the Brownings had invited Dante Gabriel Rossetti and his brother and Lord Madox Brown to meet Tennyson and listen to his reading of his new poem, "Maud," then still unpublished. During the reading Rossetti drew a caricature representing Tennyson with his hair standing on end, his eyes glowering and his hand theatrically extended, as he held a manuscript inscribed,

"I hate the dreadful hollow behind the little wood."

A reproduction of John Singer Sargent's painting, "The Gypsy Dance," bore the inscription, "To *mon ami*, Browning." From the library is a niche, decorated in gold, with memorial entablatures to the memory of Mrs. Brown-

[1] "A Study of Elizabeth Barrett Browning." Little, Brown, & Co.

ing. On the outer wall of the palace is an inscription that runs: —

"Robert Browning died in this house 12th December, 1889.

> "Open my heart and you will see
> Graven inside it 'Italy.'"

There is a sadness in the fact that this palace, consecrated to the memory of the immortal poets, husband and wife, has passed into the hands of strangers; but that is a part of the play in a world in which we have no continuing city. In the spring of 1905, Miss Sarianna Browning died in the home of her nephew, near Florence, and her body was buried in the new Protestant cemetery in that city; the old one, where all that was mortal of Elizabeth Barrett Browning was laid to rest, being now closed. Mr. Barrett Browning, in his Tuscan villa, is again dwelling near Florence, his native city, which must forever hold to him its atmosphere of consecrated beauty as the beloved home of his mother, — the noblest and greatest of all woman poets.

The centenary of Carlo Goldoni was celebrated in Venice in the spring of 1907 by the publication of all his works and a monograph on his life; an exhibition of personal relics; the presentation of one of his dramas set to music by Baldassare Galuppi, the great Venetian composer of his time, and by a procession to lay a wreath of laurel on his monument in the Campo San Bartolommeo. The drama given, entitled the "Buranello," was the last work of the author, and it was presented in the theatre Goldoni. The Municipal Council of Venice voted the sum of fifty thousand lire for the *édition de luxe*, which consists of twenty volumes, in octavo. In each volume is a different portrait of Goldoni, facsimile of manuscripts, and the reproduction of literary curiosities.

The monograph of Goldoni was issued by the press of the Venetian Institute of Graphic Art in a limited number of copies.

It contains more than three hundred printed pages and a series of very interesting illustrations. Among these are the reproductions of ancient engravings which are most rare (such as the view of the Grimani Theatre at San Giovanni Crisostomo, a famous theatre existing in the days of the Venetian republic, but now demolished), frontispieces of destroyed editions, and other personal memorials. The revival of the splendid work of the famous artist was one of the attractions of the festa of celebration. The art exhibition of Venice in this spring of 1907 was very picturesque. One special salon was allotted to the artists of Great Britain, and there was a fine loan collection of the portraits of English noblemen painted by Mr. Sargent. This salon was decorated with panels by Frank Brangwyn.

Venice forever remains a dream, a mirage, an enchantment. Has it a recognized social life, with "seasons" that come and go? Has it trade, commerce, traffic? Has it any existence save on the artist's canvas, in the poet's vision? Has it a resident population to whom it is a home, and not the pilgrimage of passionate pilgrims?

There are those who find this Venice of all the year round a society of stately nobles whose ancestral claims are identified with the history of the city and who are at home in its palaces and gondolas, but of this resident life the visitor is less aware than of that in any other city in Italy. For him it remains forever in his memory as the crowning glory of June evenings when the full, golden moon hangs over towers and walls, when gondolas freighted with Venetian singers loom up out of the shadows and fill the air with melody that echoes as in dreams, and that vanishes — one knows not when or where. Mr. Howells, in his delightful "Venetian Days," has interpreted much of that life that the tourist never recognizes, that eludes his sight; and the Dream City still, to the visitor who comes and goes, shrouds itself in myth and mystery. One of the poetic visions of Venice is that given in Robert Underwood Johnson's "Browning at Asolo" (inscribed to Mrs. Arthur Bronson), of which the opening stanzas run: —

"This is the loggia Browning loved,
　High on the flank of the friendly town;
These are the hills that his keen eye roved,
　The green like a cataract leaping down
　To the plain that his pen gave new renown.

"There to the West what a range of blue! —
　The very background Titian drew
　To his peerless Loves. O tranquil scene!
Who than thy poet fondlier knew
　The peaks and the shore and the lore between?

ITALY, THE MAGIC LAND

"See! yonder's his Venice — the valiant Spire,
   Highest one of the perfect three,
Guarding the others: the Palace choir,
The Temple flashing with opal fire —
   Bubble and foam of the sunlit sea."

Edgar Fawcett, always enchanted with his
Venetian days, pictures the northern lagoon,
some six miles from Venice, as "a revel of
pastoral greenness, with briery hedges, numberless wild flowers and the most captivating of
sinuous creeks, overarched by an occasional
bridge, so old that you greet with respect every
moss-grown inch of its drowsy and sagging
brickwork. The cathedral, the ineludible cathedral of all Italian settlements, is reached after a
short ramble, and you enter it with mingled
awe and amusement," he continues. "Some of
its mosaics, representing martyrs being devoured
by flames and evidently enjoying themselves a
great deal during this mortuary process, chal-
lenge the disrespectful smile. But others are
vested with a rude yet sacred poetry, and certain semi-Oriental marble sculptures, adjacent
to the altar, would make an infidel feel like
crossing himself for the crime of having
yielded to a humorous twinge. This duomo

dates far back beyond the Middle Ages, and
so does the small Church of Santa Fosca, only
a step away. What renders Torcello so individual among all the islands and islets of the
lagoon, I should say, is her continual contrast
between the ever-recurrent idyllicism of open
meadows or wilding clusters of simple rustic
thickets, and the enormous antiquity of these
two hoary ecclesiastic fanes. History is in
the air, and you feel that the very daisies
you crush underfoot, the very copses from
which you pluck a scented spray, have their
delicate rustic ancestries, dating back to Attila,
who is said once to have brought his de-
structive presence where now such sweet so-
lemnity of desertion and quietude unmolestedly
rules."

History and legend and art and romance meet
and mingle to create that indefinable sorcery of
Venice. It is like nothing on earth except a
poet's dream, and his poetic dream is of the
ethereal realm. The wonderful music that
floats over the "silver trail" of still waters;
the mystic silences; the resplendence of color,
— all, indeed, weave themselves into an incantation of the gods; it is the ineffable loveliness of

ITALY, THE MAGIC LAND

Paradise where the rose of morning glows "and the June is always June," and it is no more earth, but a celestial atmosphere, — this glory of June in Venice.

Dear Italy!   The sound of thy soft name
  Soothes me with balm of Memory and Hope.
  Mine, for the moment, height and sweep and slope
That once were mine.   Supreme is still the aim
            To flee the cold and gray
            Of our December day,
And rest where thy clear spirit burns with unconsuming flame.

Thou human-hearted land, whose revels hold
  Man in communion with the antique days,
  And summon him from prosy greed to ways
Where Youth is beckoning to the Age of Gold;
            How thou dost hold him near
            And whisper in his ear
Of the lost Paradise that lies beyond the alluring haze!

                    ROBERT UNDERWOOD JOHNSON.

Great ideas create great peoples. Let your life be the living summary of one sole organic idea. Enlarge the horizon of the peoples. Liberate their conscience from the materialism by which it is weighed down. Set a vast mission before them. Rebaptize them.   MAZZINI.

All parts array for the progress of souls: all religion, all solid things, arts, governments, — all that was or is apparent upon this globe, or any globe, falls into niches and comes before the procession of Souls along the grand roads of the universe. . . . . Of the progress of the souls of men and women along the grand roads of the universe, all other progress is the needed emblem and sustenance.   WALT WHITMAN.

VII

THE MAGIC LAND

More than five hundred years have passed over the country of Dante since the death of his mortal part — years of glory and of shame, of genius and intolerable mediocrity, of turbulent liberty and mortal servitude; but the name of Dante has remained, and the severe image of the poet still rules the destinies of Italian generations, now an encouragement and now a reproach. The splendor of no other genius has been able to eclipse or dim the grandeur of Dante; never has there been a darkness so profound that it could conceal this star of promise from Italian eyes; neither the profanations of tyrants and Jesuits, nor the violations of foreign invaders, have been able to efface it. *"Sanctum Poetæ nomen quod nunquam barbaries violavit."*　　　　　　　　　　　　　　　　MAZZINI.

THE true life of Italy is not read in any record of contemporary facts or statistics. Mazzini once said of Dante, in an essay on the immortal poet, that "the life, the true life of Dante does not lie in the series of the material facts of his existence. The life of Dante consists in the sufferings and aspirations of his soul; in its dominant impulses; in the ceaseless development of the idea which was at once his guide, inspiration, and consolation; in his belief as a man and as an Italian." The real life of Italy

is, by analogy, to be read in that atmosphere
of aspiration and of noble purpose which characterizes the nation rather than in the material
facts of its general progress at the present time.
As a country Italy is young. It is still less than
forty years since her unity was declared, and to
merge the large number of separate States into
one harmonious whole is a task requiring the
evolutionary progress of time; for a nation, like
a university, cannot be a matter of instanta-
neous creation. It must germinate and grow.
The country that, previous to so comparatively
a recent date as the year 1870, was, in the phras-
ing of Prince Metternich, "a geographical expression," can hardly be judged by present
national standards after an existence of only
thirty-seven years, although it need be said in
no spirit of apology; for Italy is advancing in
scientific development, in manufactures, and in
the problems involved in civil and hydraulic
engineering to a notable degree in the northern
part. Milan and Naples are separated by far
more than geographical distance. In modern
progress Milan is divided by centuries from all
Southern Italy.

Between Italy and the United States the

entente cordiale is not merely that of diplomatic
and ceremonial courtesy, but of an exceptional
degree of mutually sympathetic comprehensions.
In noble ambitions and lofty purposes Americans and Italians are closely akin. In zeal for
contemporary scientific progress, in an intense
susceptibility to the glories of art, and in hospitality to all that makes · for progress, both
nations meet in mutual recognition. Of no
people is it more deeply true than of Americans
that "each man has two countries: his own
and Italy." The average traveller sees this
fair land with a breadth and thoroughness seldom called into requisition elsewhere. In England he is usually content with London, the
tour of the cathedral towns and the lake region
of the poets. France is summed up to him in
Paris and in the chateaux of outlying districts.
But Italy beguiles the traveller into every lonely
foot-trail in the mountains; to every "piazza
grande" of lonely hamlets, isolated on a rocky
hillside; to every "fortezza" that crowns a
mountain summit. The unexplored byways of
Italy are magnetic in their fascination, and one
special source of congratulation on the part of
those fortunate tourists who travel with their

own motor car is that they are thus enabled to penetrate into untrodden byways in Italy in a manner impossible to those who must depend entirely on the regulation railroad service. All lovers of Italy are devoted to these original tours of private exploration. A recent trip to Saricinesco, in the region of Tivoli, was made by Mrs. Stetson (Grace Ellery Channing) with her husband, and in a descriptive record of the little journey into an unfrequented mountain region this paragraph occurs: —

"Roused by 'an awful rose of dawn' which turned every solemn slope to strange amber and amethyst, we left that rocky eyrie next day, returning by way of Anticoli — beloved of artists. And if the ascent had qualified us for Alpine climbers, the descent qualified us as members of the Italian cavalry corps. Pictures of officers riding down the face of cliffs will never impress us again; we know now it is the very simplest of 'stunts.' Our way down was diversified by the tinkling of thousands of sheep-bells, by the far too close proximity of bulls to Maria's crimson headdress, which nothing in the world would induce her to remove, and by sundry meetings with relations, long-unseen friends, and strangers, from whom we culled the whole register of deaths, births, marriages, and happenings for a month past. At last, beside a little bridge near the railroad station, Leonardo addressed his ten-thousandth adjuration to Beppino, whose poor little legs trembled under him. It was no longer, 'Ah, sacred one! — don't you see Anticoli!' — or 'the rock,' or whatever it might be; now he said, 'Ah, sacred one! — don't you comprehend? — the Signora descends' — and Beppino looked distinctly pleased.

"Here we demanded the reckoning, skilfully evaded hitherto.

"'Well — a franc for each beast, — and half a franc for the room, — the rest was nothing — a *sciocchezza.*'

"A franc apiece! — half a franc! — were *we* brigands that we should do this thing?"

This typical picture of idyllic days in Italy, enjoyed in the impromptu excursion and trip, reveals the delicacy of feeling and the sunny kindness that characterize the *contadini* and which imparts to any social contact with them a grace and sweetness peculiar to Italian life. There are parts of Italy where it is still the Middle Ages and no hint of the twentieth century has yet penetrated. The modern spirit has almost taken possession of Rome; it is largely in evidence in Florence and even Venice, and it dominates Milan; but in most of the "hill towns" and in the little hamlets and lonely haunts where a house is perhaps improvised out of the primeval rock, the prevailing life is still mediæval, and only awakens on festa days into any semblance of activity.

Somewhere, away up in the hills, several miles from Pegli, — on the Mediterranean coast near Genoa, — is one of these sequestered little hill towns called *Acqua Sacra*. The name is obvious, indeed, for the sound of the "sacred water" fills the air, falling from every hillside and from the fountain of the *acqua sacra* by the church. Pilgrims come from miles around to drink of these waters. Each house in this remote little hamlet is of solid stone, resembling a fortress on a small scale, and the houses cling to the hillsides like mosses to a rock. Though far up in the mountains, the hills rise around

RUINS OF THE GREEK THEATRE, TAORMINA, SICILY

Page 429

the hamlet like city walls, as if the life of all the world were kept outside. The unforeseen visit to these remote hamlets, suddenly chancing upon some small centre of happy and half-idyllic life, is one of the charms of tourist travel in this land of ineffable loveliness.

The approach to Italy, by whatever direction, by land or by sea, one enters, is one of magical beauty. Whether one enters from the Mediterranean or from the Adriatic, or by means of the Mont Cenis, the Simplon, or the St. Gothard pass, through the sublime mountain wall, each gateway is marvellous in attraction. Approaching from the seas that completely surround Italy except on one side, the almost undreamed-of splendor of Naples, Genoa, and Venice, as seen from off the shore, exceeds all power of painter or poet to reproduce. The precipitous coast of Sicily; the picturesque city of Palermo; the wonderful ruins of the Greek theatre on the heights in Taormina, — all enchant the tourist. To anchor off Naples, in the beautiful bay, serves the purpose of an hotel out at sea. It is like living in Venice — only more so! By the little rowboats one may go, at any moment, to Naples, and it is more delightful than passing the days in the city itself. For at night as one strolls or sits on deck what a picture is before the eye! All Naples, on her semicircular shores, with her terraced heights rising above, defined in a blaze of electric lights! Genoa, *la Superba*, is still more magnificent when seen from the sea; and Venice, rising dream-enchanted, completes the wonders of the approach by water.

As the new Italy has not yet achieved any homogeneous unity, Naples, Rome, Florence, Venice, and Milan differ in their characteristics to such a degree that no general interpretation of the residents of any one would appropriately describe those of another. Paris and Vienna hardly differ as much as do Milan and Rome; and Venice, Florence, and Rome, each rich in art treasures, have little else in common. Certain characteristics of each of the large cities reveal themselves prominently, even to a superficial observer. Milan, as has been said, is a centre of activity, as Florence is of culture and accomplishments. Florence has the largest and the most choice circulating library in all Italy and one that ranks among the best on the Continent. Her galleries are treasure stores of art, and her social life is unsurpassed — one might almost say unrivalled — in its fine quality. Music, philosophic culture, learning in all lines of research characterize Florentine society. Education has always been regarded in Florence as a matter of prime importance, and when the government grant of funds is insufficient the sum is made up by private contributions, so that the *Scuola del Popolo* gives free instruction, yearly, to eighteen hundred pupils, in every branch of technical and art education. This fact alone offers its own explanation of that general intelligence of the people which so impresses the visitor in Florence. But this is a municipal rather than national fact. Every special development in any direction in Italy will always be found to be the characteristic of the city or locality, not of the country as a whole; and thus the unity of Italy is still a political expression rather than a political fact. It is a theory which is not yet developed into an experience. Italy is in the making. Practically, she is the youngest of countries, with less than forty years of experimental attempt at *national* life behind her. Not until 1919 will she have attained the first half century of her united life. Educational facilities, inclusive of schools, libraries, and museums; railroads, telegraph and telephone service, electric lighting and electric trams, — all the ways and means of the modern mechanism of life are, inevitably, in a nebulous state in Italy. The political situation is extremely interesting at the present time. That the "Blacks" and the "Whites" are diametrically opposed to each other is in the nature of history rather than that of contemporary record or of prophecy; and that this is a traditional attitude in this city of the Cæsars is not a fact by any means unknown; but the situation is complicated by the third party — the Socialists — who, by allying themselves with either, would easily turn the scales and command the situation. If they were ardent Catholics and were advocates of the Papal supremacy, the temporal power of the Pope would be restored in less time almost than could be recorded, and Pius X would be in residence in the Palazzo Quirinale rather than Victor Emanuele III. But this great modern uprising in Italy — a movement that is gathering force and numbers so rapidly that no one can venture to prophesy results even in the comparatively immediate

future — this great modern movement is neither
for church nor state. The Socialist uprising is
very strong in Milan and through Northern
Italy. It is much in evidence in the Umbrian
region — in Foligno, Spoleto, Nervi, and those
towns; and from Frascati to Genzano and in
the Lake Nemi chain of villages — Rocca di
Papa, Castel Gandolpho, Ariccia, Albano —
these villages within some fifteen miles of Rome.
In these there is a veritable stronghold of Socialism, where its purposes and policy are en-
trenched. Yet when one alludes to its policy,
the term is rather too definite. If it had a
settled and well-formulated policy on which all
its adherents were in absolute accord they would
carry all before them. But Socialism is still a
very elastic term and covers, if not a multitude of sins, at least a multitude of ideas and
ideals. There is now a rumor that the situation is forcing the absolutely inconceivable union
of church and state — of the Vatican and the
Quirinale — that they may thus withstand their
common foe. A more amazing and extraordinary turn of affairs could not be imagined; and
if the rumor (which is now becoming more co-
herent in Rome) should prove to be the fore-

runner of any truth, the situation will be one of the most amazing in all history.

Epoch-making events in the course of progress are always preceded by circumstances that form to them a natural approach and chain of causation. They are the results of which the causes stretch backward in the past. One of the things that has an incalculably determining influence on the present situation is that of the character of the present Pope. His Holiness, Pius X, brings to the Papacy an entirely new element. He is no ascetic or exclusive ecclesiastic; he is no diplomat or intriguant, but rather a simple, kindly man, of a simplicity totally unprecedented in the annals of the Palazzo Vaticano. Instead of clinging with unswerving intensity of devotion to the idea of the restoration of the temporal power of the church, Pope Pius X would not be disinclined to the uniting of church and state as in England; the Vatican to remain, like the See of Canterbury, the acknowledged head of the spiritual power, while the Quirinale remained the head of the government to which the church should give its political adherence, the Quirinale in return giving to the Vatican its religious adherence. Perhaps

PONTE VECCHIO, FLORENCE
Page 430

it is not too much to say that something not
unlike this might easily become — if it is not
already — the dream of Pius X. But in the
mean time there is another factor with which to
reckon, and that is the present Papal Secretary
of State, Cardinal Merry del Val. He it is who
really holds the mystic key of St. Peter's. He
is a diplomatist, an ecclesiastic, an embodiment
of all that is severe and archaic in authority.
The Pope is by no means able to set his course
by his own watch-lights. The College of Cardinals surrounds him, and the College of Cardinals is practically one Cardinal, the keen
scholar and the all determining Cardinal Merry
del Val, whose personality dominates the court
of the Vatican. This remarkable prelate represents the most advanced and progressive
thought of the day in many ways, — as has
been noted in preceding pages, — but as a
Jesuit he is unalterably devoted to what he con-
siders the only ideal, — the restoration of the
temporal power of the Pope. Spain revealed
her attitude when King Alphonso asked of all
the monarchs of Europe that the name of each
should be borne by his infant son, the heir-
apparent; and for Italy he asked the name of

the Pope and not of the King, thus recognizing
Pius X rather than Victor Emmanuel III as
the head of the nation.

That the Socialists have very logical and
serious grounds for complaint is true. That
their leader, Signor Enrico Ferri, an Italian
journalist and a Senator, is one of the most
able men in Italy since the time of Cavour is
equally undeniable. The Socialists are fortunate, too, in other leading men. Zurati, the
editor of the *Critica Sociale*, Pantaleoni, Cola-
janni, and others are absolutely the hope of
Italy at the present time in the struggle for better conditions. For the conditions of life in
Italy, as regards taxation, the problems of transit, the government restrictions on agricultural
production and on manufactures, are absolutely
intolerable and should not be endured for a
day. The taxation is so exorbitant that it is a
marvel Italy is not depopulated. On land the tax
rate is from thirty to fifty per cent; the income
tax is not merely, as one would suppose, levied
on a legitimate income derived from a man's possessions, but is levied on salaries, ranging from
ten to twenty per cent of these, and also, not
content with this unheard-of extortion, the tax

is levied on the nature and source of his salary, and even the smallest wage is thus subject to an income tax. Again, there is a most absurd tax on salt, which, like sugar and tobacco, is held as a government monopoly. No poor person living on the seacoast in Italy is allowed to take even a pail of water from the sea to his house, as the government assumes that, by evaporation, it might yield a few grains of salt. The tax on sugar effectually checks an industry that might be made most profitable, that of putting up fruit in jams, jellies, and compote, and renders the price of these commodities absurdly high. Again, when taxes are paid the process is even worse than the unjust and exorbitant tax itself. No one is allowed to send a check or postal order; no tax gatherer calls at the home or the office. Each person must go himself or send a personal representative to a given place between certain hours. Here stand a long procession, each person in town going up, filling out pages of written formalities; talking of each item and discussing it according to the national custom, until the office hours are over for that day, and often not one-fourth of the persons waiting have been served. All then must take

their chances the next day, and perhaps even a
third or a fourth day, — a loss of time and
energy that in no other country would be tol-
erated for a moment. But time has not yet
any recognizable value in Italy. Every enterprise and manufacture is taxed in Italy, and as
the returns of these are inevitably revealed so
that no evasion is possible, and as the exactions
of the government consume nearly all the profits,
the result is that all business enterprises are dis-
couraged and that Italy swarms with a great
idle population, while nearly all articles and
supplies are imported from other countries, with
the payment of enormous duties, making their
cost far greater, proportionately, than their
value.

There are great tracts of country in Southern
Italy suitable for tobacco raising, but (as it is
one of the government monopolies) people are
forbidden to raise it; and in private gardens
only three plants are permitted. Again, all industries are crippled, if not paralyzed, by the
tax at the frontier, and also by the tax at every
gate of every city. At every *porta* in Rome
are stationed government officers who scrutinize
every box, basket, and package; and all fruit,

eggs, garden stuff, milk, and commodities of every kind are taxed as they are brought inside the walls.

The railroads of Italy are, at present, very poor in all facilities of transit. Within a year the Italian government has "taken over" these roads and better conditions are promised, which are, alas! not yet in sight. There are many "counts" to the indictment against the Italian railroads which are only suitable to adorn the very lowest circles of the Inferno described by Dante. They are uncleanly; the roadbeds are so rough that the miserably built compartments jolt and jostle over the tracks; the seats are so high that the feet can hardly touch the floor, and the facilities for light and air are as badly managed as is possible to conceive. As is well known, these are divided into first, second, and third class, these compartments all being in the same train, and between the first and second there is little difference save that of price. Curiously, the price of even second-class travelling in Italy is over half a cent a mile higher than that of the splendid trains in America, with their swift time, their smooth roadbeds, their admirable conveniences in every way.

Again, no luggage is carried free, and the prices asked for it are extortionate beyond words. One may check all his impedimenta from San Francisco to New York without extra charge; but in going from Rome to Naples, or from Florence to Genoa to sail, the same luggage will cost from six to eight dollars to convey it to the steamer. Again, these railroads pay their employés so poorly that only the most inefficient service can be retained at all; only those persons who are the absolute prisoners of poverty will consent to accept such meagrely paid service.

The Italian government consists, like that of most countries, of an upper and lower house, the Senate and the House of Deputies. But the former is rather a matter of miscellaneous honors than one of political initiative. There is no limit to the number of Senators; they are created by being named by the King, and the office is for life. If a man attracts the favorable notice of the King, — because he is a good artist, engineer, archæologist, chemist, or financier, — presto, he is liable to be made a Senator. Canova, the celebrated sculptor, was made a Senator because, indeed, he was a great artist! There

is one condition, however, that a Senator
must be one who pays annually not less than
three thousand lire in taxes. The Senators receive no salary, and their times of meeting are
uncertain and no man's presence is obligatory.
The House of Deputies has five hundred and
eight members, all of whom must be Italian
subjects over thirty years of age. They have no
salary, but are given the entire freedom of the
realm in all transit on railroads and steamers.
The Chamber of Deputies is largely made up
of professional men, and it is little wonder
that the Socialists are demanding an entire
reform in the government of the country.
There was never in any country more defective
conditions than now prevail in Italy. The very
fact that the young King is an estimable gentleman, who is personally not in the least to blame
for the prevailing status of unfortunate conditions, is in one way an added misfortune, as
the personal loyalty he justly inspires militates
by so much against the revolution in government which is so deeply a necessity of Italy
before her better and more prosperous life can
begin. It is now a country of stagnation. All
Southern and Central Italy simply lives off its

tourists; and every year prices and fees and extortion in general from the visitors to Italy become greater.

Senator Enrico Ferri, the leader of Socialism in Italy, was born in 1856 in Mantua. He had a university education, was admitted to the bar, and in 1881 was called to the chair of penal law in the University of Bologna. The Senator is a scientific Socialist, — a man of the most exceptional gifts and qualities, and the author of a noted work, entitled "Criminal Sociology," which is translated into several languages. Senators Ferri and Lombroso are special friends and also co-workers.

On taking his seat in the University of Bologna, Professor Ferri delivered a lecture, entitled "New Horizons in Penal Law," which was a most impressive effort. In it he said: —

"It was in this inaugural discourse that I affirmed the existence of the positivist school of criminal law, and assigned to it these two fundamental rules: First, while the classical schools of criminal law have always studied the crime and neglected the criminal, the object of the positivist school was, in the first place, to study the criminal, so that, instead of the crime being regarded merely as a juridical fact, it must be studied with the aid of biology, of psychology, and of criminal statistics as a natural and social fact, transforming the old criminal law into a criminal sociology. Secondly, while the classical schools, since Beccaria and Howard, have fulfilled the historic mission of decreasing the punishments as a reaction from the severity of the mediæval laws, the object of the positivist school is to decrease the offence by investigating its natural and social causes in order to apply social remedies more efficacious and more humane than the penal counteraction, always slow in its effects, especially in its cellular system, which I have called one of the aberrations of the nineteenth century."

Such is the man to whom it is no extravagance to allude as one of the present leaders of progress in Italy. He is in the early prime of mature life; he is a man of education, culture, great original gifts, and of sympathies with humanity as wise and judicious as they are liberal and all-embracing. Scientific Socialism tolerates no lawlessness, no violence, nor does it, like the so-called Christian Socialism, attempt to graft impossible conditions on society. It regards the laws of economics, and it is practicable and possible as well as considerate and just. And the great inspirer, proclaimer, and leader of scientific Socialism is Enrico Ferri.

Italy not only inspires the enthusiasm of the lover of beauty in nature and art, she inspires a vital and abiding interest in all that shall make for her true progress, and she inspires, as well, absolute faith in her ultimate future. At present her monarchy is among the most liberal and progressive of Europe. King Victor Emmanuel is a man of integrity, of intelligence, and of devotion to the best interests of his country as he understands these interests to be. If they might be better served by a more democratic form of government, it is hardly to be asked or expected that such a view should present itself to an hereditary monarch. Among the most liberal element there are not wanting men who believe that for the immediate future the present form of government is the most feasible. In their conviction Italy is by no means prepared to be a republic. The masses of the

people are uneducated; and a great work, requiring time, must be effected in the popularization of intelligence and of instruction, before
democratic government could be adopted. Yet
there is no faltering in the outlook on a glorious future. The noble words of Mazzini still
ring in the Italian air: "Walk in faith, and fear
not. Believe, and you will conquer." By way
of enforcing his convictions Mazzini said: —

"Upon a day in the sixteenth century, at
Rome, some men bearing the title of *Inquisitors*,
who assumed to derive wisdom and authority
from God himself, were assembled to decree
the immobility of the earth. A prisoner stood
before them. His brow was illumined by genius.
He had outstripped time and mankind, and revealed the secret of a world.

"It was Galileo.

"The old man shook his bold and venerable
head. His soul revolted against the absurd violence of those who sought to force him to deny
the truths revealed to him by God. But his
pristine energy was worn down by long suffering and sorrow; the monkish menace crushed
him. He strove to submit. He raised his hand,

he too, to declare the immobility of the earth. But as he raised his hand, he raised his weary eyes to that heaven they had searched throughout long nights to read thereon one line of the universal law; they encountered a ray of that sun which he so well knew motionless amid the moving spheres. Remorse entered his heart: an involuntary cry burst from the believer's soul: *Eppur si muove!* and yet it moves.

"Three centuries have passed away. Inquisitors, — inquisition, — absurd theses imposed by force, — all these have disappeared. Naught remains but the well-established movement of the earth, and the sublime cry of Galileo floating above the ages.

"Child of Humanity, raise thy brow to the sun of God, and read upon the heavens: *It moves.* Faith and action! The future is ours."

"Poetry," added Mazzini, "will teach the young the nobleness of sacrifice, of constancy, and silence; of feeling one's self alone without despairing, in an existence of suffering unknown or misunderstood; in long years of bitterness, wounds, and delusion, endured without murmur or lament; it will teach them to have faith in things to come, and to labor unceasingly to hasten their coming, even though without hope of living to witness their triumph;" and his final word in this great invocation to the new potencies of the opening future is an exhortation to believe in all greatness and goodness. "Faith," he said, "which is intellect, energy, and love, will put an end to the discords existing in a society which has neither church nor leaders; which invokes a new world, but forgets to ask its secret, its Word, from God." In universal education must lie the first national aid to the development of Italy. "*L' anima del gran mondo è l' allegria.*"

As Florence is pre-eminently the city of culture, so is Milan of activities. Her keynote is *modernité*. The visitor is at once impressed by her energy, her enterprise, and her commercial prosperity. Milan has the best municipal facilities and conveniences in all Italy. The electric lighting of streets, public buildings, and residences, the street transit, the arrangement and conduct of shops and all industrial matters, are in such contrast to any other city in Italy as to lead the sojourner to ask himself whether he can still be on the southern side of the Alpine range. In the Galleria Vittorio Emanuele Milan has the most wonderful structure in all Europe. This arcade was built in 1865, and under the magnificent glass dome it includes nearly one hundred of the most attractive and well-stocked shops, bazaars, and establishments. The dome is decorated with frescoes and caryatides, and with the statues of numbers of eminent men, among whom are Dante, Raphael, Savonarola, and Cavour. The offices and banks in Milan are centres of incessant energy.

For all this stress of activity the visitor does not, however, forget the art features; the visit to the antique Church of St. Ambrosio; to the old convent where Leonardo da Vinci's celebrated fresco, "The Last Supper," is to be seen, though so faded that it is now difficult to discern all the figures. Nor does he fail to climb the wonderful cathedral that lifts its airy grace, as if about to float upward in the skies. Every flight of the steps, in the ascent, brings one to a new vision of beauty. On the roof of this cathedral one wanders as in a very forest of sculpture. Its scheme of decoration includes more than two thousand statues, two of which are by Canova. From the summit, when the air is clear, there are beautiful views of the Alps.

To the savant and scholar the Ambrosian library in Milan is one of the special treasures of Europe. It contains some of the most rare and valuable manuscripts in the entire world, — some of Virgil's with annotations from Petrarcha; a manuscript of Dante's; drawings by Leonardo da Vinci, and other interesting matters of which no other copies exist.

The Magic Land is seen under its most bewitching spell in the region of the Italian lakes. The palace of Isola Bella; the charming gardens; the lake of Como, green-walled in hills whose luxuriant foliage and bloom form a framework for the white villas that cluster on their terraced slopes, — all form a very fairyland of ethereal, rose-embowered beauty. At night the lakes are a strange, unreal world of silver lights and shadows.

The completion of the Simplon tunnel has opened between Italy and Paris a route not only offering swifter facilities for transit, but adding another to the regions of beauty. This route has also still further increased the commercial importance of Milan, the portal and metropolis of Northern Italy. Milan has become the national centre of all scientific and technical pursuits, and it is fairly the Mecca for young men of Central and Southern Italy who are entering into the professions, or into civil and electrical engineering and other of the technical arts and industries.

Bologna, with her historic University, with the long covered arcades of the streets, the fountain, which is the work of Giovanni di Bologna, and the gallery where many of Guido's best works are placed, has its individual interest for the tourist; and Verona, Pavia, Modena, Parma, and Turin all repay a visit from the leisurely saunterer in Italy.

Pisa offers to the visitor four interesting architectural monuments in the Duomo, the Baptistery, the Leaning Tower, and the Campo Santo, all of which are unique. The cathedral has unique designs in its black and white marbles that render it almost as much an object of artistic study as is the cathedral in Siena. The view from the summit of the Leaning Tower reveals the Mediterranean six miles in the distance, gleaming like a sea of silver. The Campo Santo dates from the thirteenth

century, when the earth of which it is composed
was brought (in 1228) from the holy places
in Jerusalem, conveyed to the city (then a sea-
port) by fifty galleys sent out by the Republic
of Pisa. The interior walls of the Campo
Santo are covered with fresco paintings by
Orcagna which are one of the artistic spectacles of the country in their extravagant portrayal of theological beliefs, so realistically
presented in their dramatic scenes from Paradise and from Hades, as to leave nothing to the
imagination. The fantasies in this emblematic
sculpture of memorial monuments over a period
of seven hundred years can be seen in the
Campo Santo of Pisa, — a strange and often a
most grotesque medley.

Genoa is well named La Superba. Her
thoroughfares are streets of palaces. Her terraced gardens and villas, reached by the subterranean funicular street railway, are regions
of unique and incomparable beauty, with the
blue Mediterranean at their feet. Genoa is the
paradise for walking. The streets are largely
inaccessible to carriages, but the admirable
street electric railway penetrates every locality.
It passes in dark tunnels under the hills, reap-

pears on the high terraces, and climbs every height. From the crest of one of these Corsica can often be seen. All the hill-slopes are a dream of pictorial grandeur, with their terraces, their palaces, their sculpture, fountains, and flowers. On the summit of almost every hill there is a fortress, and often ramparts which are silhouetted, in dark masses, against the sky. Orange groves abound on the terraces, often showing the golden fruit, buds, and blossoms all at the same time.

Genoa is fairly a metropolis of sculpture. The great families have themselves perpetuated in portrait statues rather than in painted portraits. In one of the grand ducal palaces in the Via Balbi the visitor may see, not only the life-size statues and the busts of the family ancestry, but one group comprising nine figures, where three generations are represented, in both sitting and standing poses, ingeniously combined.

The churches of Genoa are among the richest in Europe. That of the Annunziati, the special monument of the Lomellini family, glitters and gleams with its gold ceilings and rich frescoes. The cathedral has the special

CAMPO SANTO, GENOA

Page 453

allurement of the emerald dish which **King**
Solomon received as a gift from the Queen of
Sheba. The little "street of the jewellers" is
an alluring place, — so narrow that one can almost stand in the centre of the road and touch
the shop windows on either hand, and these
windows dazzle the eye with their fascinating
glitter of gold and silver filigree work and their
rich jewels.

Beyond all other curious excursions that even
a Magic Land can offer is that to the Campo
Santo of Genoa. A cloistered promenade en-
closes a square, and above are terraced colonnades, each and all revealing statues, and
monuments, and groups of sculpture whose
varied beauty, oddity, or bizarre effects are a
curious study. Some memorials — as one of
an angel with outstretched wings; another of
a flight of angels bearing the soul away; another
combining the figure of Christ with the cross,
and angels hovering near — are full of beauty.
Others are a marvel of ingenious and incongruous combination. One of the latter represents
the man whose memory it commemorates as
lying on his bed in his last illness; the physician
stands by, his fingers on the patient's pulse; on

the opposite side a maid is approaching with a dish holding some article of food, and near the physician are grouped the wife, with a little child clinging to her skirts; the son, holding his hat with both hands and looking down on it, and the daughter, a young girl, with her eyes raised to heaven. Each of these figures is in life size; the bed is reproduced in marble, with the pillows and all the coverings in the most absolute realism, and the entire effect is so startling in its bizarre aspect that one could hardly believe in its existence until by personal observation he had verified so singular a monument.

Yet there is beauty and symbolic loveliness, too, in many of the memorial sculptures of this Campo Santo, and turning away from this cemetery in which lies the body of the noble Mazzini, one hears on the air the refrain of his words on Dante: —

"It appeared to him of more importance to hasten to accomplish his mission upon earth, than to meditate upon the inevitable hour which marks for all men the beginning of a new task. And if at times he speaks of weariness of life, it is only because he sees evil more and more triumphant in the places where his mission was appointed. He concerned himself, not about the length or the shortness of life, but about the end for which life was given; for he felt God in life, and knew the creative virtue there is in action."

Eighty thousand people followed Mazzini to his tomb, and his name lives in the Italy of to-day as one to be associated with that of Dante as prophet and inspirer.

The enchantment of approaching Genoa from the sea at night is an experience to remain as one of the pictorial treasures of memory. The magnificent *lanterna*, the lighthouse with its revolving light, that can be seen for fifty miles out from the coast; the brilliant illumination defining the *fortezza* on the summit of one hill; the curving lights of the terraced residential district and the illumination of the very forest of shipping clustered in the bay, — all combine into a scene not easily effaced from the memories of foreign scenes.

It is only in close relations with Italian literature that Italy can be adequately enjoyed and that the sojourner may enter into sympathetic associations with contemporary Italian life. Dr. Richard Garnett believes that the literature of Italy "is a less exhaustive manifestation than elsewhere of the intellect of the nation," and that "the best energies of the country are employed in artistic production. It is, indeed, remarkable," he continues, "that out of the nine Italians most brilliantly conspicuous in the first rank of genius and achievement, — Aquinas, Dante, Columbus, Leonardo, Michael Angelo, Raphael, Titian, Galileo, Napoleon, — only one should have been a man of letters."

Contemporary Italian literature follows the trend of the day in reflecting the life of the people. The novels of Fogazzaro, the poems of Carducci, the biography and history written by Villari, to say nothing of several other writers who, while not approaching these authors, have still a definite place in the literature of the present, offer illumination on the outer scenery of life, and offer interpretation of the life itself. Art has declined; literature has advanced in Italy, even within the past decade. The law of progress is as inevitable as is the law of gravitation.

ITALY, THE MAGIC LAND

"Onward the chariot of the Unvarying moves;
Nor day divulges him nor night conceals;
Thou hear'st the echo of unreturning hooves,
And thunder of irrevocable wheels."

The future of Italy inspires faith in the renewal of its noblest ideals of achievement. Its ineffable beauty is a heritage of joy to every visitor who comes under the indescribable spell of its attraction and finds that, in all the panorama of foreign life which haunts his memory, it is Italy which shines resplendent as the Magic Land!

INDEX

INDEX

461

INDEX

ship with Clara, 365, 367, 368; legends regarding, 370; death of, 372; miracles of, 375; tomb of, 378.

BAGOT, Richard, in Rome, 11, 13.
Baia, 241.
Baldwin, Rev. Dr., in Rome, 10, 171.
Ball, Thomas, work of, 52.
Balzac, quoted, 120.
Barberini, Cardinal, 72.
Baths of Caracalla, 139.
Baths of Diocletian, 184.
Bell, John, grave of, 216.
Bembo, Cardinal, 306.
Benedictines, 354, 365.
Benton, Dwight, grave of, 221; estimate of, 221.
Bernardino of Siena, 382, 383; quoted, 383.
Bernini, Lorenzo, work of, 22.
Besant, Mrs. Annie, 174.
Biblioteca Sarti, 48.
"Blacks," 145, 146.
Bologna, 450.
Bonaparte, Princess Christina, death of, 203.
Boni, Commendatore, opinion of, 244.
Borni, Giovanni M., 403.
Bronson, Mrs. Arthur, 409, 410.
Brooks, Rev. Phillips, in Rome, 15; quoted, 16, 39, 388, 394, 395.
Brownell, W. C., quoted, 96.
Browning, Elizabeth B., in Rome, 11; quoted, 60, 114, 125, 389; death of, 80, 408; meeting with Mrs. Bronson, 410, 411.

Browning Palace, 406, 410, 411, 412, 413.
Browning, Robert, quoted, 3, 407, 408; in Rome, 11, 70; in Venice, 406; death of, 408.
Browning, Miss Sarianna, 408, 413.
Buono, 236.
Byron, Lord, in Rome, 22; quoted, 22, 403.

CAMPAGNA, 73, 205.
Campanile, fall of, 406.
Campo Verano, 76.
Campo Santo of Pisa, 450, 451, 453.
Campidoglio, buildings on, 25.
Camprani, 237.
Canova, in Rome, 7; his genius, 33; masterpiece of, 42; realism of, 118.
Capella Sistina, 27.
Capo Miseno, 241.
Capri, island of, 262, 263, 264; roses of, 266.
Capuano, Cardinal, legends of, 256.
Capuccini, convent of, 255.
Carducci, 143.
Carter, Professor Jesse Benedict, in Rome, 169.
Carter, Mrs. Jesse Benedict, 34, 37, 169.
Casa Buonarroti, 312.
Casino Borghese, 185.
Castel d' Ischia, 292, 293, 294.
Castellammare, 250.
Castle Gondolfo, 286.
Castiglione, 306.

462

INDEX

INDEX

INDEX

Hillard, George Stillman, in Rome, 12; quoted, 23, 24, 51, 230, 248.

Holy Week, in Rome, 200.

Hosmer, Harriet, in Rome, 10, 59, 60, 61; work of, 62.

Howe, Dr. Samuel Gridley, in Rome, 12.

Howe, Julia Ward, in Rome, 12.

Howells, William Dean, in Rome, 13, 416.

Howitt, William and Mary, graves of, 216.

Hugo, Victor, 41.

Ischia, 281; romantic impressions of, 282; home of Vittoria Colonna, 282; the d' Avalos castle in, 291; as an enchanted island, 296; Vittoria's return to, 299, 305.

Italy, land of romance and song, 6; Mazzini's opinion of, 65; true life of, 423; as a youthful country, 424; relation with United States, 425; traveller in, 425; picture of idyllic days in, 427; approach to, 429; cities of, 429, 430; in the making, 431; politics of, 432; Socialistic uprising in, 433; taxation in, 436–438; railroads in, 439, 440; government of, 440, 441; future of, 444, 457; lakes of, 449; contemporary literature of, 456.

James, Henry, in Rome, 11, 13.

Jameson, Mrs., in Rome, 67; quoted, 193.

Johnson, Robert Underwood, quoted, 416, 421.

Juvenal, birthplace of, 277.

Keats, in Rome, 11, 132; memorial, 133; grave of, 216.

Kemble, Adelaide, in Rome, 68.

Kemble, Fanny, in Rome, 68.

Keynote of life, 359.

Khayyam, Omar, quoted, 1, 94.

Lacus Avernus, 240.

Lanciani, Professor, lectures by, 138, 139; opinion of, 244, 333.

Leaning Tower of Pisa, 450.

Libraries of Rome, 214, 223.

Lister, Mrs., in Rome, 172.

Liszt, Abbé, in Rome, 18, 19.

Little, Canon Knox, quoted, 347, 348, 376, 377, 380.

Lodge, Sir Oliver, quoted, 120.

Longfellow, Henry Wadsworth, in Rome, 12; quoted, 16, 17, 125, 253, 274, 279, 281, 308, 309, 310, 325, 327, 387.

Longfellow, Rev. Samuel, quoted, 18.

Lowell, James Russell, in Rome, 12.

Ludovisi collection, 185.

Luther, in Rome, 80; ascent of the Scala Santa, 156.

Margherita, Queen Mother, 140, 141; palace of, 142; quoted, 143; relations with artists, 144; at requiem mass, 179.

Marino, 286, 287.

Mazzini, 191, 192; quoted, 64, 422,

INDEX

INDEX

INDEX

in, 173; Theosophical Society of, 173, 174; demand for apartments in, 175; sight-seeing in, 183; great palaces in, 187; famous drive of, 188; birthday celebrations of, 189; Republic of, 190; rich years to artists in, 192, 193; Papal ceremonies in, 195; curious spectacle in, 198; Holy Week in, 200; Good Friday service in, 200, 201; motoring from, 204, 205; outlying towns of, 207; American Academy in, 214; libraries of, 214; Protestant cemetery of, 215; literature of, 223; modern spirit in, 428.

Rosa, Salvator, 234.

Rosenkrans, Baroness, 173.

Rota, 329.

Ruskin, in Rome, 12; quoted, 398.

Sabatier, Paul, quoted, 362, 365.

Sallust, Gardens of, 140.

Salvatico, quoted, 401.

San Agostino, church of, 198.

San Caterina di Viterbo, 314.

San Francesco, church of, 345.

San Giovanni, 153.

San Marco, 394.

San Maria della Pace, 27.

San Maria dei Frari, 405.

San Silvestre, 32.

Sansovino, Jacob, work of, 399.

Santa Anna, convent of, 314.

Santa Chiara (Clara), 365; takes vows, 366, 367; founds convent, 368; family history of, 368; friendship with St. Francis of Assisi, 368; at death of Francis,

372; personality of, 373; preservation of body of, 374.

Santa Domenica Maggiore, church of, 303, 331, 333.

Santa Maria Degli Angeli, 345, 365, 380.

Santa Maria del Popolo, 78–80.

Santa Maria della Salute, 405.

Santa Monica, tomb of, 199.

Scala di Spagna, 72.

Scala Santa, 155; Luther's ascent of, 156.

Scifi, Count Favorini, 368.

Scott, Sir Walter, in Rome, 20.

Sejanus, fall of, 263.

Sermoneta, Duke of, in Rome, 18.

Severn, Joseph, grave of, 216.

Shelley, in Rome, 22; memorial, 133; quoted, 215; grave of, 216.

Simmons, Franklin, in Rome, 10. 15, 91, 98; quoted, 29; works of, 98–112; early life, 100; degrees conferred upon, 103; marriage of, 103; latest success of, 107; studios of, 112; realism of, 119; beautiful creation of, 121; grave of, 217.

Simmons, Mrs. Franklin, in Rome, 104; death of, 112; estimate of, 112; grave of, 218.

Sindoni, Turillo, 144.

Sistine Chapel, art in, 177.

Sorrento, 251, 252.

Spearman, Frank Hamilton, in Rome, 167; work of, 168.

Spinazzola, Professor, quoted, 242, 243.

St. Ambrosio, church of, 448.

St. Andrew, 256.

INDEX

St. Benedict, work of, 270, 271; tomb of, 272; chapel of, 350.
St. Damian, chapel of, 356.
St. Gaudens, Augustus, in Rome, 10.
St. Gregory, feast of, 180.
St. Maria della Portiuncula, 351.
St. Mark's, Venice, 396, 397, 404.
St. Mark, tomb of, 397; legend regarding, 397.
St. Paola d' Orvieto, 314.
Stebbins, Emma, in Rome, 58.
Stetson, Charles Walker, in Rome, 10, 91; work of, 113.
Stetson, Mrs. Charles Walker, in Rome, 11; quoted, 426.
Stillman, Mr., quoted, 39.
Story, Julian, in Rome, 91; studio of, 97.
Story, Waldo, in Rome, 91; studio of, 97; works of, 98.
Story, William Wetmore, in Rome, 10; first visit to Italy of, 62; in Florence, 65; quoted, 70, 80, 89, 90, 286; in Palazzo Barberini, Rome, 71; works of, 81–86; estimate of, 82–90; literary work of, 90; grave of, 217.
Stowe, Harriet Beecher, in Rome, 11.
Strada Nuova di Posilipo, 239.
Symonds, John Addington, grave of, 220; estimate of, 220; quoted, 261, 264, 315, 316.

Tasso, 252, 253, 335.
Tennyson's choice of pictures in Venice, 395.
Thackeray, in Rome, 69.

Theocritus, quoted, 85.
Theosophical Society of Rome, 173.
Thomas, Edith, quoted, 82.
Thompson, Launt, in Rome, 10.
Thorwaldsen, in Rome, 7, 10; quoted, 35; realism of, 119.
Tiberius, summer palace of, 262; baths of, 263.
Tilton, J. Rollin, in Rome, 10; grave of, 219.
Titian, tomb of, 405.
Torlonia, Duca and Duchessa of, 334.
Trelawney, grave of, 216.
Trinità di Monti, church of, 133.
Tusculum, 207.

Umberto, King, 142.
Umbrians, 345.
Urbino, 285.

Vanderlyn, in Rome, 10.
Vaughn, Monsignor, 181.
Vatican, galleries of, 112.
Vatican palace, 196, 198.
Vedder, Anita, in Rome, 171.
Vedder, Elihu, in Rome, 10; art of, 91–95; appreciation of, 96; works of, 96, 97; country house of, 262.
Vedder, Mrs. Elihu, in Rome, 170.
Venice, first glimpses of, 389; Grand Canal of, 390; in June, 391; color and loveliness of, 392; art of, 395, 396; origin of, 398; first Doge of, 399; Renaissance architecture in, 399; Doge's

469

INDEX

Palace, 400–404; art in, 404; fall of Campanile in, 406; Browning Palace in, 408–413; centenary of Carlo Goldoni celebrated in, 413, 414; art exhibition in, 415; June evening in, 416; as a poet's dream, 418.

Vernet, Horace, in Rome, 10.

Verona, 311.

Veronese, Paolo, 404.

Vesuvius, 229.

Via Bonella, 45.

Victor Emmanuel III, 118, 215, 432, 444.

Villa Aldobrandini, 208.

Villa Barberini, 209.

Villa Borghese, 14, 187.

Villa Doria, 211,

Villa Falconicri, 213.

Villa Jovis, 263.

Villa Medici, 2, 134.

Villa Nazionale, 238.

Villa Pamphilia Doria, 149.

Villa Torlonia, 206.

Virgil, quoted, 241; grotto of, 242.

Visconti, 329, 330.

Vittorio Emanuele, 214.

WALDSTEIN, Dr. Charles, quoted, 245.

Ward, Mrs. Humphry, quoted, 210, 212.

Watson, William, quoted, 9, 25, 86, 87.

Wellman, Walter, 9.

West, Benjamin, in Rome, 10.

White, Mr. and Mrs. Henry, in Rome, 165.

"Whites," 145.

Whitman, Walt, quoted, 422.

Whitney, Anne, in Rome, 10, 58.

Whittier, quoted, 339.

Wilberforce, Rev. Basil, quoted, 125, 341.

Woolson, Constance Fenimore, tomb of, 219.

ZUCCARO, Federigo, 44.